THE GUGGENHEIM MUSEUM: JUSTIN K. THANNHAUSER COLLECTION

THE GUGGENHEIM MUSEUM

JUSTIN K. THANNHAUSER COLLECTION

by Vivian Endicott Barnett

The Solomon R. Guggenheim Museum, New York

Published by
The Solomon R. Guggenheim Foundation
New York, 1978

ISBN 0-89207-016-1
Library of Congress
Card Catalogue Number 78-66357

Supported by grants from the National
Endowment for the Arts in Washington,
D.C., a Federal Agency.

JUSTIN K. THANNHAUSER

on the occasion of his eightieth birthday
at The Solomon R. Guggenheim Museum,
May 7, 1972

CONTENTS

Dedicated to

DANIEL CATTON RICH
1904-1976

whose many years of Trusteeship
at the Guggenheim Museum and
whose originating role in the conception of
this catalogue are herewith commemorated.

FOREWORD

The "Guggenheim," as it is widely referred to, has a variety of meanings that relate sometimes separately, sometimes jointly, to a foundation, a museum, or a building. The Solomon R. Guggenheim Foundation is the legal entity through which my grandfather donated, in 1937, the funds to create and maintain the activities of the Museum of Non-Objective Painting, which in 1951 was renamed The Solomon R. Guggenheim Museum. The building, originally commissioned from Frank Lloyd Wright in 1943, was completed in 1959, the year of the architect's death.

These facts are recorded here to provide a background for the development that led to the incorporation of the Justin K. Thannhauser Collection into The Solomon R. Guggenheim Foundation. This process was initiated in 1965 when the Collection described in this catalogue came to us as a loan. It was completed in 1976 when, as a result of Mr. Thannhauser's death, the original loan and promised gift became the donor's bequest.

Gifts of such importance rarely come easily, and the Thannhauser Bequest to the Guggenheim is no exception. Understandably, the donor saw in the Collection the realization of his lifelong effort as a collector, while the Guggenheim looked upon the gift as a marvelous enrichment of its own treasures—one that complemented and broadened the works already in its possession. Such divergencies of perspective and differing attitudes toward details of installation occasionally tested the relationship between benefactor and beneficiary. My cousin and predecessor, Harry F. Guggenheim, in his capacity as President of The Solomon R. Guggenheim Foundation, brought about a harmonious resolution of these divergent viewpoints.

In 1972 Mr. Thannhauser's eightieth birthday was celebrated in the Guggenheim's auditorium with an unforgettable piano recital by Rudolf Serkin. A new and mutually acceptable installation of the works in the Justin K. Thannhauser Wing of the Museum and the publication of a picture book of the Collection to mark the occasion were perhaps the most tangible reminders of those birthday festivities. It was, sadly and to my deep regret, the last time I saw our old friend and benefactor, Justin.

The history of the Thannhauser gift is closely linked to the early tenure of this Museum's present director, Thomas M. Messer, whose acquaintance with Justin K. Thannhauser began in the early 1950s. Tom Messer's persuasive presence, more than any other factor, secured the Collection for the Guggenheim Museum. Harry F. Guggenheim, with the support of the Trustees of The Solomon R. Guggenheim Foundation, completed the arrangements that resulted in eventual transfer of the Thannhauser Collection as published and documented in this catalogue.

That such an agreement could be accomplished was due not only to the dedication of those already mentioned, but also to the tact and perserverance of H. Harvard Arnason, Vice President for Art Administration from 1960 to 1969; Daniel Catton Rich, a trustee of The Solomon R. Guggenheim Foundation from 1960 to 1976, the year of his death; and Dr. Louise Averill Svendsen, member of the Museum's curatorial staff since 1954, who is presently Senior Curator. Finally, we must give most emphatic credit to Hilde Thannhauser, Justin Thannhauser's widow. It is no exaggeration to say that without her strong belief in the desirability of the donation, without her active and always constructive part in the negotiations, this gift so crucial to the development of the Guggenheim Museum would never have been realized.

PETER LAWSON-JOHNSTON, *President*
The Solomon R. Guggenheim Foundation

PREFACE

The Justin K. Thannhauser Bequest to The Solomon R. Guggenheim Museum is primarily a collection of French painting from the Impressionist and Post-Impressionist eras to that part of the twentieth century dominated by the genius of Pablo Picasso. Among the seventy-five examples discussed here are also some small sculptures and numerous works on paper from the same period by artists from Degas and van Gogh to Picasso and Matisse. Part of the Thannhauser Bequest thus provides a nineteenth-century preamble, with Pissarro, Manet, Renoir, Cézanne, van Gogh, and Gauguin as its brightest stars, to the Guggenheim Museum's twentieth-century collection. The Bequest then extends into the early years of the School of Paris and particularly emphasizes Picasso's prodigious development. This latter concentration assumes its fullest significance when considered together with the Picassos that earlier entered the Guggenheim Collection and with those that are a part of Peggy Guggenheim's recent great gift to the Museum. Through the objects themselves and the relationships these establish with other Guggenheim works the Thannhauser Collection thus deepens and expands the scope and orientation of the Guggenheim Museum Collection and gives it a range and depth far beyond its original limits.

To dwell upon the importance of the Bequest is not to deny that it contains, besides its share of impressive masterpieces, items of lesser, primarily documentary interest. But the presence of secondary works, particularly within the Picasso sequence, illuminates the creative personalities of the artists represented and lends added dimension to their major examples that constitute the Collection's main strength.

Because Justin Thannhauser was able to see beyond the collection he had assembled, he left future generations free to treat his bequest as a living entity rather than a merely personal monument. Terms of the agreement are liberal enough to permit temporary display of related examples from the Thannhauser and Guggenheim collections next to one another in either the Thannhauser Wing or on the spiral ramp of the Museum's main gallery even before the merger with the Guggenheim's other holdings takes place. Thus, the integration of the Guggenheim and Thannhauser Picassos in a single presentation, or the display side by side of other works from both collections, whether by Bonnard, Vuillard, Modigliani, or Braque are among the rewards of this great Bequest. Clearly this is a benefaction which in the forty-year history of the Guggenheim Museum is comparable only to Solomon R. Guggenheim's original gifts and to Peggy Guggenheim's recent transfer of her holdings in Venice to ownership by The Solomon R. Guggenheim Foundation.

The Guggenheim Museum: Justin K. Thannhauser Collection is part of an on-going series of related publications which will ultimately document the Guggenheim Museum's collection. The present catalogue, researched and written by Vivian Endicott Barnett, follows two previously published volumes by Angelica Zander Rudenstine devoted to the Guggenheim's paintings of 1880 to 1945. The next book, now in preparation by Mrs. Rudenstine, will consider the Peggy Guggenheim Collection.

Vivian Barnett, the Guggenheim's Curatorial Associate, began the present book in congenial collaboration with Daniel Catton Rich. This cooperative effort ended tragically, however, with Mr. Rich's death and resulted in the assumption of increased responsibility by Mrs. Barnett, who is the author of the entire manuscript. The catalogue, nevertheless, imparts Dan Rich's vision and concept, and Mrs. Barnett relied greatly upon his profound knowledge of French painting. Mrs. Barnett also received assistance from her curatorial colleagues and from many other departments of this Museum. None of these contributions, however, detracts from the originality of her research and the distinction of her authorship, which remain the ultimate determinants of her achievement as well as the measure of our indebtedness to her.

Research and production of a publication as ambitious as *The Guggenheim Museum: Justin K. Thannhauser Collection* are not only laborious and time-consuming but also extremely demanding financially. We are therefore particularly grateful to the National Endowment for the Arts for grants received in support of this project.

With the publication of *The Guggenheim Museum: Justin K. Thannhauser Collection,* the Bequest described in this volume enters a new and more fluid phase. Placement, framing, and lighting, already modified during Mr. Thannhauser's lifetime, have been further altered. The formerly static installation will benefit from temporary additions of works from other sources which will create evocative and stimulating visual juxtapositions. The autonomy and identity of Justin K. Thannhauser's gift to the Guggenheim Museum will, however, remain unimpaired and stand as a reminder and example of an invaluable and most generous public benefaction for many years to come.

THOMAS M. MESSER, *Director*
The Solomon R. Guggenheim Museum

INTRODUCTION AND ACKNOWLEDGMENTS

Since the works from the Thannhauser Collection are on permanent view, this catalogue is written not only for scholars and students of nineteenth- and twentieth-century art but also for interested visitors to the Museum. For every object in the Thannhauser Bequest, the catalogue entry provides specific information on the medium, support, dimensions, inscriptions, provenance, exhibition history, and, when necessary, condition of the work. Comprehensive bibliographic references have been included to shed light on the history of Justin K. Thannhauser's collection. The text itself focuses on objective, factual issues related to the work in question such as problems of dating and iconography, the identification of the subject, and a discussion of related works. Biographies of the artists, the development of an artist's oeuvre, and stylistic analysis of each work have been omitted.

Every effort has been made to include all the factual information known about each object since so much of the history of the works remains unknown or is irrevocably lost. For the most part, J. K. Thannhauser's records do not exist nor do those of the family's Moderne Galerie. Our knowledge is far from complete and, ironically, record of when a work was on view at the Thannhauser's galleries is most conspicuously lacking.

Justin K. Thannhauser possessed a keen memory and shared his recollections with Daniel Catton Rich in notes (December 1972) and conversations (March 1975) which are frequently cited as the source of information in catalogue entries. The present volume would not exist without the information he graciously and tirelessly provided. A brief history of J. K. Thannhauser's life and the family gallery illuminates the context in which the Thannhauser Collection at the Guggenheim should be seen and offers a fascinating perspective on the history of taste.

Justin K. Thannhauser was born on May 7, 1892, in Munich, Germany. His father was the prominent art dealer Heinrich Thannhauser (1859-1935). Since 1906 the elder Thannhauser was an associate of F. J. Brakl in Munich. On November 1, 1909, he opened the Moderne Galerie in the Arco-Palais at Theatinerstrasse 7 in Munich with an exhibition of Impressionist paintings. It was about this time that Justin assisted his father with exhibitions. Beginning in 1911 Justin K. Thannhauser studied art history, philosophy, and psychology in Paris, Munich, Berlin, and Florence. He particularly recalled his studies with Henri Bergson, Adolf Goldschmidt, and Heinrich Wölfflin.

The first exhibition of the *Neuekünstlervereinigung München,* an association of Munich artists which was founded by Vasily Kandinsky and others, was held at the Moderne Galerie from December 1-15, 1909. It included thirteen works by Kandinsky, eleven by Alexej Jawlensky, and several by Adolf Erbslöh, Alexander Kanoldt, Alfred Kubin, Gabriele Münter, and Marianne von Werefkin. A second exhibition of the *Neuekünstlervereinigung* was held at Thannhauser's Moderne Galerie from September 1-14, 1910, at which time paintings by Braque, Picasso, Derain, Rouault, van Dongen, and Vlaminck as well as Jawlensky, Kandinsky, Kubin, Münter, and von Werefkin were shown. Also in 1910 the Moderne Galerie mounted exhibitions of forty paintings by Manet from the Pellerin collection (May), twenty or more pictures by Gauguin (August), and paintings by Pissarro and Sisley (November).

One of the first exhibitions of Franz Marc's work was held in May 1911, followed by a Paul Klee show in June. Later, in December of that year, one hundred works by Ferdinand Hodler were shown.

At the same time as the third *Neuekünstlervereinigung* exhibition, *Der Blaue Reiter, die erste Ausstellung der Redaktion* took place at the Moderne Galerie from December 18, 1911, to January 1, 1912. The Blue Rider was founded by Kandinsky and Marc; its first exhibition included their work as well as that of Robert Delaunay, Auguste Macke, Gabriele Münter, Henri Rousseau, Arnold Schönberg, and others.

When Walt Kuhn was in Europe locating works of art for the *International Exhibition of Modern Art,* he contacted Heinrich Thannhauser, who lent several works including two Hodlers and a Vlaminck to the Armory Show, which opened in New York in February 1913.

The Moderne Galerie presented works by Renoir in January 1912 followed by those of Edvard Munch in February. A Futurist show opened October 27, 1912, and paintings by Paul Cézanne were exhibited in December 1912. February 1913 saw the first major exhibition of paintings by Pablo Picasso, for which Justin Thannhauser wrote the foreword to the catalogue. Picasso's *Woman Ironing,* now in the Thannhauser Collection at the Guggenheim, was included. A Kandinsky exhibition took place in January 1914.

During World War I the Moderne Galerie curtailed its activities considerably. Following the war Justin K. Thannhauser assumed the dominant role. The gallery added a branch in Lucerne, Switzerland (1919-37). January 1927 marked the opening of the Galerien Thannhauser in Berlin (1927-37), and a large exhibition to commemorate the occasion was held at the Künstlerhaus. The *Erste Sonderausstellung in Berlin* included several pictures now at the Guggenheim: van Gogh's *Mountains at Saint-Rémy,* Manet's *Before the Mirror,* Pissarro's *The Hermitage at Pontoise,* and Renoir's *Woman with Parrot* and *Still Life: Flowers.* The original Moderne Galerie in Munich continued to do business until 1928.

The gallery held a Picasso exhibition in Munich in June 1922, a Gauguin show in Berlin in October 1928, and a large Matisse exhibition in Berlin in February-March 1930. Justin K. Thannhauser played a prominent role in the organization of the 1932 Picasso exhibition at the Kunsthaus Zürich. His friendship with the artist continued and is attested to by the many Picassos in the Collection.

Justin K. Thannhauser was forced to leave Germany in 1937 and reestablished his gallery in Paris at 35, rue de Miromesnil the same year. He had to flee the Nazis again in 1939. On Christmas Eve 1940 Justin Thannhauser left from Lisbon for

New York. By April 1941 he was living at 165 East 62nd Street. Later his home and private gallery were located at 12 East 67th Street. Justin Thannhauser lost his sons Heinz (1918-1944) and Michel (1920-1952) and his first wife Kate (1894-1960). His elder son was the first to research and publish the letters and drawings by van Gogh in the Thannhauser Collection (see catalogue numbers 18-23 and 25). Justin K. Thannhauser and his second wife Hilde moved to Bern in 1971. He died December 26, 1976, and she alone survives.

In the preparation of this catalogue each painting and piece of sculpture was examined carefully by either Orrin Riley, Conservator, or Lucy Belloli, Associate Conservator, and all works on paper were studied by Christa Gaehde. The works which were placed on permanent view in 1965 as a loan from the Thannhauser Foundation have to date received only such conservation treatment as specifically authorized by the trustees of the Thannhauser Foundation. Upon becoming the property of the Solomon R. Guggenheim Museum it is expected that each work will be subject to renewed conservation attention.

I am grateful to Orrin Riley, Lucy Belloli, Dana Cranmer, and Saul Fuerstein for their expert assistance in examining the works and to Robert E. Mates and Mary Donlon for virtually all the photography. I was fortunate to have the advice of two skillful and perceptive editors. Carol Fuerstein worked on preliminary sections of the catalogue, and Joanne Greenspun edited the entire final manuscript and saw it through the presses. Margit Rowell kindly advised me in translating the titles into French; Audrey Helfand also assisted in translations.

I am indebted to Angelica Rudenstine for providing the model for this catalogue in her two volumes, *The Guggenheim Museum Collection: Paintings 1880-1945*, and for her advice on many questions. Louise Averill Svendsen's knowledge of the paintings, drawings, and sculptures in the Thannhauser Collection and her friendship with Mr. and Mrs. Thannhauser have been especially valuable. I am most grateful to Thomas M. Messer for his personal interest in the Thannhauser Collection catalogue, his careful and perceptive reading of the manuscript, and his support of my endeavor.

This catalogue began as a collaboration with Daniel Catton Rich, and it could not have been written without his guidance and encouragement. His sense of style, clarity, and precision set a standard to emulate. During years of working with Dan Rich, I admired the scope of his knowledge and the acuity of his intuition.

Much of the research has been conducted in libraries. I wish to thank Mary Joan Hall and Marion Wolf of The Solomon R. Guggenheim Museum library, and members of the staff of the Frick Art Reference Library, The Museum of Modern Art library, the Thomas J. Watson Library of The Metropolitan Museum of Art, and The New York Public Library. On occasion the facilities of the Fine Arts Library at the Fogg Art Museum and the Harry Elkins Widener Memorial Library at Harvard University in Cambridge and the Sterling Memorial Library at Yale University in New Haven have been extremely useful. We are grateful for access to the Bibliothèque Nationale, the Bibliothèque d'Art et d'Archéologie (Jacques Doucet), and the library of the Musée National d'Art Moderne in Paris; the Witt Library, The Courtauld Institute of Art in London; the Archivo Histórico de la Ciudad in Barcelona; and the Zentralinstitut für Kunstgeschichte in Munich.

We particularly appreciate the extensive original contributions made by the following individuals: Morris Appelman, London; R. G. Appleyard, The Art Gallery of South Australia, Adelaide; Wilhelm Arntz, Haag/Oberbayern; Merete Bodelsen, Copenhagen; Victor Carlson, The Baltimore Museum of Art; Ralph F. Colin, New York; Douglas Cooper, Monte Carlo; Pierre Daix, Paris; M. G. Dortu, Paris; Charles Durand-Ruel, Paris; Mme Georges Duthuit, Paris; Richard S. Field, Wesleyan University, Middletown, Conn.; Ann Galbally, University of Melbourne; Donald E. Gordon, University of Pittsburgh; Gilbert Gruet, Bernheim-Jeune, Paris; Georges Bernstein Gruber, Paris; Maurice Jardot, Galerie Louise Leiris, Paris; Daniel-Henry Kahnweiler, Galerie Louise Leiris, Paris; Marilyn McCully, Princeton University; Charles W. Millard, The Hirshhorn Museum and Sculpture Garden, The Smithsonian Institution, Washington, D.C.; Margaret Potter, New York; Theodore Reff, Columbia University; John Rewald, The Graduate Center of the City University of New York; John Richardson, New York; Nicole Mangin de Romilly, Galerie Maeght, Paris; Alexandre Rosenberg, Paul Rosenberg and Co., New York; Robert Rosenblum, The Institute of Fine Arts, New York University; Isabelle Rouault, Paris; Antoine Salomon, Paris; Rosa Maria Subirana, Museo Picasso, Barcelona; Oriol Vals, Museo de Arte Moderno, Barcelona; Bogomila Welsh-Ovcharov, Erindale College, University of Toronto; Barbara E. White, Tufts University, Medford, Mass.; Daniel Wildenstein, Paris. I am grateful to them and to other individuals mentioned in specific catalogue entries for their answers to our questions and for their knowledgeable opinions.

I am most deeply indebted to Justin K. Thannhauser and Daniel Catton Rich who knew and respected each other over many years. They worked together on this catalogue but neither lived to see its completion.

VIVIAN ENDICOTT BARNETT, *Curatorial Associate*
The Solomon R. Guggenheim Museum

EXPLANATORY NOTES

Titles:

If the artist's title is known, it is given first in English. Since this is rarely the case, the title corresponds with that in a catalogue raisonné or an accurate title commonly used to refer to the work. Generally the title in French and other titles by which the work has been known follow in parentheses. Most of the titles are those designated by J. K. Thannhauser; any changes have been indicated in the catalogue entry.

Medium:

In the discussion of related works where no medium is specified, oil on canvas is understood.

Measurements:

The dimensions are given in inches followed by centimeters. Height precedes width followed by depth, where applicable. For paintings, the dimensions are those of the painted surface. For works on paper, the dimensions are those of the support.

Inscriptions:

All inscriptions and signatures on the reverse of a work are recorded in the entry and, in most cases, reproduced. Unless otherwise indicated, all inscriptions are in the artist's hand.

Condition:

The absence of condition notes signifies that the work is in good condition, and that there is no evidence of any prior treatment. If a painting has been lined or is unvarnished, such information is always noted. Com-

ments are intended to provide further information about the medium and the support, to explain what is visible in the work itself, and to indicate what cannot be readily observed (i.e., changes in composition and old repairs). Since 1965 the works have received only such conservation treatment as specifically authorized by the trustees of the Thannhauser Foundation. Christa Gaehde treated certain works on paper at the date given in parentheses. The date at the end of the condition notes indicates when the work was examined.

Exhibitions:

All works from the Thannhauser Collection have been on permanent view at the Guggenheim Museum since 1965. The exhibition histories are as complete as possible considering the fact that the records of the Thannhauser galleries no longer exist (see Introduction).

References:

References are comprehensive and, like exhibition histories, often include in parentheses the title, date, or collector's name relevant to the discussion in the text.

Right and Left:

The terms refer to the spectator's right and left unless otherwise stated.

ABBREVIATIONS

Blunt and Pool, 1962:

A. Blunt and P. Pool, *Picasso: The Formative Years*, Greenwich, Conn., 1962.

Cirici Pellicer, 1946:

A. Cirici Pellicer, *Picasso antes de Picasso*, Barcelona, 1946.

Cirici Pellicer, 1950:

A. Cirici Pellicer, *Picasso avant Picasso*, trans. M. de Floris and V. Gasol, Geneva, 1950.

Cirlot, 1972:

J.-E. Cirlot, *Picasso: Birth of a Genius*, New York and Washington, 1972.

CLVG:

The Complete Letters of Vincent van Gogh, Greenwich, Conn., 1958, vols. I-III.

Daix and Boudaille, 1967: D-B.

P. Daix and G. Boudaille, *Picasso: The Blue and Rose Periods*, trans. P. Pool, Greenwich, Conn., 1967.

Daix, 1965:

P. Daix, *Picasso*, New York, 1965.

Daix, 1977:

P. Daix, *La Vie de peintre de Pablo Picasso*, Paris, 1977.

Daulte, 1971:

F. Daulte, *Auguste Renoir: catalogue raisonné de l'oeuvre peint*, Lausanne, 1971, vol. I.

de la Faille, 1928:

J.-B. de la Faille, *L'Oeuvre de Vincent van Gogh*, Paris and Brussels, 1928, vols. I-IV.

de la Faille, 1939:

J.-B. de la Faille, *Vincent van Gogh*, Paris, 1939.

de la Faille, 1970:

J.-B. de la Faille, *The Works of Vincent van Gogh: His Paintings and Drawings*, rev. ed., Amsterdam, 1970.

Duncan, 1961:

D. D. Duncan, *Picasso's Picassos,* New York, 1961.

Gordon, 1974:

D. E. Gordon, *Modern Art Exhibitions 1900-1916,* Munich, 1974, vols. I-II.

Lemoisne, 1946:

P. A. Lemoisne, *Degas et son oeuvre,* Paris, 1946, vols. I-IV.

Masterpieces, 1972:

The Solomon R. Guggenheim Museum, *A Picture Book of 19th and 20th Century Masterpieces from the Thannhauser Foundation,* New York, 1972.

Penrose, 1958:

R. Penrose, *Picasso: His Life and Work,* London, 1958.

Rewald, 1944:

J. Rewald, *Degas: Works in Sculpture, A Complete Catalogue,* New York, 1944.

Rewald, 1956:

J. Rewald, *Degas Sculpture: The Complete Works,* rev. ed., New York, 1956.

Rewald, 1962:

J. Rewald, *Post-Impressionism: From van Gogh to Gauguin,* 2nd ed., New York, 1962.

Venturi, 1936:

L. Venturi, *Cézanne: son art, son oeuvre,* Paris, 1936, vols. I-II.

Wildenstein, 1964:

G. Wildenstein and R. Cogniat, *Gauguin,* Paris, 1964.

Zervos, 1932-77: Z.

C. Zervos, *Pablo Picasso,* vol. I, Paris and New York, 1932; vols. II-XXXII, Paris, 1942-77.

Georges Braque

Born May 1882, Argenteuil
Died September 1963, Paris

1

I

Landscape near Antwerp. 1906
(Paysage près d'Anvers; La Rivière; The River)

Oil on canvas, 23⅝ x 31⅞ (60 x 81)

Signed l.l.:[1] *G Braque*   Not dated.

PROVENANCE:

Purchased from an unknown private collection in Paris by Robert Lebel, c. 1935; purchased from Lebel by J. K. Thannhauser, 1950-51 (correspondence with Lebel, Mar. 1974).

CONDITION:

Support is fine-weave canvas that was glue lined at an unknown date prior to 1965. Flattening of the pigment especially in area of sky. Scattered minor areas of abrasion (Jan. 1975).

Braque spent the summer of 1906 in Antwerp, his only visit to the city. He went there with Emile-Othon Friesz (1879-1949), who had already been in Antwerp the previous summer. Braque had grown up in Le Havre, where he became friends with Raoul Dufy and Friesz. Friesz was slightly older than Braque and, at that time, farther along in his career. In Antwerp Braque and Friesz lived in a *pension* near the port and rented an abandoned casino as a studio on the banks of the Scheldt River. From the balcony of the studio they had a view of the harbor and the river traffic (H.R. Hope, *Georges Braque,* New York, 1949, p. 23; Oppler, p. 51, fn. 3).

In his Fauve period, which began that summer in Antwerp, Braque often made more than one version of the same composition (unpublished research by Margaret Potter). Nicole de Romilly finds that when there are two pictures of the same view it is possible to postulate which one was done in front of the motif and which one was probably done later in the studio (conversation, May 1977). Braque painted two variations of the scene near Antwerp depicted in the present picture: *Landscape near Antwerp* (16½ x 19¾ in., 42 x 50 cm., 1906, signed, private collection, Paris; J. Russell, *Georges Braque,* New York, 1959, color pl. 3) and *Marine* (19⅝ x 24 in., 50 x 61 cm., signed and dated 1906, private collection, Paris; Galerie Schmit, *Cent Ans de peinture française,* no. 19).

Although the former is extremely close to the present work in terms of what is represented, it displays none of the stylized brushwork found in the Thannhauser painting. In addition, the palette has more blues and greens than in the present picture. The predominance of pale yellow and lavender tones in the Thannhauser version would indicate a development in Braque's Fauve style and leads to the hypothesis that our version was painted after the *Landscape near Antwerp* in a private collection, Paris (de Romilly concurred in conversation, May 1977). In *Marine,* the sky is decidedly blue, the left foreground area has more orange, and the right foreground area contains more green than in the present picture. Furthermore, the colors

1. R. Lebel remembers that when he acquired it about 1935, the painting was unsigned and that he took it soon thereafter to Braque, who then signed it (correspondence with D. C. Rich, Mar. 1974). Braque signed most of his early works years after he painted them. An example of an early signature is found on the related painting, *Marine* (Paris, Galerie Schmit, *Cent Ans de peinture française,* exh. cat., 1969, no. 19, color repr.). Likewise, Braque only rarely dated his early pictures and often added dates at a later time (J. Elderfield, *The "Wild Beasts": Fauvism and Its Affinities,* exh. cat., The Museum of Modern Art, New York, 1976, p. 158, fn. 107).

become more expressive in *Marine*. Here, the artist has omitted the large background building found at the left in the present work and in the related *Landscape near Antwerp* (private collection, Paris) and has added a pier in the foreground suggestive of that in *L'Estaque* (19⅝ x 23⅝ in., 50 x 60 cm., Musée National d'Art Moderne, Paris). While the use of color in *Marine* also suggests that it was painted after the Thannhauser version, no conclusive evidence exists to place the canvases in a sequence.

Although Braque and Friesz often painted the identical view, no corresponding picture by Friesz has been located. There are similar distant buildings in Friesz's *La Cale rouge* (A. Salmon, *Emile-Othon Friesz*, Paris, 1920, p. 25, repr.) and *Anvers* (M. Gauthier, *Othon Friesz*, Geneva, 1957, pl. 16).

The palette of the Thannhauser work resembles that in another of Braque's paintings of Antwerp, *The Mast* (18⅞ x 14 in., 48 x 35.5 cm., 1906, Wally Findlay Galleries, New York; Russell, pl. 1) and that of his *Still Life with Pitchers* (20¾ x 25 in., 52.5 x 63.5 cm., signed and dated 1906, private collection, Switzerland; J. Elderfield, *Fauvism*, 1976, p. 128, color repr., where the author gives a date of 1906-7).

Braque is said to have executed over a dozen paintings that he thought worth keeping during that summer of 1906 (Hope, p. 24). Georges Isarlov ("Georges Braque," *Orbes*, no. 3, spring 1932, pp. 79-80) lists ten Antwerp paintings but includes neither the Thannhauser picture nor the two versions related to it. The Thannhauser painting (60 x 81 cm.) is larger than any works catalogued by Isarlov under 1906, although some canvases executed in 1907 measure 60 x 81 and 65 x 81 cm.

Following his stay in Antwerp, Braque was in Paris during September and part of October. He spent the rest of the autumn at L'Estaque with Friesz. Braque continued to work in a Fauve manner through 1907, when he lived in the south of France and in Paris.

John Elderfield (correspondence, May 1976) considers the present picture more advanced stylistically than the Antwerp harbor paintings and even some Paris paintings but points out that Braque's development is by no means a clear progression, a conclusion also arrived at by de Romilly (conversation, May 1977). The brushwork of *Landscape near Antwerp* is stylized in a manner not common to the summer of 1906. However, the colors are not as extreme as those found in the work of 1907. Ellen Oppler agrees on a date of 1906 (correspondence, Jan. 1977). Potter thinks it likely that Braque painted the Thannhauser picture in his studio when he was no longer in Antwerp (conversation, Apr. 1975).

EXHIBITIONS:

Paris, Galerie Pierre, *Georges Braque: Paysages de l'epoque fauve (1906)*, Feb. 4-21, 1938;[2] New York, Marie Harriman Gallery, *Les Fauves,* Oct. 20-Nov. 22, 1941, no. 27 *(La Rivière,* 1906); New York, Buchholz Gallery (Curt Valentin), *Early Work by Contemporary Artists,* Nov. 16-Dec. 4, 1943, no. 3 *(The River,* 1906, lent by Lebel); New York, Mortimer Brandt Gallery, *Color and Space in Modern Art Since 1900,* Feb. 19-Mar. 18, 1944, no. 10; Boston, Institute of Modern Art, *Pioneers,* Mar. 28-Apr. 30, 1944, no. 1; The Toledo Museum of Art, *The Spirit of Modern France: An Essay on Painting in Society 1745-1946,* Nov.-Dec. 1946,

---

2. According to a list of exhibitions given by Lebel to Thannhauser. A copy of the catalogue has not been found if, in fact, one existed.

no. 67, traveled to The Art Gallery of Toronto, Jan.-Feb. 1947; Venice, XXV Esposizione Biennale Internazionale d'Arte, *Mostra dei Fauves*, 2nd ed., 1950, no. 6 bis (?)[3] *(Riviera [sic], 1906, coll. Robert Lebel, New York)*; New York, Sidney Janis Gallery, *Les Fauves*, Nov. 13-Dec. 23, 1950, no. 2 *(River, 1906, lent by Lebel)*; The Art Institute of Chicago, on loan from J. K. Thannhauser (correspondence with W. D. Bradway, Dec. 1973), May-Aug. 1955; Pasadena Art Museum, *Georges Braque*, Apr. 20-June 5, 1960, no. 2 *(Landscape, 1906)*.

REFERENCES:

H. H. Arnason, *History of Modern Art*, New York, 1968, pp. 122 and 123, repr.; *Masterpieces*, 1972, p. 78, repr.; E. C. Oppler, *Fauvism Reexamined*, New York, 1976, p. 52, fn. 2 (photo reprint of Ph. D. dissertation, Columbia University, 1969).

3. In a list of exhibitions for the present picture given to Thannhauser, Lebel included the 1950 Biennale exhibition, citing the painting as no. 6 bis. On the other hand, he stated (in correspondence, Mar. 1974) that another Fauve Braque, which he still owns, was exhibited there and the present painting was not. The presence of a sticker from "XXV Biennale Internazionale d'Arte di Venezia—1950" on the reverse of the stretcher of the Thannhauser work would favor the former alternative.

---

2   Teapot on Yellow Ground. 1955
(Théière sur fond jaune)

Oil on canvas, 13¾ x 25⅝ (35 x 65)

Signed at bottom left of center: *G Braque*
Not dated.

PROVENANCE:

Purchased from the artist by Galerie Maeght, Paris, 1955; purchased from Maeght by J. K. Thannhauser, Feb. 1956 (correspondence with N. de Romilly, Mar. 1974).

CONDITION:

The support is sized but unprimed linen. The canvas has tack holes on the top and right sides, and it has been cut on the bottom and left sides. On the reverse is a fragment of a Cubist landscape painted on commercially primed canvas.

Small losses above the handle and spout of the teapot (Jan. 1975).

A related version from the same year is *La Théière grise* (7½ x 23⅝ in., 19 x 60 cm., Galerie Rosengart, Lucerne; Mangin, pl. 99). The still-life arrangement with teapot first appears in 1942 (Mangin, *Catalogue de l'oeuvre de Georges Braque 1942-1947*, Paris, 1960, vol. II, pls. 16-19, 21-24) and recurs from time to time, especially around 1950.

On the reverse of the present picture is an earlier attempt (fig. a) which Nicole de Romilly (formerly Mangin) considers to be almost certainly a work of 1910 (correspondence, Mar. 1976). She does not know of another fragment from the same period used in the same manner. However, throughout his life Braque sometimes painted on the reverse of a canvas he had already begun (correspondence with de Romilly, Mar. 1976).

REFERENCES:

N. Mangin, *Catalogue de l'oeuvre de Georges Braque 1948-1957*, Paris, 1959, vol. I, pl. 98 *(Théière sur fond jaune)*; *Masterpieces*, 1972, p. 79, repr.

fig. a.
Reverse of *Teapot on Yellow Ground*.

Paul Cézanne

Born January 1839, Aix-en-Provence
Died October 1906, Aix-en-Provence

3   Still Life: Flask, Glass and Jug. c. 1877
     *(Fiasque, verre et poterie; La Bouteille
     paillée; La Bouteille treillissée; Le Pichet)*

Oil on canvas, 18 x 21¾ (45.7 x 55.3)

Not signed or dated.

PROVENANCE:

Eugène Murer, Auvers-sur-Oise;[1] purchased
from Murer by Bernheim-Jeune family
collection, Paris, c. 1907 (correspondence
with G. Gruet, May 1977); purchased from
Bernheim-Jeune by Joseph Brochier, Lyons,
probably after 1934;[2] acquired from Brochier by J. K. Thannhauser, c. 1957 (notes by
D. C. Rich from conversation with Thannhauser, Mar. 1975).

CONDITION:

Glue lined at an unknown date before 1965
and edges trimmed. *Pentimenti* reveal that
the rim of the glass has been lowered by approximately one and one-half inches. Indication of reworking in area of jug and flask
(Dec. 1974).

Still Life: Flask, Glass and Jug has been dated c. 1877 by Lionello Venturi, Lawrence
Gowing, John Rewald (correspondence with D. C. Rich, Feb. 1975), Douglas Cooper
(correspondence, Mar. 1977), Robert W. Ratcliffe (correspondence, June 1977), and
Theodore Reff (correspondence, Nov. 1977). At that time Cézanne lived at 67, rue de
l'Ouest in Paris. Georges Rivière was the first to associate the background wallpaper
in the still lifes with the apartment Cézanne occupied in Paris from late 1876 to early
1878 and again for a short while in 1879 (*Cézanne: le peintre solitaire,* Paris, 1933,
p. 126). The present work is included as no. 139 in Vollard's photo archive, where
it is annotated 1874 (Rewald correspondence, Feb. 1975). Rewald finds the Thannhauser still life close in style to two pictures known to have been painted in 1877:
a portrait of Victor Chocquet (Venturi 373) and a still life (Venturi 494; see "A propos
du catalogue raisonné de l'oeuvre de Paul Cézanne et de la chronologie de cette
oeuvre," *La Renaissance,* XXe année, Mar.-Apr. 1937, p. 54).

Venturi (vol. I, p. 112) grouped together five still lifes (nos. 209, 210, 212, 213, and
214) and two portraits of Mme Cézanne (nos. 291 and 292) where the background
wallpaper has the same pattern: a blue lozenge motif repeated on an olive-yellow
background. *The Plate of Apples* (Venturi 210; The Art Institute of Chicago) has the
same dimensions as the present picture. Comparison of the two demonstrates how
the artist adapted the lozenge pattern of the wallpaper to correspond with the composition of the still life. In the Thannhauser still life the lozenges are arranged hori-
zontally and are closer together than in the Chicago painting. Likewise, there are
similar discrepancies between the wallpaper patterns in the *Portrait of Madame
Cézanne* in The Museum of Fine Arts in Boston (Venturi 292; 28½ x 22 in., 72.5
x 56 cm.) and *Madame Cézanne Sewing* in the Nationalmuseum, Stockholm (Venturi 291; 23⅝ x 19⅝ in., 60 x 49.7 cm.).

1. According to J. Rewald (correspondence with D. C. Rich, Feb. 1975), Murer may have acquired the present picture directly from the artist or from his friend Dr. Gachet, who could
   have purchased it from Cézanne. Murer died in 1906.
2. The picture was returned to Josse Bernheim after the exhibition at Alex Reid and Lefevre,
   Ltd., in June 1934 (correspondence with D. L. Corcoran, Aug. 1977).

EXHIBITIONS:

Paris, 1912;[3] London, Alex Reid and Lefevre, Ltd., *Renoir, Cézanne, and Their Contemporaries,* June 1934, no. 3, repr. (*La Bouteille paillée,* 1883); Paris, Bernheim-Jeune, *Quelques Tableux d'Ingres à Gauguin,* June 11-July 13, 1935, no. 3 (acc. to Venturi); Paris, Paul Rosenberg, *Exposition Cézanne organisée à l'occasion de son centenaire,* Feb. 21-Apr. 1, 1939, no. 5, repr. (1877, coll. Joseph Brochier); London, Wildenstein and Co., Ltd., *Homage to Paul Cézanne,* July 1939, no. 20 (correspondence with L. Foster, Nov. 1973); Musée de Lyon, *Centenaire de Paul Cézanne,* 1939, no. 19 and pl. viii; Musée de Lyon, *Exposition de peinture française de l'Impressionisme à nos jours,* May 1942, no. 6; Aix-en-Provence, Musée Granet, *Cézanne,* 1953, no. 7, traveled to Nice; Saint-Etienne, Musée d'Art et d'Industrie, *Nature mortes de Géricault à nos jours,* 1955, no. 15, repr.; Aix-en-Provence, Pavillon de Vendôme, *Exposition pour commemorer le cinquantenaire de la mort de Cézanne,* July 21-Aug. 15, 1956, no. 16, repr. (private coll., Lyons); The Cleveland Museum of Art, summer 1962 (lent by J. K. Thannhauser; correspondence with T. Hinson, Jan. 1974).

REFERENCES:

Paul Cézanne Mappe, Munich, 1912, no. 2 *(Stilleben mit Weinflasche);* A. J. Eddy, *Cubists and Post-Impressionism,* Chicago, 1914, opp. p. 36, repr.; O. Mirbeau et al., *Cézanne,* Paris, Bernheim-Jeune, 1914, pl. xxxv; *L'Art moderne et quelques aspects de l'art d'autrefois: cent-soixante-treize planches d'après la collection privée de MM. J & G. Bernheim-Jeune,* Paris, 1919, vol. I, p. 90 and pl. 31 *(Le Pitchet);* A. Zeisho, *Paul Cézanne,* Tokyo, 1921, pl. 5; J. Meier-Graefe, *Cézanne und sein Kreis,* Munich, 1922, p. 190, repr.; G. Rivière, *Le Maître Paul Cézanne,* Paris, 1923, p. 211 (*La Bouteille treillissée,* 1883); E. Bernard, *Souvenirs sur Paul Cézanne,* Paris, 1926, opp. p. 61, repr.; *Samleren,* vol. 6, no. iii, 1929, p. 138, repr.; C. Z[ervos], "Les Expositions," *Cahiers d'Art,* 9e année, no. 5-8, 1934, p. 127, repr. (*La Bouteille paillée,* 1883); M. Raynal, *Cézanne,* Paris, 1936, pl. lxxxvi; Venturi, 1936, vol. I, p. 113, no. 214, and vol. II, pl. 58 *(Fiasque, verre et poterie,* c. 1877); R. O. Dunlop, "Modern Still Life Painting in Oils," *The Artist,* vol. XIII, May 1937, p. 67, repr.; W. Gaunt, "P. Cézanne: An Essay in Valuation," *The London Studio,* vol. 16, Sept. 1938, p. 148, repr. (*La Bouteille paillée,* 1883); L. Gowing, "Notes on the Development of Cézanne," *The Burlington Magazine,* vol. XCIII, June 1956, p. 188 (1877); R. W. Ratcliffe, *Cézanne's Working Methods and Their Theoretical Background,* Ph. D. dissertation, Courtauld Institute of Art, University of London, 1960, pp. 140, 158, 290, 383 fn. 35, and 430 fn. 151; L. Brion-Guerry, *Cézanne et l'expression de l'espace,* Paris 1966, pp. 91 and 276, no. 21; M. Schapiro, "Les Pommes de Cézanne," *Revue de l'Art,* no. 1-2, 1968, p. 80, fn. 44; A. Gatto and S. Orienti, *L'opera completa di Cézanne,* Milan, 1970, p. 96, repr., no. 212; *Masterpieces,* 1972, p. 18, repr.

3. Rewald (correspondence, Feb. 1975) agrees that the reference might be to *Exposition d'art moderne* at Galerie Manzi-Joyant et Cie., Paris, at an unknown date in 1912 where nos. 1, 3, 12, 13, 20, 21, or 23 could be the present picture (Gordon, 1974, vol. II, p. 530).

4   Still Life: Plate of Peaches. 1879-80
     (Assiette de pêches; L'Assiette bleue)

Oil on canvas, 23½ x 28⅞ (59.7 x 73.3)
Not signed or dated.

PROVENANCE:
Egisto Fabbri, Florence;[1] purchased from
Fabbri by Paul Rosenberg, Paris, 1928 (cor-
respondence with A. Rosenberg, Nov.
1973); acquired from Rosenberg by J. K.
Thannhauser, 1929 (notes, Dec. 1972).

CONDITION:
Glue lined at an unrecorded date before
1965 and margins trimmed. Considerable
reworking in tablecloth and in background.
Especially true in area over table where
there is impasto and visible evidence of four
pieces of fruit that have been painted over
by the artist. The effect of emerging background shapes is augmented by the leaf
wallpaper (Dec. 1974).

1. Egisto Fabbri (1866-1933) was an early collector of Cézanne's work. He lived in Paris for
   many years before returning to Florence late in life. He owned sixteen works as of May
   1899. L. Venturi's catalogue raisonné lists twenty-six paintings that once belonged to
   Fabbri. He probably purchased his Cézannes from Vollard (correspondence with Rewald,
   Feb. 1975 and with Cooper, Mar. 1977).

The background in the present picture is gray-blue wallpaper with sprays of leaves. It occurs in thirteen still lifes (Venturi 337-48 and 353) as well as in the portraits of Louis Guillaume (Venturi 374) and Mme Cézanne (Venturi 369). Lionello Venturi (vol. I, p. 138) stated that the leaf-patterned wallpaper was from either the house in Melun, where Cézanne lived in 1879 and 1880, or from his apartment at 32, rue de l'Ouest, where he lived in 1881 and 1882. No documentary evidence has emerged to resolve the question.

John Rewald thinks that the wallpaper decorated Cézanne's lodgings in Melun (correspondence with D. C. Rich, Feb. 1975). Cézanne was in Melun from April 1879 through March 1880 (Rewald, *Paul Cézanne: A Biography*, New York, 1948, p. 218). Robert W. Ratcliffe places the Thannhauser still life in the winter of 1879-80 (correspondence, June 1977) while Theodore Reff prefers a date of c. 1880 (correspondence, Nov. 1977).

Although Douglas Cooper dates the present picture c. 1879, he thinks that it was painted in Paris, probably in the summer. He refers to similarities with *Bridge at Maincy* (Venturi 396) and to the fact that the latter was painted during the summer of 1879 (correspondence, Mar. 1977). While Maincy is near Paris, it is far closer to Melun. Cézanne's letters give the distinct impression that he was in Melun all summer (Rewald, ed., *Paul Cézanne's Letters,* trans. M. Kay, Oxford, 1946, Letters LXI-LXX, esp. LXV).

EXHIBITIONS:

Paris, Bernheim-Jeune, *Exposition Cézanne*, Jan. 10-22, 1910, no. 20;[2] Venice, XII Esposizione Internazionale d'Arte della città di Venezia, French Pavillion, *Mostra individuale di Cézanne,* 1920, nos. 4, 5, or 6;[3] Basel, Kunsthalle, *Maîtres du XXe siècle,* Sept. 27-Oct. 25, 1931, no. 2 (correspondence with M. Suter, Dec. 1973); The Art Institute of Chicago, *Cézanne,* Feb. 7-Mar. 16, 1952, no. 25, repr., traveled to New York, The Metropolitan Museum of Art, Apr. 1-May 16; Kansas City, William Rockhill Nelson Gallery of Art, *Summer Exhibition,* 1955 (label on reverse); New York, The Solomon R. Guggenheim Museum, *Cézanne and Structure in Modern Painting,* June-Aug. 1963.

REFERENCES:

L. Henraux, "I Cézanne della raccolta Fabbri," *Dedalo,* no. 1, 1920, p. 67, repr.; "La Collection Egisto Fabbri," *L'Amour de l'Art,* Vᵉ année, Nov. 1924, p. 340, repr.; Venturi, 1936, vol. I, p. 113, no. 347, and vol. II, pl. 96 (*Assiette de pêches,* 1879-82; A. Gatto and S. Orienti, *L'opera completa di Cézanne,* Milan, 1970, p. 107, repr., no. 455; *Masterpieces,* 1972, p. 19, repr. (1879-82).

2. According to G. Gruet of Bernheim-Jeune (correspondence, Dec. 1973), it was no. 20 and not 19 as stated in the catalogue.

3. The *Mostra individuale di Cézanne* included twenty-four paintings from the collection of Egisto Fabbri. Comparing the Biennale catalogue to Venturi's catalogue raisonné, all but nos. 4-6 ("*Tre Nature Morte*") and nos. 15, 16, and 22 (landscapes) in the Biennale can be readily identified. Venturi catalogues four still lifes which belonged to Fabbri (193, 220, 221, and 347) of which three must have been in the Biennale. Of the four, only the present picture has a reference to the Biennale in Venturi.

A coeval article on the Fabbri collection in *Dedalo* reproduces fourteen pictures (including the present one). Venturi catalogues each of these as having been exhibited at the Biennale, and all but the Thannhauser painting can be associated with a specific catalogue number. Thus, it seems certain that the present picture was exhibited.

5 Madame Cézanne. 1885-87

Oil on canvas, 21⅞ x 18 (55.6 x 45.7)
Not signed or dated.

PROVENANCE:
Ambroise Vollard, Paris;[1] probably purchased from Vollard by Marie Harriman, New York, by 1933; purchased from Marie Harriman by J. K. Thannhauser, Jan. 1946 (conversation with A. Sardi, July 1974); purchased from Thannhauser by Vladimir Horowitz, New York, 1946-47 (correspondence with B. Stein, Feb. 1974); purchased from Horowitz by The Cincinnati Art Museum, 1947; acquired through exchange by J. K. Thannhauser, 1955 (correspondence with P. R. Adams, Nov. 1973).

CONDITION:
Glue lined at an unknown date prior to 1965 and edges trimmed. Considerable soil on surface (Dec. 1974).

The sitter is Hortense Fiquet, who was to become Mme Cézanne. She was born in 1850 in the region of the Jura Mountains in France near the Swiss border. The artist met her about 1869 in Paris and their son Paul was born there in January 1872 (J. Rewald, "Cézanne and His Father," *Studies in the History of Art,* 1971-72, p. 52). They were married April 28, 1886, in Aix-en-Provence. During the three years before their marriage, Cézanne lived in Provence while Hortense stayed in Paris most of the time, although in 1886 Cézanne spent much of the year with her in Gardanne. The same pattern persisted after their marriage with visits and occasional trips together (J. Rewald, *Paul Cézanne: A Biography,* New York, 1948, pp. 113-14, 131, and 218-19). Photographs of Mme Cézanne at a later age can be found in W. Andersen, *Cézanne's Portrait Drawings,* Cambridge, 1970, p. 113, figs. 91 a and b. Mme Cézanne was buried May 6, 1922, in Père-Lachaise Cemetery, Paris (conversation with Rewald, Oct. 1977).

When they were together Cézanne frequently painted her portrait. These portraits have always been dated on the basis of style in the absence of documentary evidence. A system of dating has also been proposed based on the fashion of Mme Cézanne's clothes, the date a new style appeared providing a *terminus post quem* (Ann H. van Buren, "Madame Cézanne's Fashions and the Dates of Her Portraits," *The Art Quarterly,* vol. XXIX, no. 2, 1966, pp. 111-27). Mme Cézanne wears the navy blue jacket with upright collar which came into fashion in the spring of 1886 in the *Portrait of Mme Cézanne* (Venturi 523; 31¹⁵⁄₁₆ x 25⅝ in., 81 x 65 cm., Musée du Louvre, Galerie du Jeu de Paume, Paris, Bequest of Jean Walter-Paul Guillaume; Paris, Musée de l'Orangerie, exh. cat., 1974, p. 16, color repr. of face), and either the same jacket or a dress with wide vertical pleats in the *Portrait of Mme Cézanne* (Venturi 524; 18⅛ x 15 in., 46 x 38 cm., Collection J. V. Pellerin; van Buren, p. 119). In the Thannhauser sketch (Venturi 525), she appears to wear the same style of dress and hairdo as in the above pictures. Thus, by implication, van Buren would date the present work no earlier than 1886. However, the lack of description in the present work rules out conclusive proof. In the Thannhauser version and in the Pellerin portrait, the artist has painted the sitter's head tipped at a slight angle so that only one ear is visible.

1. Vollard first saw Cézanne's work at Père Tanguy's shop in 1892 and, three years later, gave an exhibition of Cézanne's paintings at his own gallery in the rue Laffitte (G. Rivière, *Le Maître Paul Cézanne,* Paris, 1923, p. 111).
   According to John Rewald, a photograph of the Thannhauser work is not in Vollard's photo archive (correspondence with D. C. Rich, Feb. 1975).

Lionello Venturi dated the present picture 1885-87, the same as the Pellerin work, and gave 1885-90 for the picture in the Walter-Guillaume Bequest. John Rewald suggested a date of c. 1885(?) for the Thannhauser work (correspondence with D. C. Rich, Feb. 1975).

Douglas Cooper (correspondence, Mar. 1977) prefers a date of c. 1883 for the present work and three he relates to it: *Portrait of Mme Cézanne* in the Walter-Guillaume Bequest; *Madame Cézanne in the Conservatory* (Venturi 569; The Metropolitan Museum of Art, New York); and the pencil drawing from page vii of the *Album* owned by Paul Mellon (Venturi 1303; Chappuis, vol. I, p. 246, no. 1068). The Metropolitan's painting has also been dated c. 1890 by Venturi and c. 1891 by Georges Rivière and Rewald.

Rewald (conversation, Oct. 1977) disagrees with suggestions that the Thannhauser picture is a study for the portrait in the Walter-Guillaume Bequest or a reworking of it (Paris, Musée de l'Orangerie, exh. cat. 1966, no. 11, and 1974, no. 35).

EXHIBITIONS:

New York, Marie Harriman Gallery, *French Paintings,* opened Feb. 21, 1933, no. 2 *(Tête de femme)*;[2] Philadelphia, Pennsylvania Museum of Art, *Cézanne,* Nov. 10-Dec. 10, 1934, no. 34[3] *(Head of a Woman,* c. 1890-91, 22 x 18¼ in., lent by Marie Harriman Gallery); San Francisco Museum of Art, *Opening Exhibition,* from Jan. 18, 1935, no. 1[4] *(Head of a Woman,* 1890-91, lent by Marie Harriman Galleries); New York, Marie Harriman Gallery, *Paul Cézanne, André Derain, Walt Kuhn, Henri Matisse, Pablo Picasso, Auguste Renoir, Vincent van Gogh,* Feb. 1936, no. 5 *(Study: Madame Cézanne);* San Francisco Museum of Art, *Paul Cézanne,* Sept. 1-Oct. 4, 1937, no. 22, repr. *(Portrait of Madame Cézanne,* lent by Marie Harriman Gallery); New York, Marie Harriman Gallery, *Cézanne Centennial Exhibition,* Nov. 7- Dec. 2, 1939, no. 12 (1885-87); Lynchburg (Va.), Randolph-Macon Woman's College, *Modern French Paintings,* May 6-June 5, 1940, no. 1 *(Portrait de Mme Cézanne);* Oberlin (Ohio), Allen Memorial Art Museum, *Modern Paintings,* Nov. 1-27, 1940;[5] New York, The Museum of Modern Art, *Advisory Committee Exhibition: Techniques of Painting,* Aug. 4-Oct. 15, 1941 (no cat.; MOMA Registrar's Files 41.1423); New York, Wildenstein and Co., *Cézanne,* Mar. 27-Apr. 26, 1947, no. 38 (lent by Mr. and Mrs. Vladimir Horowitz); Raleigh, The North Carolina Museum of Art, *French Painting of the Last Half of the Nineteenth Century,* June 15-July 29, 1956, repr. (lent by J. K. Thannhauser); New York, The Solomon R. Guggenheim Museum, *Cézanne and Structure in Modern Painting,* June-Aug. 1963.

REFERENCES:

Venturi, 1936, vol. I, p. 177, no. 525, and vol. II, pl. 163 (1885-87); *Cincinnati Art Museum News,* vol. II, no. 7, Nov. 1947, p. i, repr. (1885-87); Paris, Musée de l'Orangerie, *Collection Jean Walter-Paul Guillaume,* exh. cat., 1966, no. 11 (suggests Venturi 524 and 525 are studies for 523); T. Reff, review of "Album de Paul Cézanne," *The Burlington Magazine,* vol. CIX, Nov. 1967, p. 653 (relates Venturi 525 to p. 7 of *Album);* A. Gatto and S. Orienti, *L'opera completa di Cézanne,* Milan, 1970, p. 110, repr., no. 532; *Masterpieces,* 1972, p. 20, repr.; A. Chappuis, *The Drawings of Paul Cézanne: A Catalogue Raisonné,* Greenwich, 1973, vol. I, p. 246, no. 1068 (refers to Reff); Paris, Musée d l'Orangerie, *Cézanne dans les musées nationaux,* exh. cat., 1974, p. 92, no. 35 (Venturi 525 is "esquisse" or "reprise" for 523).

2. Information from Frick Art Reference Library photograph (no. 522-9/c).

3. Confirmed by information on Frick Art Reference Library photograph and in *Cincinnati Art Museum News,* vol. II, no. 7, Nov. 1947, p. i.

4. *Ibid.*

5. *Ibid.*

6   Bibémus. c. 1894-95
*(Bibémus: rochers rouges; Die
roten Felsen bei Gardanne)*

Oil on canvas, 28⅛ x 35⅜ (71.5 x 89.8)

Not signed or dated.

PROVENANCE:
Ambroise Vollard, Paris; purchased from
Vollard by J. K. Thannhauser, Nov. 1929
(notes by D. C. Rich from conversation with
Thannhauser, Mar. 1975).

CONDITION:
Glue lined at an unknown date prior to
1965 and edges trimmed. Smoothly and
very thinly painted, with drawing visible.
At upper left, unpainted areas in sky (Dec.
1974).

Discussion of the present picture focuses on the questions of where and when the landscape was painted. Lionello Venturi identified the site as Bibémus. John Rewald (correspondence with D. C. Rich, Feb. 1975) thinks that the landscape resembles the area, and Robert W. Ratcliffe (correspondence, June 1977) agrees that it recalls the terrain. By now the foliage has grown so as to obscure the sites around the Bibémus quarry, and even in the late 1920s Erle Loran found it difficult to photograph them.

The rugged and remote area of Bibémus lies a short distance to the east of Aix-en-Provence off the road to Vauvenarges. It is slightly north of Le Château Noir and Le Tholonet (see J. Rewald, "The Last Motifs at Aix," in *Cézanne: The Late Work,* exh. cat., The Museum of Modern Art, New York, 1977, pp. 93-97). The quarry, which was abandoned when Cézanne painted there, is said to date from Roman times (E. Loran [Johnson], "Cézanne's Country," *The Arts,* vol. XVI, Apr. 1930, pp. 520-51). One of Loran's photographs bears a strong resemblance to the Thannhauser painting (*Cézanne's Composition: Analysis of His Form with Diagrams and Photographs of His Motifs,* Berkeley and Los Angeles, 1959, p. 113).

With the probable identification of the landscape as Bibémus, the question of date arises since Cézanne's first recorded payment of rent for a hut at the quarry dates from November 1, 1895. Evidence compiled by Ratcliffe would place the artist's work at Bibémus between that date and September 1899 (*Cézanne's Working Methods and Their Theoretical Background,* Ph.D. dissertation, Courtauld Institute of Art, University of London, 1960, pp. 22-26). Yet Cézanne certainly could have painted in the area of the Bibémus quarry before the autumn of 1895. Furthermore, Rewald (conversation, Oct. 1977) points out that it is impossible to know if the rent paid November 1, 1895, was for past or future use of the hut and even if it was actually the first payment Cézanne made. Rewald dates the Thannhauser picture c. 1894 (correspondence, Feb. 1975) allowing that it could have been painted in 1895 (conversation, Oct. 1977).

Ratcliffe (correspondence, June 1977) tentatively places the Thannhauser picture not later than 1896-97. He finds it close in style to *Arbre et pigeonnier provençal* (Venturi 300; Boerlage collection, Laren), which is painted from the plateau that is pierced by the Bibémus quarry, and to *Le Rocher rouge* (Venturi 776; Collection Jean Walter-Paul Guillaume, Musée du Louvre, Paris). Theodore Reff also dates the present picture 1895-97 (correspondence, Nov. 1977).

In his catalogue, Venturi listed nine works as representing Bibémus (nos. 767, 772, 773, 777, 778, 781, 782, 785, and 786). He dates none earlier than 1898 and most, including the present picture, c. 1900.

The Thannhauser landscape is closely related to *Corner of Quarry* in The Barnes Foundation, Merion, Pa. (Venturi 782; 17¾ x 21½ in., 45.1 x 54.6 cm.) with which it shares similar palette, brushwork, and terrain. Similarities in style can also be detected in the upper portion of *Bibémus Quarry* (Venturi 767; Museum Folkwang, Essen), which Rewald considers one of Cézanne's earliest views of the quarry (*Cézanne: The Late Work,* p. 390, no. 11).

In contrast, Douglas Cooper (correspondence, Mar. 1975) thinks that the Thannhauser painting does not represent Bibémus. He finds the subject, palette, and style close to Renoir and prefers a date of 1883-84, soon after Cézanne worked with Renoir in the south of France in 1882-83. Cooper places the present picture with *Le Grand pin et les terres rouges* (Venturi 459; Lecomte collection, Paris) and *La Ferme au Jas de Bouffan* (Venturi 461), both of which he dates c. 1885, and *Edge of a Wood in Provence* (Venturi 446; National Museum of Wales, Cardiff), which he dates slightly later.

EXHIBITIONS:

Frankfurt, Städelsches Kunstinstitut, *Von Abbild zum Sinnbild,* June 3-July 3, 1931, no. 25 (*Die roten Felsen bei Gardanne,* lent by Galerie Thannhauser; correspondence with P. Eich, Nov. 1973); Paris, Grand Palais, Société des Artistes Indépendants, *Centenaire du peintre indépendant Paul Cézanne,* Mar. 17-Apr. 10, 1939, no. 47 *(Bibémus: rochers rouges);* Musée de Lyon, *Centenaire de Paul Cézanne,* 1939, no. 37 *(Rochers rouges à Bibémus);* Adelaide, The National Art Gallery, *Exhibition of French and British Contemporary Art,* opened Aug. 21, 1939, no. 24 *(Rochers rouges à Bibémus,* c. 1900), traveled to Melbourne, Town Hall, opened Oct. 16, and Sydney, David Jones, opened Nov. 20;[1] The Art Institute of Chicago, *Cézanne,* Feb. 7-Mar. 16, 1952, no. 105, repr. *(Bibémus,* c. 1900), traveled to New York, The Metropolitan Museum of Art, Apr. 1-May 16; San Francisco Museum of Art, *Art in the 20th Century: Commemorating the Tenth Anniversary of the Signing of the United Nations Charter,* June 17-July 10, 1955, p. 5, repr.; New York, The Solomon R. Guggenheim Museum, *Cézanne and Structure in Modern Painting,* June-Aug. 1963.

REFERENCES:

Venturi, 1936, vol. I, p. 232, no. 781, and vol. II, pl. 258 *(Bibémus,* c. 1900); A. Gatto and S. Orienti, *L'opera completa di Cézanne,* Milan, 1970, p. 118, repr., no. 709; *Masterpieces,* 1972, p. 21, repr. (1900); T. Reff, "Painting and Theory in the Final Decade," in *Cézanne: The Late Work,* exh. cat., The Museum of Modern Art, New York, 1977, p. 24.

1. The exhibition was brought to Adelaide by *The Advertiser* and the French section was arranged under the auspices of the *Association française d'action artistique.* Information on the exhibition has kindly been provided by R. Appleyard (Nov. 1973 and June 1975) and A. Dixon (Nov. 1973).

After Honoré Daumier

7   The Chess Players
(Les Joueurs d'échecs; Schachspieler)

Oil on cradled wood panel, 9⅝ x 13
(24.4 x 33)
Signed l.l.: *h. Daumier*   Not dated.

PROVENANCE:

Collection Weiler, Frankfurt (J. K. Thannhauser notes, Dec. 1972); Galerie Caspari,
Munich (acc. to Thannhauser); Moderne
Galerie (Heinrich Thannhauser), Munich,
by 1918.

CONDITION:

Under strong light, an area over the head of
each man is significantly darker than rest of
background. An X-ray of the area revealed
an earlier composition in which the men's
heads were approximately one inch higher.
The placement of the chessmen and the
hand at the bottom edge of the painting co-
incides in both the visible painted surface
and in the painted sketch revealed by X-ray
(Jan. 1975).

The painting is an almost exact copy of *The Chess Players* in the Musée du Petit Palais, Paris (oil on wood panel, 9⅝ x 12¾ in., 24.5 x 32.5 cm., signed l.l.: h. Daumier; Maison, no. I-168; R. Rey, *Honoré Daumier,* New York, 1965, p. 137, color repr.). It was in the Musée des Beaux-Arts de la Ville de Paris in 1899 and is dated 1864-65 by Karl Eric Maison (p. 143).

Maison includes the present picture with "sketches and unfinished paintings by Daumier either definitely or probably completed by later hands" (p. 183). He explains that "the painting is listed here because of the possibility that it was completed from a thinly laid-on authentic sketch which Daumier discarded" (p. 200). See above CONDITION. At the present time it has not been possible to identify with certainty the authorship of the sketch or the completed painting.

EXHIBITIONS:

Berlin, Künstlerhaus (organized by the Galerien Thannhauser), *Erste Sonderausstellung in Berlin,* Jan. 9-Feb. 15, 1927, no. *63 (Schachspieler);* Raleigh, The North Carolina Museum of Art, *French Painting of the Last Half of the Nineteenth Century,* June 15-July 29, 1956 [p. 10], repr.

REFERENCES:

Munich, Moderne Galerie (Heinrich Thannhauser), *Nachtragswerk III,* 1918, pp. 8, repr., and 118 *(Schachspieler);* E. Klossowski, *Honoré Daumier,* Munich, 1923, p. 118, no. 350A, and pl. 120 ("Genaue Wiederholung" of Paris *Chess Players);* H. Osborn, "Klassiker der Französischen Moderne," *Deutsche Kunst und Dekoration,* vol. 59, Mar. 1927, p. 334; *Kunst und Künstler,* Jg. 25, Mar. 1927, p. 224, repr.; E. Fuchs, *Der Maler Daumier,* Munich, 1927, p. 47 ("eine Wiederholung im Besitz von Heinr. Thannhauser"); London, Tate Gallery (organized by the Arts Council of Great Britain), *Daumier,* exh. cat., 1961, p. 33 (under no. 34: "painting identical in subject and size is in the J. K. Thannhauser Collection"); K. E. Maison, *Honoré Daumier,* Greenwich, 1968, vol. I, pp. 199-200, no. II-31, and pl. 192 (" a very nearly exact replica of I-168"); *Masterpieces,* 1972, p. 9, repr. (c. 1863).

Hilaire-Germain-Edgar Degas

Born July 1834, Paris
Died September 1917, Paris

8

8   Dancer Moving Forward, Arms Raised.
1882-95
*(Danseuse s'avançant, les bras levés;
Tänzerin vorschreitend, Arme erhoben)*

Bronze, height 13¾ (35)

Signature incised at left side of base: *Degas;*
stamp of the founder in relief on base near
model's right foot: CIRE PERDUE/A.A.
HEBRARD; incised identifying mark near
model's right foot: 19.   Not dated.
                          ――
                          D

PROVENANCE:

Galerie Hébrard, Paris; Walther Halvorsen[1]
(notes by J. K. Thannhauser, Dec. 1972);
J. K. Thannhauser, probably 1926.

After Degas' death, about one hundred and fifty pieces of sculpture were found scattered about his atelier. Ranging in date from the 1870s to 1911, many of the models had been executed in wax or wax and plastilene and occasionally in clay. Many of the sculptures were in pieces and needed restoration, and half of them were damaged beyond repair (see Millard, 1976, pp. 25-26). None had been cast in bronze during the artist's lifetime and only three in plaster. Soon after the discovery, a decision was made to have seventy-three wax statues cast in bronze. These wax figures were taken to the cellar of the founder Adrien A. Hébrard (Millard, 1976, pp. 30-32). At the end of World War I, Hébrard's master founder, Albino Palazzolo, returned from his native Italy and prepared the waxes for casting. The casting was done according to a variation of the lost-wax *(cire-perdue)* method so that the originals were not destroyed. Work was probably begun toward the end of 1919.

Jean Adhémar described the process as follows: "Palazzolo covered the figures with earth, then he enveloped the whole with a coat of plaster, then he removed the earth and poured in its place a specially prepared gelatine, which he then allowed to harden, thus obtaining a gelatine mold. He extracted the original wax figures unharmed and poured wax into the mold reinforcing it with a central core of sand. The duplicate wax figure, being expendable, was cast by the ordinary lost-wax method with the advantage that the resulting bronze cast could be compared with Degas' original wax and given the same tone and finish" ("Before the Degas Bronzes," trans. M. Scolari, *Art News,* vol. 54, Nov. 1955, p. 70). Most of the extant original wax figures came to light in 1955 and belong to Paul Mellon, Upperville, Virginia (sixty-four waxes); he gave four additional ones to the Louvre.

The founders decided to make a bronze master cast (marked *modèle*) from each duplicate wax figurine (first mentioned by Adhémar, 1955, p. 70). The entire set of master casts remained with Hébrard's heirs until 1976, when it was exhibited at the Lefevre Gallery in London and acquired by The Norton Simon Museum of Art, Pasadena.

1. According to his widow, Halvorsen destroyed all his correspondence before his death in 1972. She remembers that her husband sold the remainder of his collection to Flechtheim, Berlin, before leaving Paris in 1920 (correspondence with Anita Halvorsen, Nov. 1976). It appears likely that the bronzes went from Halvorsen to Flechtheim and/or Thannhauser c. 1926. It is not known whether Halvorsen owned the complete set D. Bronze nos. 23, 52, 65, 68, and 72 from set D belonged to Halvorsen and then Thannhauser (see New York, Parke Bernet, *Modern and Other French Paintings,* Apr. 12, 1945) as well as bronze nos. 20 and 46 (cat. nos. 9 and 10).

From each master cast twenty-two casts were made: twenty were for sale, lettered A to T, and two were reserved for the founder and Degas' heirs. The bronzes marked *modèle* are generally one percent larger, vary slightly in their markings, and have more clearly defined forms and crisper details than those of other casts (conversation with Arthur Beale, July 1977). This practice of *surmoulage,* making a cast from another cast, was common in the nineteenth century.

One complete set of bronzes was ready for exhibition at the Galerie A. A. Hébrard in May 1921 (Millard, 1976, p. 33). The titles by which the statuettes are known were assigned at this time by Hébrard and Joseph Durand-Ruel with the assistance of Paul-Albert Bartholomé (Millard, 1976, p. 5, fn. 13). Yet Palazzolo recalled that all casting was not completed until 1932 (Adhémar, p. 70).

Nearly complete or intact lettered sets can be found at The Metropolitan Museum of Art, New York (A); Musée du Louvre, Galerie du Jeu de Paume, Paris (P); Ny Carlsberg Glyptotek, Copenhagen (R); and the Museu de Arte, São Paulo.

The present work (like cat. nos. 9 and 10) belongs to set D. *Dancer Moving Forward, Arms Raised* bears bronze number 19. It has been dated within the middle range, 1882-95, of Degas' sculptures by John Rewald and Charles Millard (1971, Appendix I, c. 1889). Michèle Beaulieu dates it c. 1898-1900 on the basis of a group of pastels of dancers in the same pose (Lemoisne 1336-39 and 1386-90). Theodore Reff thinks that pastels and sculptures cannot reliably be given coeval dates (conversation, Apr. 1977). In this case, it appears that Degas modeled the figure in wax before treating the pose several times in pastel.

Degas represented full-length female figures without ballet costumes, with the left leg forward and both arms raised, in a charcoal drawing entitled *Trois danseuses en maillot, les bras levés* (30¾ x 20⅛ in., 78 x 51 cm., Second Sale of Degas' Studio, Dec. 11-13, 1918, no. 259). Degas' *impression,* or counterproof, of *Deux femmes nues, les bras levés* (25⅝ x 16¹⁵⁄₁₆ in., 65 x 43 cm., Fourth Sale of Degas' Studio, July 2-4, 1919, no. 350; Rewald, 1944, p. 76, repr.) displays similar figures, although the right leg assumes a forward position.

The attitude of the present statue is found in a larger version, *Dancer Moving Forward, Arms Raised, Right Leg Forward* (bronze no. 72, Rewald no. xxvi). Hébrard identified the latter as "second state," a distinction that Rewald chose not to adopt (1944, p. 16).

As to Degas' source, Millard finds the statuette similar in pose to the Naples *Dancing Faun* and suggests that Degas may have known smaller-scale plaster casts like that owned by Gustave Moreau as well as the original statue (1976, p. 69).

Attempts were made in the casting process to retain the color of the wax originals. While the bronze marked *modèle* has a decidedly greenish-black color, it is less evident in the present work.

EXHIBITIONS:
Berlin, Galerie Flechtheim, *Das Plastische Werk von Edgar Degas,* May 1926, no. 18 (*Tänzerin vorschreitend, Arme erhoben* [Erster Zustand]), traveled to Munich, Moderne Galerie (Thannhauser), July-Aug., and Dresden, Galerie Arnold, Sept.

REFERENCES:
C. Glaser and W. Hausenstein, *Das Plastische Werk von Edgar Degas,* Berlin, 1926, p. 13, no. 18 (*Danseuse s'avançant, les bras levés* [Premier état]); Rewald, 1944, pp. 22 and 76, repr., no. xxiv (1882-95); New York, M. Knoedler and Co., *Edgar Degas: Original Wax Sculp-*

tures, exh. cat., 1955, no. 24 (wax original); Rewald, 1956, p. 146, no. xxiv, and fig. 8 (original: greenish-black wax); M. Beaulieu, "Les Sculptures de Degas: Essai de chronologie," *Revue du Louvre,* 19ᵉ année, no. 6, 1969, p. 377, fn. 69; Paris, Musée de l'Orangerie, *Degas: Oeuvres du Musée du Louvre,* exh. cat. by M. Beaulieu, 1969, no. 268 (c. 1898-1900; another cast); C. W. Millard, *The Sculpture of Edgar Degas,* Ph.D. dissertation, Harvard University, 1971, p. 126, fig. 100, and Appendix I (author gives date of 1889); *Masterpieces,* 1972, p. 13, repr.; London, The Lefevre Gallery, *The Complete Sculptures of Degas,* exh. cat., 1976, p. 37, repr., no. 18 (*modèle* cast); C. W. Millard, *The Sculpture of Edgar Degas,* Princeton, 1976, p. 69 and fig. 97.

---

9   Spanish Dance. 1896-1911
     (Danse espagnole; Spanischer Tanz)

Bronze, height 16 (40.5)

Signature incised at left side of base: *Degas;* stamp of the founder in relief on base near model's left foot: CIRE PERDUE/A.A.HEB-RARD; incised identifying mark near model's left foot: 20. Not dated.
     D

PROVENANCE:
Galerie Hébrard, Paris; Walther Halvorsen (see cat. no. 8, fn. 1); J. K. Thannhauser, probably 1926.

Spanish Dance is not the artist's title. As indicated in cat. no. 8, all titles for Degas' sculpture (with the exception of *Little Dancer*) were decided upon by Adrien A. Hébrard and Joseph Durand-Ruel with the help of Paul-Albert Bartholomé at the time the bronzes were first exhibited at the Galerie Hébrard in 1921 (C. W. Millard, *The Sculpture of Edgar Degas,* Princeton, 1976, p. 5, fn. 13).

There is another version of the *Spanish Dance* (bronze no. 45, Rewald no. xlvii) which is an inch higher and smoother in execution than the present statuette. Degas had the larger version (height 17 in., 43.2 cm.) cast in plaster around 1900 (see Rewald, 1944, p. 104, and Millard, 1976, fig. 73). Hébrard referred to the present one (bronze no. 20) as the first state and the other one (bronze no. 45) as the second state. John Rewald considers the present version to date from 1896-1911 because of its rather summary but expressive treatment of the surface. He places the larger *Spanish Dance* earlier, from the years 1882-95 (Rewald, 1944, pp. 16 and 25).

Degas first treated the pose of the *Spanish Dance* in the mid-1880s not only in sculpture but also in pastels (Lemoisne 689, *Danseuse espagnole* and Lemoisne 690, *Danseuse au tambourin;* both are dated c. 1882). A charcoal drawing (23⅝ x 18⅛ in., 60 x 46 cm., present whereabouts unknown; Rewald, 1944, p. 131, repr., and T. Reff, "The Degas of Detroit," *Bulletin of the Detroit Institute of Arts,* vol. 53, no. 1, 1974, p. 41, where it is dated c. 1890) shows the figure in both front and back views; another drawing is a study for the legs (present whereabouts unknown; Millard, 1976, fig. 74). In the bronze the dancer's right leg is longer than the left.

Millard (1976, p. 67) suggests a variety of sources for the pose of Degas' *Spanish Dance:* the Herculaneum bronze of a *Dancer* in Naples; the *Marsyas* from the Lateran Museum, Rome; and the standard representation of Siva Nataraja popularized by Indian bronzes. He gives the statuette a date of after 1890 (correspondence, Aug. 1977).

See cat. no. 8 for general information about Degas' bronzes.

EXHIBITIONS:

Berlin, Galerie Flechtheim, *Das Plastische Werk von Edgar Degas,* May 1926, no. 16 (*Spanischer Tanz* [Erster Zustand]), traveled to Munich, Moderne Galerie (Thannhauser), July-Aug., and Dresden, Galerie Arnold, Sept.; Houston, Museum of Fine Arts, *House of Art,* Oct. 17-Nov. 28, 1954, no. 65, repr. (*Danse espagnole,* lent by J. K. Thannhauser).

REFERENCES:

C. Glaser and W. Hausenstein, *Das Plastische Werk von Edgar Degas,* Berlin, 1926, p. 13, no. 16 (*Danse espagnole* [Premier état]); Rewald, 1944, pp. 27 and 130, repr., no. lxvi (1896-1911); New York, M. Knoedler and Co., *Edgar Degas: Original Wax Sculptures,* exh. cat., 1955, no. 62, repr. (wax original); Rewald, 1956, p. 156, no. lxvi, and pl. 51 (original: greenish wax, pieces of wire appear in left hand); M. Beaulieu, "Les Sculptures de Degas: Essai de chronologie," *Revue du Louvre,* 19ᵉ année, no. 6, 1969, p. 375; Paris, Musée de l'Orangerie, *Degas: Oeuvres du Musée du Louvre,* exh. cat. by M. Beaulieu, 1969, no. 254 (1882; another cast); C. W. Millard, *The Sculpture of Edgar Degas,* Ph.D. dissertation, Harvard University, 1971, Appendix I (1892); *Masterpieces,* 1972, p. 16, repr.; London, The Lefevre Gallery, *The Complete Sculptures of Degas,* exh. cat., 1976, p. 35, repr., no. 16 (*modèle* cast).

10   Seated Woman Wiping Her Left Side.

1896-1911

*(Femme assise, s'essuyant le côté gauche;
Frau im Sessel Sitzend, sich die linke Seite
trocknend)*

Bronze, height 13¾ (35)

Signature incised on base near model's left
foot: *Degas;* stamp of the founder in relief
on base in back of chair: CIRE PERDUE/
A.A. HEBRARD; incised identifying mark also
on base in back of chair: 46. Not dated.

D

PROVENANCE:

Galerie Hébrard, Paris; Walther Halvorsen
(see cat. no. 8, fn. 1); J. K. Thannhauser,
probably 1926.

Degas' sculptural series of seated women bathing and drying themselves is generally placed late in his career. John Rewald dates this group 1896-1911, and Charles Millard tentatively proposes more precise dates within this time span (see New York, The Metropolitan Museum of Art, *Degas in the Metropolitan,* exh. checklist, 1977).

The present work (bronze no. 46) resembles the sculpture *Seated Woman Wiping Her Left Hip* (bronze no. 54, Rewald no. lxxi; dated 1896-1911 by Rewald and 1900-1912 by Millard). However, in the latter, the support on which she sits is clearly defined as a chair; in addition, the woman's pose is slightly different from the Thannhauser version, especially noticeable in the placement of the head.

The sitter's pose closely resembles an earlier pastel, *Femme s'essuyant* (Lemoisne 886; 21⅝ x 28 in., 55 x 71 cm., Collection James Archdale, Birmingham, England; Cooper, no. 25, color repr.), which is dated c. 1886 by Paul André Lemoisne and Douglas Cooper. Degas executed another version in pastel c. 1895, *Après le bain* (Lemoisne 1179; 32¼ x 28 in., 82 x 71 cm., The Hermitage, Leningrad).

While two-dimensional representations frequently predate their sculptural counterparts (Millard, 1976, p. 46, fn. 19), such a general observation is not without exception (see cat. no. 8).

EXHIBITIONS:

Berlin, Galerie Flechtheim, *Das Plastische Werk von Edgar Degas,* May 1926, no. 67 *(Frau im Sessel Sitzend, sich die linke Seite trocknend),* traveled to Munich, Moderne Galerie (Thannhauser), July-Aug. and Dresden, Galerie Arnold, Sept.; New York, Buchholz Gallery (Curt Valentin), *Degas: Bronzes, Drawings, Pastels,* Jan. 3-27, 1945, no. 48 *(Seated Woman,* Rewald no. lxix).

REFERENCES:

C. Glaser and W. Hausenstein, *Das Plastische Werk von Edgar Degas,* Berlin, 1926, p. 15, no. 67 *(Femme assise dans un fauteuil s'essuyant le côté gauche);* A. Zweig, "Degas als Plastiker," *Der Querschnitt,* Jg. VI, 1926, opp. p. 177, repr.; Rewald, 1944, pp. 28 and 135, repr., no. lxix (1896-1911); D. Cooper, *Pastels d'Edgar Degas,* Basel, 1952, p. 25 (after 1895); New York, M. Knoedler and Co., *Edgar Degas: Original Wax Sculptures,* exh. cat., 1955, no. 65, repr. (wax original); Rewald, 1956, p. 157, no. lxix, and pls. 85, 86, 87, 88 (original: red wax with large pieces of cork and wood visible from behind); Paris, Musée de l'Orangerie, *Degas: Oeuvres du Musée du Louvre,* exh. cat. by M. Beaulieu, 1969, no. 287 *(Femme assise s'essuyant la hanche gauche,* c. 1884; another cast); *Masterpieces,* 1972, p. 17, repr.; London, The Lefevre Gallery, *The Complete Sculptures of Degas,* exh. cat., 1976, p. 84, repr., no. 67 *(modèle* cast); C. W. Millard, *The Sculpture of Edgar Degas,* Princeton, 1976, p. 109 and pl. 133 (another cast).

11   Dancer in Repose. c. 1897-1900
      (Danseuse au repos; Danseuse en jaune)

Pastel on laid paper, 21⁵⁄₁₆ x 17⅜
(54.1 x 44.1)

Black signature stamp l.l.:[1] *degas*   Not
dated.

PROVENANCE:

Included in the Second Sale of Degas'
Studio, Paris, Galerie Georges Petit, *Cata-*
logue des tableaux, pastels et dessins par
Edgar Degas et provenant de son atelier,
Dec. 11-13, 1918, no. 361 *(Danseuse en*
jaune); purchased at sale by Gustave Pellet,
Paris;[2] inherited by Pellet's son-in-law,
Maurice Exteens, Paris, c. 1919; acquired
from Exteens by J. K. Thannhauser, c. 1929.

Dancer in Repose is the mirror image of a pastel (fig. a) in the Cone Collection at the
Baltimore Museum of Art (Lemoisne 1302). In the Baltimore version, the dancer's
bodice is blue and her skirt yellow and green; however, both have orange highlights.
The model's hair is red and her tights are lavender. The column is orange and the
background is quite red as opposed to the yellow-green coloration of the present
work.

fig. a.
Degas, *Dancer,* c. 1897-1900, pastel on paper,
22 x 17¾ in., 55.9 x 45.1 cm., The Baltimore
Museum of Art, The Cone Collection, formed
by Dr. Claribel and Miss Etta Cone of
Baltimore, Maryland.

1. The signature stamp was used on works in Degas' studio sales with black ink for the *im-*
   pressions.
2. Pellet (1859-1919) was Toulouse-Lautrec's publisher and printer. He acquired many works
   at the Degas sales. At the time of his death, Pellet left his collection and publishing business
   to his son-in-law (sale cat. of Klipstein et Kornfeld, Bern, *Archives de la maison Gustave*
   Pellet, May 24, 1962).

The reversal may be accounted for by the fact that the Thannhauser version is an *impression*, or counterproof, made by transfer. A pastel or charcoal drawing is placed on another sheet of paper, both are put in a press, and a fainter replica of the original is transferred to the clean sheet, producing a base for the addition of more pastel. The artist often retouched the original work with more pastel as well (see Rouart, p. 63, and T. Reff, *Degas: The Artist's Mind,* New York, 1967, p. 282).

At the time of the studio sale in 1918, the present work was listed under "Impressions en couleurs retouchées par Edgar Degas." However, Paul André Lemoisne catalogued it incorrectly as "pastel sur monotype" (vol. III, no. 1303). Eugenia Parry Janis has pointed out that the Thannhauser example does not have a plate mark, but that the paper support does have fine creases (at center right) indicating the use of a press and a transfer process. Furthermore, she finds the work too late in date to correspond to the monotype period and too large in scale (correspondence with E. P. Janis, Mar. 1976).

In view of the fact that there are several studies for the pastel in the Cone Collection (Lemoisne 1299, 1300, 1300 bis, and 1301), it was probably executed first, and the Thannhauser pastel seems to be a counterproof taken from it (confirmed by Janis in correspondence, Apr. 1977). Furthermore, in the present work, the outlines are less distinct than in the Baltimore version. Degas depicted the pose of the dancer in the Cone Collection pastel about 1894 (Lemoisne 1158) and returned to it about 1901 (Lemoisne 1398).

Other pastels reversing a pose and related by the same technical method are *Danseuse assise* (Lemoisne 1203) and *Danseuse au repos* (Lemoisne 1203 bis). Like the Thannhauser pastel they can be dated in the mid to late 1890s, when Degas experimented with counterproofs.

REFERENCES:

D. Rouart, *Degas à la recherche de sa technique,* Paris, 1945, p. 74, fn. 89; Lemoisne, 1946, vol. III, pp. 758 and 759, repr., no. 1303 (pastel sur monotype, c. 1897-1900); L. Browse, *Degas Dancers,* New York, 1949, p. 402 and pl. 203 (*Danseuse en jaune assise,* c. 1890-1900); F. Russoli and F. Minervino, *L'opera completa di Degas,* Milan, 1970, p. 136 (compared with Lemoisne 1302; 1897-1900); *Masterpieces,* 1972, p. 14, repr.

12   Dancers in Green and Yellow. c. 1903
(Danseuses vertes et jaunes; Four Dancers;
Quatre danseuses; Vier Tänzerinnen)

Pastel on several pieces of paper mounted on board, 38⅞ x 28⅛ (98.8 x 71.5)

Red signature stamp l.l.:[1] *degas*   Not dated.

PROVENANCE:
Included in the First Sale of Degas' Studio, Paris, Galerie Georges Petit, *Catalogue des tableaux, pastels et dessins par Edgar Degas et provenant de son atelier,* May 6-8, 1918, no. 167 *(Danseuses [Jupes vertes et jaunes]);* purchased at sale by Paul Rosenberg, Paris

(conversation with A. Rosenberg, Feb. 1977); acquired by J. K. Thannhauser, probably by 1926.

CONDITION:
Large piece of paper (32¼ x 26¾ in., 82 x 68 cm.) was cut by hand at left edge. Strips of the same kind of paper were added: four inches at the top and one and one-quarter inches at the bottom. The pastel has not been fixed, and it appears to have been done in a wet technique (Jan. 1975).

The composition of four dancers waiting in a line in the wings occurs several times around 1903 in Degas' pastels and drawings. The Thannhauser example is decidedly more vertical in format than the other six pastels closely related to it. They are *Quatre danseuses* (Lemoisne 1431 bis; 31½ x 35¼ in., 80 x 89.6 cm.; Paris, Galerie Schmit, *Degas,* exh. cat., 1975, no. 46, color repr.); *Quatre danseuses* (Lemoisne 1431 ter; 33 x 28¾ in., 84 x 73 cm.; D. C. Rich, *Degas,* New York, 1951, p. 127, color repr.); *Quatre danseuses* (Lemoisne 1432; 36¼ x 31½ in., 92 x 80 cm.; Lemoisne, vol. III, p. 819, repr.); *Danseuses (Jupes jaunes)* (Lemoisne 1433; 32¼ x 36¼ in., 82 x 92 cm.; P. Cabanne, *Edgar Degas,* Paris and New York, 1958, no. 148, repr.); *Danseuses* (Lemoisne 1434; 29½ x 24 in., 75 x 61 cm.; Basel, Galerie Beyeler, *Autour de l'Impressionisme,* exh. cat., 1966, no. 12, color repr.); and *Quatre danseuses dans les coulisses* (Lemoisne 1435; 37½ x 31½ in., 95 x 80 cm.; Lemoisne, vol. III, p. 821, repr.). Of the works in this group, Degas has added strips of paper at the top and bottom only to the present work and to *Quatre danseuses dans les coulisses* (clearly visible in a photograph at Durand-Ruel, Paris).

Among the related versions listed above, *Danseuses (Jupes jaunes)* appears to be closest to the present work not only because of the dancers' yellow and orange skirts but because of the identical position of the dancers' arms and legs. A charcoal drawing of *Trois danseuses en maillot* (33⅞ x 30 in., 86 x 76 cm., Collection Durand-Ruel, Paris; First Degas Sale, May 6-8, 1918, no. 318, and L. Browse, *Degas Dancers,* New York, 1949, no. 250, repr.) is perhaps a sketch for the present work. This drawing contains visible evidence of how the artist has rubbed out the charcoal in places to alter the dancers' poses so that they correspond with the poses found in the Thannhauser pastel. In this drawing and a close variant (First Degas Sale, May 6-8, 1918, no. 319, repr.) the dancers wear only *maillots* rather than the costumes found in the present picture.

1. A stamp of Degas' signature was used with red ink on pastels and drawings included in the studio sales held after the artist's death.

Daniel Catton Rich agreed with Paul André Lemoisne's date of c. 1903 (conversation, May 1976). In contrast, Lillian Browse would appear to place it later since she dates the charcoal drawing discussed above 1905-12 and places within the same years a pastel, *Trois danseuses dans les coulisses,* in The Museum of Modern Art, New York (Browse no. 231 and Lemoisne 1429, where it is dated 1903). A definitive chronology of Degas' late work has yet to be established.

EXHIBITIONS:

Munich, Moderne Galerie (Thannhauser), *Edgar Degas: Pastelle, Zeichnungen, Das Plastische Werk,* July-Aug. 1926, no. 20[2] *(Vier Tänzerinnen);* Lucerne, Galerie Thannhauser, *Mâitres français du XIXe siècles,* 1927, no. 72.[3]

REFERENCES:

Lemoisne, 1946, vol. III, p. 818 and 819, repr., no. 1431 *(Danseuses vertes et jaunes [Quatre danseuses],* c. 1903); F. Russoli and F. Minervino, *L'opera completa di Degas,* Milan, 1970, p. 137, repr., no. 1149 (c. 1903); *Masterpieces,* 1972, p. 15, repr.

2. J. K. Thannhauser (notes, Dec. 1972) confirmed this reference.

3. According to J. K. Thannhauser's notes. No catalogue has been located, and it is not known if one was even produced.

André Derain

Born June 1880, Chatou
Died September 1954, Garches (Seine-et-Oise)

13   Still Life: Fruit. c. 1925
      (Nature morte: fruits)

Oil on paper mounted on canvas, 5⅞ x 13⅜
(15 x 34)

Signed l.r.: *a derain*   Not dated.

PROVENANCE:
J. K. Thannhauser, probably since late
1920s.[1]

CONDITION:
Support is thin reddish-pink paper mounted
on canvas which, in turn, has probably been
lined with a second canvas at an unknown
date before 1965. Painted surface has taken
on texture of canvas (Jan. 1975).

The *Still Life* can be placed with others of grapes and pears that Derain painted in the
mid-1920s: for example, *Still Life with Glass of Wine* (14⅛ x 19¾ in., 36 x 50 cm., c.
1925; Paris, Musée de l'Orangerie, *Collection Jean Walter-Paul Guillaume,* exh. cat.,
1966, no. 72, repr.).

    Michel Kellerman dated the present picture 1926-28 (correspondence, Feb. 1974).
However, the presence of a customs sticker on the reverse of the stretcher would place
the painting even earlier. Works in oil on paper are rarely found in Derain's mature
period (conversation with R. Stoppenbach, Sept. 1975).

EXHIBITIONS:
Chicago, The Arts Club, *Exhibition of Paintings by André Derain,* Jan. 3-25, 1947, no. 27;
The Minneapolis Institute of Arts, *Twentieth Century French Painters,* May 3-June 1, 1947
(no. cat.; correspondence with S. L'Heureaux, Jan. 1975).

REFERENCE:
Masterpieces, 1972, p. 43, repr. (c. 1927-28).

1. The reverse of the stretcher bears a label from the Galerien Thannhauser when there were
   three branches: Berlin, Lucerne, and Munich. Since the Berlin branch opened in 1927 and
   the Munich one closed in 1928, the date at which the label originated can be specified as
   1927-28. The customs sticker dated 1926 is corroborating evidence.

Ida Fischer

Born October 1883, Vienna
Died January 1956, New York

14   Abstraction. 1945-49

Watercolor and gouache on paper, 18⅞ x
23¾ (47.9 x 60.3)

Not signed or dated.

PROVENANCE:
Acquired from the artist by J. K. Thannhauser, New York.

Fischer came to this country at the age of nine. She was a music teacher at Morris High School in the Bronx until her retirement at the age of fifty, when she began a new career. While on sabbatical in 1932, she traveled to China and began to paint under the instruction of a Chinese artist in Peking. Continuing her travels, she studied ceramics at the Kunstgewerbeschule in Vienna and painting with Sybil Andrews in London. On her return to this country she studied with I. Rice Pereira and Hans Hofmann (information from obituary in *The New York Times,* Jan. 23, 1956, p. 25, and E. de Kooning's press release for the Hansa Gallery, New York, Jan. 17-Feb. 6, 1955).

By late 1945-46 Fischer and her close friend, Frances Eckstein, were members of the Jane Street Group, an early cooperative gallery devoted to modern art whose membership was predominantly ex-Hofmann students. During the period of the Jane Street Group (1945-49), Fischer did abstractions similar to the Thannhauser example (correspondence with N. Blaine, Jan. 1975 and conversation with I. Bolotowsky, Feb. 1977). Prior to the early 1940s she painted in a realistic manner (correspondence with Milton Rindler, Oct. 1974). Later, into the 1950s, she worked in a wide variety of styles including mosaic collage. A large collection of her work is at the Roy R. Neuberger Museum at The State University of New York at Purchase, the gift of J. K. Thannhauser.

Sponsored by Nell Blaine, she joined the American Abstract Artists in 1947 and from 1953-55 was secretary of that group (Archives of American Art, microfilm roll N69-97).

REFERENCE:
Masterpieces, 1972, p. 38, repr. (c. 1945-48).

Paul Gauguin

Born June 1848, Paris
Died May 1903, Atuana, The Marquesas

15

15   In the Vanilla Grove, Man and Horse.

1891

(Dans la Vanillère homme et cheval; In the Vanilla Field, Man and Horse; Le Rendez-Vous; The White Horse; Pferdeführer; Mann mit Pferd im Walde)

Oil on burlap, 28¾ x 36¼ (73 x 92)

Signed and dated l.l.: *P Gauguin.91*

PROVENANCE:

Galerie Barbazanges, Paris, by 1923; Vignier, Paris, by 1928; Wildenstein and Co., New York; purchased from Wildenstein by Baron Eduard von der Heydt, Zandvoort, The Netherlands, and Ascona, Switzerland, c. 1935 (correspondence with M. R. Fisher, Jan. 1978); S. Wright Ludington, Santa Bar-bara, by Jan. 1941 and until Dec. 1942; purchased from Ludington by J. K. Thannhauser, 1942 (conversation with D. C. Rich, Mar. 1975).

CONDITION:

Glue lined at an unrecorded date before 1965. The support is identical with *Haere Mai* (cat. no. 16) but the application of pigment is heavier. Active cleavage in green foliage at upper left and in center (Dec. 1974).

Gauguin's list of paintings on page 2R of the *Carnet de Tahiti* (1891 into 1892) includes "Dans la Vanillère homme et cheval." Surely Gauguin intended the word "vanillière," which means a place where vanilla is grown. The present picture is the single known work by the artist representing a vanilla grove as well as a man and horse. Richard Field (p. 305) was the first to identify the present picture with the title "Dans la Vanillère homme et cheval," a conclusion with which Merete Bodelsen and Bengt Danielsson agree (conversation between Bodelsen and Danielsson kindly transmitted in correspondence with Bodelsen, May 1977). In addition, Bodelsen finds no narrative or symbolic meaning in the present picture (correspondence, July 1976 and May 1977).

Douglas Cooper thinks that there is insufficient proof to identify the present painting with the title "Dans la Vanillère homme et cheval" in Gauguin's *Carnet*. He prefers the title *Le Rendez-Vous* to refer to a meeting between the man and woman depicted (correspondence, May 1977).

However, the background trees in the Thannhauser picture conceal not one but two female figures who are picking or otherwise tending the vanilla plants. Vanilla, a creeping plant with flowers and pods which climbs up poles and sometimes on trees, is grown not in fields but in groves (kindly brought to my attention by Cooper, Mar. 1977). Photographs of vanilla growing in Tahiti around the turn of the century bear a resemblance to the background of the present picture (Gilbert Bouriquet, *Le Vanillier et la vanille dans le monde,* Paris, 1954, p. 455, fig. 171 and pls. vi-ix).

Gauguin arrived in Tahiti in early June of 1891 and soon left the capital city of Papeete for the countryside, where he spent much of his time in the district of Mataiea. Evidence compiled by Field (pp. 20-22) indicates that he began to paint about September-October. Field places the present picture in October-November of the same year.

A pencil drawing of *Man and Horse in a Landscape* (8½ x 10 ⅝ in., 21.6 x 27 cm., Collection M. Français, Paris; Rewald, 1962, p. 494, repr.) is related to the present painting in the juxtaposition of man and horse and in the pose of the man's legs and torso. However, in the drawing, the man's left arm is raised so as to recall *Man with an Axe* (Wildenstein 430; 36¼ x 27¼ in., 92 x 70 cm., signed and dated 1891, Collection Alex M. Lewyt, New York; Rewald, 1962, p. 495, color repr.).

fig. a.
Slab N from C. Yriarte, *Les Frises du Parthénon*,
Paris, 1868.

The source for the man and horse is the West Frieze of the Parthenon as suggested by Alfred Langer (p. 53) and Theodore Reff (review of A. Blunt and P. Pool, *Picasso: The Formative Years, The Art Bulletin*, vol. XLVIII, June 1966, p. 266) and not the Column of Trajan as proposed by Samuel Wagstaff (Field, p. 41) and William M. Kane (p. 357). Field agrees that the figures came from the Parthenon frieze (correspondence, Aug. 1974).

The hypothesis proposed by the present writer is that Gauguin knew the specific part of the frieze from Slab N of *Les Frises du Parthénon* (Paris, 1868; fig. a) which contained an essay by Charles Yriarte and twenty-two phototypes of casts taken by Gustave Arosa, Gauguin's close friend and former guardian. In his Tahitian works, Gauguin used figures from Slabs M, N, O, and U of this portfolio. Significantly, the *Man with an Axe* represents Slab U. At the sale of Gauguin's possessions from Tahiti, Victor Segalen purchased several photographs, including one of Slab O, which now belong to his daughter, Mme Anne Joly-Segalen, Bourg-la-Reine (correspondence with A. Joly-Segalen, Nov. 1976).

Before his trip, in the autumn of 1890, Gauguin wrote to Odilon Redon: "*Gauguin est fini pour ici, on ne verra plus rien de lui. Vous voyez que je suis un égoiste. J'emporte en photographies, dessins, tout un petit monde de camarades qui me causeront tous les jours*" (R. Field, "Plagiaire ou créateur?" in *Gauguin*, Paris, 1961, p. 123). ("Gauguin is finished here, you'll see nothing more of him. You see that I am an egotist. I am taking away with me in photographs and drawings a whole small world of friends who will chat with me every day.") Gauguin's use of photographs as the source of figures in the Tahitian paintings has been well-documented.

Near the end of his life, in *Avant et après,* Gauguin refers to the horses of the Parthenon: *"Quelquefois je me suis raculé* [sic] *bien loin, plus loin que les chevaux du Parthénon . . . jusqu'au dada de mon enfance, le bon cheval de bois"* (facsimile ed., Copenhagen [1948], p. 16). ("Sometimes I stepped very far back, farther than the horses of the Parthenon...back to the hobbyhorse of my childhood, the good wooden horse.")

EXHIBITIONS:
Basel, Kunsthalle, *Paul Gauguin,* July-Aug. 1928, no. 65 or 76 (depending on cat. ed.), repr. *(Mann mit Pferd im Walde,* coll. Vignier, Paris); Berlin, Galerien Thannhauser, *Paul Gauguin,* Oct. 1928, no. 51, repr. *(Mann mit Pferd im Walde);* London, Wildenstein and Co., Ltd., *Nineteenth Century Masterpieces,* May 9-June 15, 1935, no. 12, repr. (*The White Horse,* coll. Baron von der Heydt); The Art Gallery of Toronto, *Loan Exhibition of Paintings,* Nov. 1935, no. 177 (Wildenstein); New York, Wildenstein and Co., *Paul Gauguin,* Mar. 20-Apr. 18, 1936, no. 18 (von der Heydt); Cambridge, Mass., The Fogg Art Museum, *Paul Gauguin,* May 1-21, 1936, no. 16; The Baltimore Museum of Art, *Paul Gauguin,* May 24-June 5, 1936, no. 11; San Francisco Museum of Art, *Paul Gauguin,* Sept. 5-Oct. 4, 1936, no. 15, repr.; Los Angeles County Museum, *Aspects of French Painting from Cézanne to Picasso,* Jan. 15-Mar. 2, 1941, no. 22 (*The White Horse,* coll. S. Wright Ludington); New York, Wildenstein and Co., *Paul Gauguin,* Apr. 3-May 4, 1946, no. 21, repr. (J. K. Thannhauser).

REFERENCES:
E. Wiese, *Paul Gauguin,* Leipzig, 1923, n.p., repr. *(Pferdeführer,* Galerie Barbazanges, Paris); Paris, Galerie Marcel Guiot, *Gauguin: Documents Tahiti,* exh. cat., 1942, p. 38 (incorrectly lists Basel exhibition as Bremen); L. van Dovski, *Paul Gauguin,* Basel, 1947, pl. 19 *(Homme avec un cheval dans la fôret,* coll. Vignier); M. Malingue, *Gauguin,* Paris, 1948, pl. 166 *(Le Rendez-Vous);* L. van Dovski, *Paul Gauguin oder die Flucht vor der Zivilisation,* Bern, 1950, p. 348, no. 253 (J. K. Thannhauser); J. Taralon, *Gauguin,* Paris, 1953, p. 6, no. 32, repr.; B. Dorival, *Carnet de Tahiti,* facsimile ed., Paris, 1954, p. 2R and text pp. 18-19, 37; A. Blunt and P. Pool, *Picasso: The Formative Years,* Greenwich, 1962, pl. 166; A. Langer, *Paul Gauguin,* Leipzig, 1963, pp. 53, 54 (detail repr.), and 87; R. S. Field, *Paul Gauguin: The Paintings of the First Voyage to Tahiti,* Ph.D. dissertation, Harvard University, 1963, pp. 21, 38-41, 304, 312, no. 8 (*The White Horse,* Oct.-Nov. 1891); Wildenstein, 1964, p. 175, repr., no. 443 *(Le Rendez-Vous);* W. M. Kane, "Gauguin's *Le Cheval Blanc:* Sources and Syncretic Meanings," *The Burlington Magazine,* vol. CVIII, July 1966, pp. 357, 359, and fig. 27; G. M. Sugana, *L'opera completa di Gauguin,* Milan, 1972, p. 102, repr., no. 258; *Masterpieces,* 1972, p. 25, repr. *(In the Vanilla Field, Man and Horse);* L. S. Dietrich, *A Study of Symbolism in the Tahitian Painting of Paul Gauguin: 1891-1893,* Ph.D. dissertation, University of Delaware, 1973, pp. 234 and 274.

16   Haere Mai. 1891
(Haere temai; Les Deux cochons airani;
Tahitian Landscape with Black Hogs)

Oil on burlap, 28½ x 36 (72.4 x 91.4)

Signed and dated l.l.: *P Gauguin 91;*
inscribed l.r.: HAERE MAI.

PROVENANCE:

Ambroise Vollard, Paris;[1] purchased from
Vollard by J. K. Thannhauser, June 1934.

CONDITION:

Worn at edges, especially upper right
corner. In 1968 the painting was lined with
wax resin after a small hole was repaired in
the head of the pig at bottom right of center
(Dec. 1974).

The third entry, "Les 2 cochons airani," of Gauguin's list on page 2R of the *Carnet de Tahiti* refers to *Haere Mai.* Presumably by "airani" is intended the French word "airain," which means bronze or metals of which copper is the base.

Since Gauguin inscribed the Tahitian words "Haere Mai" on the canvas, they are retained here as the title. According to Bengt Danielsson, "Haere Mai" is a very common phrase meaning "Come here!" (*The Burlington Magazine,* p. 230). Common also in Tahiti is the sight of black pigs running loose (*Gauguin in the South Seas,* trans. R. Spink, London, 1965, pp. 288-89, fig. 59). Gauguin knew very little Tahitian during his first year there, but he used words in his paintings to make them appear more exotic to the Parisian public. Thus the expressions inscribed on paintings are ordinary ones which do not relate closely to the content of the paintings (correspondence with M. Bodelsen summarizing her conversation with Danielsson, May 1977).

Gauguin's Tahitian sketchbook contains several drawings of pigs: those on pages 37V and 39V resemble those in *Haere Mai.* A sketch for the palm tree is on page 71V. Richard Field dates the present picture October-November 1891.

Gauguin had treated the theme earlier in Brittany (Wildenstein 255; *The Swineherd,* 29 x 36½ in., 73 x 93 cm., signed and dated 1888, Collection Norton Simon, Los Angeles). Landscapes related by subject and date are *The Black Hogs* (Wildenstein 446; 35⅞ x 28⅜ in., 91 x 72 cm., signed and dated 1891, The Museum of Fine Arts, Budapest) and *Tahitian Landscape* (Wildenstein 442; 25⅜ x 18⅝ in., 64 x 47 cm., The Metropolitan Museum of Art, New York). However, the colors of *Haere Mai,* bolder and brighter than in the latter, anticipate *Tahitian Landscape* (Wildenstein 504; 26¾ x 36⅜ in., 68 x 92.5 cm., 1893, The Minneapolis Institute of Arts; R. Goldwater, *Paul Gauguin,* New York, 1958, p. 107, color repr.).

1. The original document of sale from Vollard, dated June 1934, was in the possession of J. K. Thannhauser.

    It has not been possible to determine conclusively whether the picture was exhibited with others owned by Vollard at the Moderne Galerie (Heinrich Thannhauser) in Munich in Aug. 1910 and the following month at the Galerie Arnold in Dresden (mentioned by Field, 1963, p. 312, and further discussed in correspondence, Aug. 1974). Rich, Gordon, and Field were unable to locate a copy of the catalogue. Contemporary newspaper accounts mention as many as seventeen of the twenty-one paintings exhibited and none resembles *Haere Mai* (D. E. Gordon, "Kirchner in Dresden," *The Art Bulletin,* vol. XLVIII, Sept.-Dec. 1966, p. 356, fn. 124). Thus it was probably not exhibited at the Moderne Galerie in 1910.

EXHIBITIONS:

London, Grafton Galleries, *Manet and the Post-Impressionists,* Nov. 8, 1910-Jan. 15, 1911, no. 44A (*Les Cochons noirs dans la prairie,* lent by Vollard; confirmed by D. Cooper, correspondence, Mar. 1977); Prague, Spolku Výtvarných Umělců Mánes, *Výstava francouzského umění XIX a XX století [French Art of the 19th and 20th century],* May-June 1923, no. 183 (Vollard); Amsterdam, Stedelijk Museum, *Honderd Jaar Fransche Kunst,* July 2-Sept. 25, 1938, no. 125, repr. (J. K. Thannhauser)); Buenos Aires, Museo Nacional de Bellas Artes, *La pintura francesca de David a nuestros días,* July-Aug. 1939, no. 57, traveled to Montevideo, Ministero de Instruccion Publica, Apr.-May 1940, and Rio de Janeiro, Museu Nacional de Belas Artes, June 29-Aug. 15; San Francisco, M. H. De Young Memorial Museum, *The Painting of France Since the French Revolution,* Dec. 1940-Jan. 1941, no. 41, repr.; Los Angeles County Museum, *Aspects of French Painting from Cézanne to Picasso,* Jan. 15-Mar. 2, 1941, no. 19; The Art Institute of Chicago, *Masterpieces of French Art,* Apr. 10-May 20, 1941, no. 64; The Portland Art Museum, *Masterpieces of French Painting from the French Revolution to the Present Day,* Sept. 3-Oct. 5, 1941, no. 42; Washington, D. C., The National Gallery of Art, on loan from Feb. 1942-July 1946 (correspondence with P. Davidock, Nov. 1973); Pittsfield (Mass.), The Berkshire Museum, *French Impressionist Painting,* Aug. 2-31, 1946, no. 10; New York, Wildenstein and Co., *Gauguin,* Apr. 5-May 5, 1956, no. 20, repr.

REFERENCES:

J. Rewald, *Gauguin,* Paris, 1938, p. 105, color repr. (*Haere Temai*); M. Malingue, *Gauguin,* Paris, 1948, no. 170, repr.; L. van Dovski, *Paul Gauguin oder die Flucht vor der Zivilisation,* Bern, 1950, p. 347, no. 244 (*Haere Temai*); B. Dorival, *Carnet de Tahiti,* facsimile ed., Paris, 1954, p. 2R and text pp. 18, 23, 28, 37, 40; L.-J. Bouge, "Traduction et interprétation de titres en langue tahitienne . . . ," in *Gauguin: sa vie, son oeuvre,* Paris, 1958, p. 162, no. 14 (*Haere Mai*); R. S. Field, *Paul Gauguin: The Paintings of the First Voyage to Tahiti,* Ph.D. dissertation, Harvard University, 1963, pp. 21, 38, 39, 304, 311, no. 7 (Oct.-Nov. 1891); Wildenstein, 1964, p. 177, repr., no. 447 (*Haere Mai Venez!*); M. Bodelsen, "The Wildenstein-Cogniat Gauguin Catalogue," *The Burlington Magazine,* vol. CVIII, Jan. 1966, p. 38 (correcting error of ex. coll. Fayet); C. Sterling and M. M. Salinger, *French Paintings: A Catalogue of the Collection of the Metropolitan Museum of Art,* New York, 1967, vol. III, p. 174; B. Danielsson, "Gauguin's Tahitian Titles," *The Burlington Magazine,* vol. CIX, Apr. 1967, p. 230, no. 16 (*Haere Mai*); G. M. Sugana, *L'opera completa di Gauguin,* Milan, 1972, p. 102, repr., no. 259; *Masterpieces,* 1972, p. 24, repr.

Vincent van Gogh

Born March 1853, Groot-Zundert, The Netherlands
Died July 1890, Auvers-sur-Oise

17   Roadway with Underpass. 1887
(Le Viaduc; The Viaduct; Viaduct at Asnières;
Tunnel)

Oil on cardboard mounted on panel,
12⅞ x 16⅛ (32.7 x 41)

Not signed or dated.

PROVENANCE:
Unknown Russian collector acting for
Galerie Charpentier, Paris;[1] Galerie Hans
Bamman, Düsseldorf, by 1927; J. K. Thann-
hauser, Berlin, by 1937.

CONDITION:
At an unrecorded date before 1965 the
cardboard was mounted with glue onto a
paper-veneered panel with wood center.
Panel has a double warp. Cracks in pigment
and some abrasion (Jan. 1975).

1. According to de la Faille (1970, p. 616), the unknown Russian collector mentioned as the
   first owner acted in fact for the Galerie Charpentier. However, according to R. Nacenta
   (correspondence, May 1975) it was never at the Galerie Charpentier.

Van Gogh must have painted *Roadway with Underpass,* formerly titled *The Viaduct,* in the early autumn of 1887. Although J.-B. de la Faille (1928, vol. I, p. 71) recognized the foliage as autumnal, the recent edition of de la Faille (1970, p. 122) places the picture in the early summer. According to Bogomila Welsh-Ovcharov (correspondence, Oct. 1977), the systematic dotting and parallel brushwork found in the Thannhauser painting cannot predate 1887. The dots of red and green pigment in the foliage at the upper left imply van Gogh's knowledge of Divisionist technique.

Welsh-Ovcharov has identified the subject of the picture as the fortifications between Montmartre and Asnières, where Vincent painted several watercolors in the summer of 1887 (de la Faille 1401, 1402, 1403, and 1410). More specifically it represents a *poterne,* or covered masonry underpass. Originally there were approximately ninety underpasses allowing entrance to or exit from Paris through these fortifications. Frequently a tollhouse or guardhouse structure, complete with chimneys for heating, was located on the city side of the underpass. The presence of two chimneys in the Thannhauser oil would confirm Welsh-Ovcharov's identification of the site. Although the *poternes* no longer exist, a photograph of a *poterne* from the turn of the century displays two chimneys, a lantern, and lateral embankments similar to those in the present work. In the Thannhauser painting the view is toward Paris. (I am indebted to Bogomila Welsh-Ovcharov for providing all of the above information.)

The present picture brings to mind *The Railway Bridge over Avenue Montmajour* (de la Faille 480; Arles, Oct. 1888) or *The Iron Bridge at Trinquetaille* (de la Faille 481; Oct. 1888) and even foreshadows *A Passage at Saint Paul's Hospital* (de la Faille 1529; May-early June 1889, The Museum of Modern Art, New York).

EXHIBITIONS:

New York, Wildenstein and Co., *Van Gogh,* Mar. 24-Apr. 30, 1955, no. 21, repr.; The Art Center in La Jolla (Calif.), *Great French Paintings 1870-1910,* June 15-July 26, 1956, no. 24, repr.; San Antonio, The Marion Koogler McNay Art Institute, *A Summer Exhibition,* June-Aug. 1961, no. iv, repr.; New York, The Solomon R. Guggenheim Museum, *Van Gogh and Expressionism,* July 1-Sept. 13, 1964 [p. 3].

REFERENCES:

J.-B. de la Faille, "Unbekannte Bilder von Vincent van Gogh," *Der Cicerone,* Jg. XIX, Feb. 1927, pp. 102 and 104, repr. (*Tunnel,* c. 1887, coll. Hans Bamman, Düsseldorf); de la Faille, 1928, vol. I, p. 71, no. 239, and vol. II, pl. lxiv (*Le viaduc,* coll. Hans Bamman, Düsseldorf); de la Faille, 1939, p. 280, repr., no. 385 (Galerie Thannhauser, Berlin); de la Faille, 1970, pp. 122, 123, repr., and 620, no. 239 *(The Viaduct);* P. Lecaldano, *L'opera pittorica completa di Van Gogh,* Milan, 1971, vol. I, p. 114, repr., no. 385; *Masterpieces,* 1972, p. 27 *(The Viaduct);* B. Welsh-Ovcharov, *Vincent van Gogh: His Paris Period 1886-1888,* Utrecht and The Hague, 1976, p. 234 *(The Viaduct:* colors of the painting suggest an autumn date).

18   Letter to John Peter Russell.   April 1888

Ink on laid paper, 8 x 10¼ (20.3 x 26)

No watermark.

Not dated.

PROVENANCE:
Received from the artist by John Peter Russell (d. 1931), 1888; inherited from Russell

by his daughter, Jeanne Jouve, Paris, probably 1931-32; acquired from Jouve by J. K.
Thannhauser, Paris, probably 1938-39
(notes Dec. 1972).

My dear Russell,[1] I ought to have answered your letter ever so long ago[2] but working
pretty hard every day at night I feel so often too weary to write. As it rains to day I avail
myself of the opportunity. Last Sunday I have met Macknight[3] and a Danish painter[4]
and I intend to go to see him at Fonvieille[5] next Monday. I feel sure I shall prefer him
as an artist to what he is as an art critic his vieuws as such being so narrow that they
make me smile.

I heartily hope for you that you will be able to leave Paris for good soon and no
doubt leaving Paris will do you *a world of good* in all respects.[6] As for me I remain
enraptured with the scenery here am working at a series of blooming orchards.[7] And
unvoluntarily I thought often of you because you did the same in Sicily.[8] I wished
you would one day or another when I shall send over some work to Paris exchange a
Sicilian study with me — in case you should have one to spare —

1. The letter is transcribed as van Gogh wrote it. H. Thannhauser (*L'Amour de l' Art*, p. 285,
   fn. 2) states that Russell's name was crossed out by his son-in-law.
2. See Letter 466 (*CLVG*, II, pp. 528-29). In Letter 473 (dated c. Apr. 1, by Hulsker, 1960,
   p. 334), van Gogh tells Theo: "I think that Russell is trying to reconcile me with [Alex-
   ander] Reid, and that he wrote the letter expressly for that purpose. I shall certainly write
   Russell and tell him that I have told Reid frankly that he made a foolish mistake in loving
   dead pictures and completely neglecting living artists, and that moreover I hoped to see
   him change, at least in that respect" (*CLVG*, II, p. 540).
3. Hulsker (p. 332) thinks that "last Sunday" must be Apr. 22, 1888. The American painter,
   Dodge MacKnight (1860-1950), arrived in Paris at the end of 1883 and studied at Cormon's studio in 1884. According to D. Adlow (Boston, Museum of Fine Arts, *Dodge
   MacKnight*, exh. cat., 1950, pp. 9-11), MacKnight first met van Gogh at Cormon's. Van
   Gogh mentions the American painter in Letters 479-82, 485, 498, 502, 505, 506, 514, 516,
   and 528 and frequently refers to him as Russell's friend.
4. Christian Vilhelm Mourier-Petersen (1858-1945). Van Gogh made his acquaintance in
   March, and Mourier-Petersen left late in May for Paris, where he stayed with Theo. He is
   mentioned in Letters 468, 469, 474, 476, 482, 488-90, 496, 498, 502, 507, and 515.
5. Fontvieille, where MacKnight stayed, is 9 km. from Arles.
6. Russell left Paris in the summer of 1888 to live at Belle-Ile (correspondence with Galbally,
   Oct. 1976).
7. For example, de la Faille 404, 405, and 552-56. Compare with Letter IV to Bernard
   (D. Lord, pseud. for D. Cooper, ed., *Vincent van Gogh: Letters to Emile Bernard*, London,
   1938, p. 29, fn. 8).
8. Russell was in Sicily in the autumn of 1886.

Sicily Monticelli gives us not neither
serious by serious local colour or even local
truth. But gives us something passionate
and eternal — the rich colour and rich sun
of the glorious South in a true colourists way
parallel with Delacroix conception of the South
Viz that the South be represented now by
contraste simultané of colours and
their derivations and harmonies and
not by forms or lines in themselves
as the ancient artists did formerly
by pure form greeks & michel Ange
or by pure line or delineation Rafael
Mantegna   Venetian primitifs
(Botticelli Cimabue Giotto Bellini)
Contrariwise the thing undertaken
by P. Veronese & Titian — Colour
the thing undulated by Velasquez and
Goya to be continued and —
more fully or rather more universally done
by the more universal knowledge
we have a power of the
colours of the prism and their proprieties
hoping to write to you again and
to hear of y   pretty soon
yours very truly
Vincent

my dear   I ought to have
answered your letter ever so long ago
but working pretty hard every day at
night I feel so often too weary to
write. As it rains to day I avail myself
of the opportunity. Last sunday I have
met Macknight and a Danish painter
and I intend to go to see him at Fonvieille
next monday. I feel sure I shall
prefer him as an artist to what he
is as an art critic — his views as such
being so narrow that they make me
smile. I heartily hope for you that you will
be able to leave this for good soon
and no doubt leaving Paris will
do you a world of good in all
respects. As for me I remain
enraptured with the scenery here
am working at a series of blooming
orchards. & I involuntarily
thought often of you because you
did the same in Sicily. I
wished you would one day or
another when I let go
over some work to Paris exchange
a Sicilian study with me — in
case you should have one to
spare.

You know I thought and I think
such a deal of those of yours.
I don't gainsay that your
portraits are more serious
and higher art — but I think
it meritory in you and a
rare quality that together with
a perfection as appeared to me
the Fabian and McKnight portraits
you are at the same time able
to give a Scherzo the
adagio con espressione the
gay note in one word together
with more manly conceptions
of a higher order. And I so heartily
hope that you will continue to
give us simultanément
both the grave and elaborate works
and those aforesaid scherzos —
Then let them say if they like
that you are not always serious
or that you have done works
of a lighter sort — So much the
worse for the critics & the better for you.
I have heard nothing of
our friend McKnight. I felt rather
anxious on his account because
I feel sure that he was on a false
track. My brother has received a letter
from him but pretty unsatisfactory.

I was very much taken in by him during
the first 6 weeks or 2 months but after
that period he was in pecuniary difficulty
and in the same acted in a way
that nobody
me the impression that he had lost his
wits.
Which I still think was the case and
consequently he not responsible
even if his doings then were
pretty unfair. He is very nervous
— as we all are — and can't help
being so — He is sprung to act
in his crisis of nerves to make money
— — — whilst painters would
make pictures . . . . .
So much to say that I saw
the dealer stronger in him than
the artist though there be a battle
in his conscience concerning this
of which I do not know the issue.
So much — pour ta gouverne —
as I had the pleasure of introducing
him to you I feel bound to warn
you with the same sympathy however
for him because I found him artistic
in pleading the monticelli cause
in the which I took and take my part
Witnessing the very scenery which
inspired Monticelli I maintain
his rights to public though
too late appreciation.

You know I thought and think such a deal of those of yours I don't gainsay that your portraits are more serious and higher art but I think it meritory in you and a rare quality that together with a perfection as appeared to me the Fabian and McKnight portraits[9] you are at the same time able to give a Scherzo the adagio con expressione the gay note in one word together with more manly conceptions of a higher order. And I so heartily hope that you will continue to give us simultanément both the grave and elaborate works and those aforesaid scherzos.—Then let them say if they like that you are *not always* serious or that you *have* done work *of a lighter sort*—So much the worse for the citics [critics] & the better for you.

I have heard nothing of our friend Mr. Reid.[10] I felt rather anxious on his account because I feel sure that he was on a false track. My brother has received a letter of him but pretty unsatisfactory.

I was very much taken in by him during the first 6 weeks or 2 months but after that period he was in pecuniary difficulties and in the same acted in a way that made on me the impression that he had lost his wits.[11]

Which I still think was the case and consequently he not responsable even if his doings then were pretty unfair. He is very nervous—as we all are—and can't help being so—He is prompted to act in his crisis of nerves to make money . . . whilst painters would make pictures. . . .

So much to say that I consider *the dealer stronger* in him than *the artist* though there be a battle in his conscience concerning this—of the which battle I do not yet know the result. So much— pour votre gouverne— as I had the pleasure of introducing him to

9. Russell's *Portrait of Fabian* (25½ x 24⅞ in., 64.8 x 63.2 cm.) was given to The Fogg Art Museum, Harvard University, Cambridge, Mass., in 1956 by Mr. and Mrs. Justin K. Thannhauser in memory of their son Heinz H. Thannhauser. According to MacKnight's letters to Russell, Fabian was a Spanish painter (*L'Amour de l'Art*, p. 285, fn. 6). He appears in a photograph taken at Cormon's atelier c. 1883-85, where he probably met Russell (see B. Welsh-Ovcharov, *Vincent van Gogh: His Paris Period 1886-1888*, Utrecht and The Hague, 1976, pp. 22, 56 fn. 26, and fig. Ib, and M. Joyant, *Henri de Toulouse-Lautrec 1864-1901*, Paris, 1926, p. 58). Van Gogh and Fabian may have exchanged paintings since a landscape, *Roadway with Fence*, bearing Fabian's signature belonged to Theo (Welsh-Ovcharov, fig. Ic, and Amsterdam, Stedelijk Museum, *Collectie Theo van Gogh*, exh. cat., 1960, no. 34).

   Russell's *Portrait of Dodge MacKnight* (22 x 19 in., 55.9 x 48.2 cm.) belongs to the latter's niece, Mrs. George W. Bruce, West Barnstable, Mass. (correspondence, Sept. 1976).

10. Alexander Reid (1854-1928) went to Paris in 1887 and joined the firm of Boussod et Valadon with which Theo van Gogh was associated. Vincent undoubtedly met Reid through his brother, and he painted the Scot's portrait twice in 1887 (de la Faille 270 and 343). After returning to Glasgow in 1889, Reid opened a gallery, La Société des Beaux-Arts. Van Gogh refers to Reid in Letters 464, 465, 472, 473, 482, 506, 511, 512, and 597.

11. See also Letter 464 in which van Gogh mentions that Reid had been "right good company for the first few months" (*CLVG*, II, p. 526).

   It is said that Vincent and Reid shared rooms together for a time until one evening Vincent proposed a suicide pact and Reid left soon thereafter (see T. J. Honeyman, "Van Gogh: A Link with Glasgow," *The Scottish Art Review*, vol. II, no. 2, 1948, p. 17, and R. Pickvance, "A Man of Influence: Alex Reid," *The Scottish Art Review*, vol. XI, no. 3, 1968, p. 6).

you feel bound to warn you with the same sympathy however for him because I found him artistic in pleading the monticelli cause.[12]

In the which I took and take my part Witnessing the very scenery which inspired Monticelli I maintain this artists rights to public though too late appreciation.[13]

Surely Monticelli gives us not neither pretends to give us local colour or even local truth. But gives as something passionate and eternal—the rich coulour and rich sun of the glorious South in a true colourists way parallel with Delacroix conception of the South Viz that the South be represented now by contraste simultané of colours and their derivations and harmonies and not by forms or lines in themselves as the ancient artists did formerly by pure *form* greeks & Michel Ange or by pure line or delineation Rafael Mantegna Venetian *primitifs* (Botticelli Cimabue Giotto Bellini.)

Contrariwise the thing undertaken by P. Veronese & Titian—Colour. The thing undertaken by Velasquez and Goya to be continued and—more fully or rather more universally done by the more universal knowledge we have & possess of the colours of the prism and their properties.

Hoping to write to you again and to hear of you pretty soon!

Yours very truly,

Vincent

The painter John Peter Russell was born in Sydney in 1858 of wealthy Australian parents. He went to Paris in 1885 following three years of study in London. It is most likely that Russell and van Gogh first met at the atelier of Fernand-Anne Piestre, called Cormon, at 104, boulevard de Clichy (Galbally, p. 29). Russell had been at Cormon's atelier since the beginning of 1885 and van Gogh was there in the spring and/or autumn of 1886 (see B. Welsh-Ovcharov, *Vincent van Gogh: His Paris Period 1886-1888*, Utrecht and The Hague, 1976, pp. 12-13 and 209-12). Vincent lived with his brother Theo at 54, rue Lepic which was near Russell's home at 73, boulevard de Clichy and his studio at 15, impasse Hélène which was part of the Villa des Arts (correspondence with Galbally, Oct. 1976). Russell knew Anne Marie Mattiocco from c. 1885 and decided in 1886 to have a house built on Belle-Ile off the coast of Brittany. He actually left Paris to live on Belle-Ile in 1888. Russell invited several painters to

12. Van Gogh refers frequently to Adolphe Monticelli (1824-1886). A letter written to Theo from Arles makes it clear that both he and Reid were interested in purchasing works by Monticelli and that they were competitors rather than partners in their efforts to obtain works by Monticelli (*CLVG*, II, Letter 464, p. 526). For references to Monticelli, see Letters 463, 464, 471, 478, 496, 507, 508, 541, 542, 550, 558a, and 574. Van Gogh had seen Monticelli's paintings first at the gallery of Joseph Delarebeyrette at 43, rue de Provence and then at Boussod et Valadon. Theo owned five pictures by Monticelli in addition to the one given to him by Reid. See A. M. Alauzen and P. Ripert, *Monticelli: sa vie et son oeuvre*, Paris, 1969, pp. 441-48.

13. Monticelli lived in Marseilles; thus, the south of France is intended. In Letters 541 and 558a Vincent expresses his own sense of continuing Monticelli's work. In Letter 558a he asks Theo: "What do De Haan and Isaäcson say about Monticelli? Have they seen other pictures of his than those in your house? You know that I myself still have the pretension to continuing the job that Monticelli started here" (*CLVG*, III, p. 97).

visit him there: Monet and Matisse as well as van Gogh (who never went). Russell returned to Australia in 1921 with his second wife, and he died there in 1931 (information from Galbally, 1976, and D. Finley in *John Peter Russell,* exh. cat., Wildenstein and Co., Ltd., London, 1965 [pp. 2-6]).

Russell's *Portrait of van Gogh* (23⅝ x 17¾ in., 60 x 45 cm., Rijksmuseum Vincent van Gogh, Amsterdam; *CLVG,* II, p. 548, color repr.) probably dates from 1886, after van Gogh arrived in Paris (by early March) and became acquainted with Russell but before Russell's departure for Italy that autumn. The following year the two artists were both in Paris in the late spring-early summer and the rest of 1887 until van Gogh left for Arles in February 1888 (Galbally, p. 32).

From Vincent's letters to Theo it is evident that he wrote many letters to Russell. Justin Thannhauser's son Henry estimated that Russell must have destroyed at least a dozen letters from van Gogh (*The Burlington Magazine,* p. 96). There are no letters from van Gogh among the surviving Russell papers (correspondence with Galbally, Aug. 1976).

Henry Thannhauser, who was the first to write about van Gogh's letters to the Australian, pointed out that "though one of his [van Gogh's] motives was the desire to help Gauguin by persuading Russell to buy one of the latter's paintings, the correspondence in general shows a continuity of friendship which is a moving trait in the lonely Van Gogh: a trait well known to us already through the letters to Van Rappard and Emile Bernard" (*The Burlington Magazine,* p. 96). Letters 466, 467, 494a, 496, 506, 514-16, and 536 all refer to persuading Russell to purchase a painting by Gauguin.

Two of the letters in the Thannhauser Collection are written in English. Van Gogh's correspondence in English is otherwise extremely rare and limited to two postcards (Letters 196 and 203), a letter to the English painter Levens (Letter 459a), a letter to Van Rappard (R5), and his sermon (*CLVG,* I, pp. 87-91). Scattered phrases and sentences in English appear in letters primarily written in French or Dutch. Van Gogh lived in England for periods of time between 1873 and 1876 but he knew English even before the trips (*CLVG,* I, p. 3).

The present letter dates from April 1888 not long after van Gogh went to Arles. Hulsker places it after Letter 479, that is, about April 24-28. Henry Thannhauser dated it early in April (*The Burlington Magazine,* p. 97, fn. 24). MacKnight's letters, which might validate a more precise date, were known to Thannhauser in 1938 but probably no longer exist.

EXHIBITION:

New York, Wildenstein and Co., *Van Gogh,* Mar. 24-Apr. 30, 1955, no. 110.

REFERENCES:

H. Thannhauser, "Documents inédits: Vincent van Gogh et John Russell," *L'Amour de l'Art,* XIXᵉ année, Sept. 1938, pp. 285-86 (early April); H. Thannhauser, "Van Gogh and John Russell: Some Unknown Letters and Drawings," *The Burlington Magazine,* vol. LXXIII, Sept. 1938, pp. 96-97 (early April); H. Graber, ed., *Vincent Van Gogh: Briefe an Emile Bernard, Paul Gauguin, John Russell, Paul Signac und Andere,* Basel, 1941, pp. 119-22 (German trans.); *CLVG,* 1958, vol. II, Letter 477a, pp. 546-48; J. Hulsker, "Van Gogh's Extatische Maanden in Arles," *Maatstaf,* Jg. 8, Aug.-Sept. 1960, pp. 332 and 334 (c. Apr. 24-28, 1888); *Masterpieces,* 1972, p. 28, repr.; A. Galbally, "Amitie: Russell and Van Gogh," *Art Bulletin of Victoria,* 1976, p. 32.

19 Letter to John Peter Russell.
Late June 1888

Ink on wove paper, 8 x 10⅜ (20.3 x 26.3)

Watermark: L-J D L&C°

Not dated.

PROVENANCE:

Received from the artist by John Peter Russell (d. 1931), 1888; inherited from Russell

by his daughter, Jeanne Jouve, Paris, probably 1931-32; acquired from Jouve by J. K. Thannhauser, Paris, probably 1938-39 (notes Dec. 1972).

My dear Russell[1] for ever so long I have been wanting to write to you—but then the work has so taken me up. We have harvest time here at present and I am always in the fields.[2]

And when I sit down to write I am so abstracted by recollections of what I have seen that I leave the letter.[3] For instance at the present occasion I was writing to you and going to say something about Arles as it is—and as it was in the old days of Boccaccio.—

Well instead of continuing the letter I began to draw on the very paper the head of a dirty little girl[4] I saw this afternoon whilst I was painting a view of the river with a greenish yellow sky.[5]

This dirty "mudlark" I thought yet had a vague florentine sort of figure like the heads in the monticelli pictures,[6] and reasoning and drawing this wise I worked on the letter I was writing to you. I enclose the slip of scribbling. that you may judge of my abstractions and forgive my not writing before as such.

1. The letter is printed as van Gogh wrote it and differs slightly from the transcription in *CLVG,* II, pp. 592-94. Russell's name has been crossed out in ink in the same manner as in the earlier letter (see cat. no. 18, fn. 1).

2. Van Gogh mentions working in the fields in Letters 496 and 498 as well as in Letter 501 (dated June 29 or 30 by Hulsker). For drawings of the harvest, see M. Roskill, "Van Gogh's Blue Cart," *Oud Holland,* Jg. LXXXI, no. 1, 1966, pp. 3-19. In Letter 507 (dated c. July 7 by Hulsker), van Gogh wrote that "during the harvest my work was not any easier than what the peasants who were actually harvesting were doing" (*CLVG,* II, p. 607).

3. The meaning becomes clear if "distracted" is substituted for "abstracted." See also fn. 16. H. Thannhauser (*The Burlington Magazine,* p. 98) discusses possible meanings of "abstractions" and suggests that van Gogh may have been making an excuse for his delay in writing to Russell.

4. This refers to cat. no. 20. R. Pickvance ("The new De La Faille," *The Burlington Magazine,* vol. CXV, Mar. 1973, p. 178) points out that it is "a" dirty little girl rather than "the" as given in *CLVG,* II, p. 592 and de la Faille, 1970, p. 523.

5. The painting referred to is probably *The Bridge at Trinquetaille* (de la Faille 426; 25½ x 32 in., 65 x 81 cm., June-July 1888, Collection André Meyer, New York). A drawing of the same subject exists (de la Faille 1507; 9½ x 12¼ in., 24 x 31 cm., The Metropolitan Museum of Art, New York, The Robert Lehman Collection).

6. See cat. no. 18, fn. 12 for Monticelli. Theo owned several paintings by Monticelli including *L'Italienne* (A. M. Alauzen and P. Ripert, *Monticelli: sa vie et son oeuvre,* Paris, 1969, fig. 476). However, faces like those described in the letter appear in many paintings by Monticelli.

I heard Rodin had a beautiful head at the Salon.

I have been to the seaside for a week and very likely am going thither again soon. - Flat shore sands - fine figures there like Cimabue - straight stylish. Am working at a Sower:

The great field all violet the sky & sun very yellow. It is a hard subject to treat. Please remember me very kindly to Mrs Russell - and in thought I heartily shake hands.

Yours very truly

Vincent

My dear ████ for ever so long I have been wanting to write to you - but then the work has so taken me up. We have harvest time here at present and I am always in the fields.

And when I sit down to write I am so abstracted by recollections of what I have seen that I leave the letter. For instance at the present occasion I was writing to you and going to say something about Arles as it is - and as it was in the old days of Boccaccio. -

Well instead of continuing the letter I began to draw on the very paper the head of a dirty little girl I saw this afternoon whilst I was painting a view of the river with a greenish yellow sky.

This dirty "mudlark" I thought yet had a vague florentine sort of figure like the heads in the monticelli pictures. and reasoning and drawing this wise I worked on the letter

I was writing to you. I enclose the slip of scribbling. that you may judge of my abstractions and forgive my not writing before as such.

Do not however imagine I am painting old florentine scenery - no I may dream of such - but I spend my time in painting and drawing landscapes or rather studies of colour.

The actual inhabitants of this country often remind me of the figures we see in Zola's work.

And Manet would like them as they are and the city as it is?

Bernard is still in Brittany and I believe he is working hard and doing well.

Gauguin is in Brittany too. but has again suffered of an attack of his liver complaint. I wished I were in the same place with him or he here with me.

My brother has an exhibition of 10 new pictures by Claude Monet - his latest works. for instance a landscape with red sun set and a group of dark firtrees by the seaside.

The red sun casts an orange or blood red reflection on the blue green trees and the ground. I wished I could see them.

How is your house in Brittany getting on - and have you been working in the country.

I believe my brother has also another picture by Gauguin which is as I heard say very fine. two negro women talking. it is one of those he did at martinique.

McKnight told me he had seen at Marseilles a picture by monticelli flowerpiece.

Very soon I intend sending over some things to Paris and then you can, if you like, choose one for our exchange.

I must hurry off this letter for I feel some more abstractions coming on and if I did not quickly fill up my paper I would again set to drawing and you would not have your letter. -

Do not however imagine I am painting old florentine scenery—no I may dream of such—but I spend my time in painting and drawing landscapes or rather studies of colour.

The actual inhabitants of this country often remind me of the figures we see in Zola's work.[7]

And Manet would like them as they are and the city as it is.

Bernard is still in Brittany and I believe he is working hard and doing well.[8]

Gauguin is in Brittany too but has again suffered of an attack of his liver complaint.[9] I wished I were in the same place with him or he here with me.[10]

My brother has an exhibition of 10 new pictures by Claude Monet—his latest works.[11] for instance a landscape with red sun set and a group of dark firtrees by the seaside. The red sun casts an orange or blood red reflection on the blue green trees and the ground. I wished I could see them.

How is your house in Brittany getting on—[12] and have you been working in the country.

I believe my brother has also another picture by Gauguin which is as I heard say very fine two negro women talking. it is one of those he did at Martinique.[13]

McKnight told me he had seen at Marseilles a picture by Monticelli, flowerpiece.[14]

Very soon I intend sending over some studies to Paris and then you can, if you like, choose one for our exchange.[15]

7. Zola (1840-1902) is mentioned in Letters 497, 498, 514, 519, 524, 525, and 543.

8. Bernard stayed at Saint-Briac on the northern coast of Brittany until early Aug., when he went to Pont-Aven, where Gauguin was staying. See D. Lord, pseud. for D. Cooper, ed., *Vincent van Gogh: Letters to Emile Bernard*, New York, 1938, Letter XIV, p. 72, fn. 1.

9. Gauguin was at Pont-Aven from Feb.-Oct. 1888.

10. On Oct. 23, 1888, Gauguin joined van Gogh at Arles.

11. Theo was manager of Boussod et Valadon, 19, boulevard Montmartre in Paris. According to J. Rewald, Theo bought the ten Monets on June 4, 1888, and immediately arranged for a small exhibition ("Theo van Gogh, Goupil, and the Impressionists," *Gazette des Beaux-Arts*, vol. LXXXI, Jan. 1973, p. 23). The exhibition is listed as being open in *Journal des Arts,* June 15, 1888, p. 2, but the exact date that it began is not known (correspondence with F. Daguet, Fondation Wildenstein, Paris, July 1976).

12. Russell was having a house built on Belle-Ile-en-Mer, off the coast from Quiberon in Brittany. The house, "Le Château de l'Anglais," was begun in 1887 and completed by the summer of 1888 (correspondence with A. Galbally, Oct. 1976).

13. Rewald (*Gazette des Beaux-Arts*, Jan. 1973, p. 61, fn. 33) points out that van Gogh had not seen the Gauguin in question, *Négresses causant à la Martinique* (Wildenstein 227; 24 x 29^{15}/16 in., 61 x 76 cm., dated 1887, private collection, Switzerland). Boussod et Valadon had the painting on consignment at that time; they purchased the work from Gauguin on June 22, 1889, having actually sold it four days earlier (Rewald, *Gazette des Beaux-Arts,* Jan. 1973, p. 21, and Feb. 1973, p. 91). Van Gogh states in Letter 514, which is dated July 29, that Russell did not have time to see the painting.

14. A Monticelli flower piece that Dodge MacKnight had seen is also referred to in Letter 496.

15. It is very doubtful that an exchange of pictures took place since Russell's name is not mentioned in the provenance of paintings in de la Faille, 1970. However, van Gogh did send twelve drawings after paintings to Russell (see cat. no. 21).

I must hurry off this letter for I feel some more abstractions coming on[16] and if I did not quickly fill up my paper I would again set to drawing and you would not have your letter.

I heard Rodin had a beautiful head at the salon.[17]

I have been to the seaside for a week and very likely am going thither again soon.[18] Flat shore sands— fine figures there like Cimabue— straight stylish.[19]

Am working at a Sower:[20]

the great field *all violet* the sky & sun very yellow. it is a hard subject to treat.[21]

Please remember me very kindly to Mrs. Russell— and in thougt I heartily shake hands.

> Yours very truly
> Vincent

16. Although H. Thannhauser (*The Burlington Magazine*, p. 98) states that "abstractions" in this form were not alluded to elsewhere, Letter 507, which describes the artist's method of working rapidly in a single long sitting, reports: "But when I come home after a spell like that, I assure you my head is so tired that if that kind of work keeps recurring, as it has done since the harvest began, I become hopelessly absent-minded and incapable of heaps of ordinary things" (*CLVG*, II, p. 606). Significantly, in the original, the last phrase reads: ". . . *je deviens absolument abstrait et incapable d'un tas de choses ordinaires*" (*Lettres de Vincent van Gogh à son frère*, Paris, 1937, pp. 203-4). Van Gogh's use of the word "abstraction" derives from his translation of the French *"abstrait."*

    Later in 1889, in a letter to Bernard, van Gogh discusses "abstractions" as opposed to paintings based upon a study of nature (*CLVG*, III, pp. 522-25; *Lettres de Vincent van Gogh à Emile Bernard*, Paris, 1911, p. 133).

17. *"No. 4592 Portrait de Mme. M.V. . . . ; buste, marbre"* was Rodin's only piece in the Salon, which opened May 1, 1888 (Paris, Société des artistes français, *Salon de 1888,* 2nd ed., p. 365). The 1884 portrait of Mme Luisa Lynch de Morla Vicuña was purchased by the French government at the Salon of 1888 (J. L. Tancock, *The Sculpture of Auguste Rodin,* Philadelphia, 1976, no. 89).

18. The visit to Saintes-Maries-de-la-Mer took place during the week of June 17-24, 1888 (C. W. Millard, "A Chronology for Van Gogh's Drawings of 1888," *Master Drawings,* vol. 12, summer 1974, pp. 159, 163, fn. 33). It appears to have been Vincent's only trip to Saintes-Maries.

19. Van Gogh wrote to Bernard: "There, at Saintes-Maries, were girls who reminded one of Cimabue and Giotto—thin, straight, somewhat sad and mystic" (*CLVG*, III, Letter B6, p. 490).

EXHIBITION:

New York, Wildenstein and Co., *Van Gogh,* Mar. 24-Apr. 30, 1955, no. 110.

REFERENCES:

H. Thannhauser, "Documents inédits: Vincent van Gogh et John Russell," *L'Amour de l'Art,* XIXe année, Sept. 1938, p. 286; H. Thannhauser, "Van Gogh and John Russell: Some Unknown Letters and Drawings," *The Burlington Magazine,* vol. LXXIII, Sept. 1938, pp. 97-98 and 102, pl. IIIc (end of June or early July); H. Graber, ed., *Vincent Van Gogh: Briefe an Emile Bernard, Paul Gauguin, John Russell, Paul Signac und Andere,* Basel, 1941, pp. 122-24 (German trans.); *CLVG,* 1958, vol. II, Letter 501a, pp. 592-94 (*Sower,* repr.); F. Elgar, *Van Gogh,* trans. J. Cleugh, New York, 1958, p. 191; J. Hulsker, "Van Gogh's Extatische Maanden in Arles," *Maatstaf,* Jg. 8, Aug.-Sept. 1960, pp. 332, 334 (c. June 27 and before Letter 501); H. R. Graetz, *The Symbolic Language of Vincent Van Gogh,* New York, 1963, pp. 96-97, repr.; *Masterpieces,* 1972, p. 29, repr.

20. The painting referred to is *The Sower* (de la Faille 422; 25¼ x 31¾ in., 64 x 80.5 cm., Rijksmuseum Kröller-Müller, Otterlo; de la Faille, 1970, p. 234, color repr.). Drawings related to the sower in the present letter are: a sketch in Letter VII to Emile Bernard (B7; dated c. June 28 in de la Faille), de la Faille 1441 (9⅝ x 12⅝ in., 24.5 x 32 cm., Rijksmuseum Vincent van Gogh, Amsterdam), and de la Faille 1442 (9⅞ x 12³⁄₁₆ in., 25 x 31 cm., present whereabouts unknown, ex. coll. Thannhauser, Berlin).

   Van Gogh first treated the subject of the sower in 1880 (Letter 134) and did approximately thirty versions of it during his lifetime. According to R. L. Herbert, Millet's *Sower* had been popularized with the engraving executed by Paul LeRat (or Lerat, 1849-1892) for Durand-Ruel in 1873 (Paris, Grand Palais, *Jean-François Millet,* exh. cat., 1975, p. 92). LeRat's engraving was the source for van Gogh's drawing of 1881 (de la Faille 830) and painting of Oct. 1889 (de la Faille 689).

21. Van Gogh sketched the sower in Letter VII to Bernard and wrote: "Here is a sketch of a sower: large plowed field with clods of earth, for the most part frankly violet. A field of ripe wheat, yellow ocher in tone with a little carmine. The sky, chrome yellow, almost as bright as the sun itself, which is chrome yellow No. 1 with a little white, whereas the rest of the sky is chrome yellow Nos. 1 and 2 mixed. So very yellow. The Sower's shirt is blue and his trousers white. Size 25 canvas, square" (*CLVG,* III, pp. 491-92).

   Letter 501, which closely parallels the present letter and is placed a few days later than it by Hulsker (June 29 or 30), states: "A plowed field, a big field with clods of violet earth—climbing toward the horizon, a sower in blue and white. On the horizon a field of short ripe corn. Over it all a yellow sky with a yellow sun. . . . And the sketch, such as it is—a size 25 canvas—torments me, making me wonder if I shouldn't attack it seriously and make a tremendous picture of it" (*CLVG,* II, p. 591).

   When the artist wrote Letter 503 (dated c. July 6 by Hulsker), the picture had been altered so that the sky was yellow and green and the ground violet and orange.

20   Head of a Girl. Late June 1888

Ink on wove paper (lozenge), 7⅛ x 7¹¹⁄₁₆
(18 x 19.5)

Watermark: L-J D

Not signed or dated; inscribed by the artist
on reverse (fig. a):

*Have you been working in the country
lately and is the house you are building getting on. It appears that Claude Monet has
done fine things my brother writes to say
that he has at present an exhibition of 10
new pictures. One representing pine trees
at the seaside with a red sunset casting a red
glow over some branches foliage and the
ground. It is a marvel I hear. Bernard is
doing good things I believe he is taking a lot
of trouble. Gauguin is still at Pont-Aven and
suffering of his liver complaint [bu]t working nevertheless.*

PROVENANCE:

Received from the artist by John Peter Russell (d. 1931), 1888; inherited from Russell
by his daughter, Jeanne Jouve, Paris, probably 1931-32; acquired from Jouve by J. K.
Thannhauser, Paris, probably 1938-39
(notes Dec. 1972).

CONDITION:

Small loss of support at upper right. Old repair of five and one-half inch cut in support
on right side from top to bottom through
figure's hair and left shoulder. Work deacidified and rehinged by C. Gaehde (June
1973). Horizontal and vertical grid of graph
paper visible only on reverse.

This drawing was enclosed with the letter van Gogh sent to John Russell late in June
1888 (cat. no. 19). Vincent identifies the subject as "a dirty little girl I saw this afternoon whilst I was painting a view of the river." He refers to her as "this dirty 'mudlark'" and makes it clear that the present drawing was done from memory.

The same model appears in a painting, *The Girl with the Ruffled Hair* (de la Faille
535; 14 x 9¾ in., 35.5 x 24.5 cm., private collection, Switzerland; de la Faille, 1970,
p. 229, repr. [June 1888]). Henry Thannhauser (*The Burlington Magazine*, p. 98) was
the first to point out that the female model in *The Girl* had been incorrectly identified
as *L'Homme aux cheveux ébouriffés* (de la Faille, 1928, vol. I, p. 153).

The foreground figure in *The Bridge at Trinquetaille* (de la Faille 426) and in a
drawing of the same subject (de la Faille 1507) resemble the *Head of a Girl* (see cat.
no. 19, fn. 5).

REFERENCES:

H. Thannhauser, "Documents inédits: Vincent van Gogh et John Russell," *L'Amour de l'Art,*
XIXᵉ année, Sept. 1938, p. 284, repr.; H. Thannhauser, "Van Gogh and John Russell: Some
Unknown Letters and Drawings," *The Burlington Magazine,* vol. LXXIII, Sept. 1938, pp. 98
and 102, pl. IIIa; *CLVG,* 1958, vol. II, pp. 593, repr., and 665 (June 1888); de la Faille, 1970,
p. 523, repr., no. 1507a; M. Roskill, "Van Gogh's Exchanges of Work with Emile Bernard
in 1888: Appendix A," *Oud Holland,* Jg. LXXXVI, no. 2-3, 1971, p. 169 (late June); *Masterpieces,* 1972, p. 32, repr.; R. Pickvance, "The new De La Faille," *The Burlington Magazine,*
vol. CXV, Mar. 1973, p. 178.

fig. a.
Reverse of *Head of a Girl*.

21   Boats at Saintes-Maries.

      End of July-early August 1888

Pencil and ink on wove paper, 9%6 x 12%6
(24.3 x 31.9)

No watermark.

Not signed or dated.

PROVENANCE:

Received from the artist by John Peter Russell (d. 1931), 1888; inherited from Russell

by his daughter, Jeanne Jouve, Paris, probably 1931-32; acquired from Jouve by J. K.
Thannhauser, Paris, probably 1938-39
(notes Dec. 1972).

CONDITION:

Deacidified, flattened, and rehinged by
C. Gaehde (June 1973).

During July and early August of 1888, van Gogh made many drawings after recent
paintings and then sent the sketches to his brother Theo and to his friends, John Peter
Russell and Emile Bernard, both painters.

In Letter 516 (dated c. July 31 by Jan Hulsker, "Van Gogh's Extatische Maanden in
Arles," *Maatstaf,* Jg. 8, Aug.-Sept. 1960, p. 335), van Gogh writes: "I am working
hard for Russell, I thought that I would do him a series of drawings after my painted
series; I believe that he will look upon them kindly, and that, at least I hope so, will
help him to make a deal" (*CLVG,* II, p. 623). He had mentioned Russell in Letters 514
and 515 (placed July 29-30 by Hulsker) but without reference to the drawings. In Letter 517 (dated c. August 3 by Hulsker) van Gogh informs his brother that he had "sent
Russell 12 drawings after painted studies" (*CLVG,* II, p. 625). Thus all these drawings were completed before August 3.

Since the paintings from which *Boats at Saintes-Maries* and *The Zouave* (cat. no. 23) were copied date from June, it is possible that the drawings were done before the period of late July to early August. However, the letters cited above and the rapidity with which van Gogh worked at the time suggest a date of very late July into the first days of August. Ronald Pickvance specifies July 31-August 3, 1888 ("The new De La Faille," *The Burlington Magazine*, vol. CXV, Mar. 1973, p. 180). The twelve drawings in question are: *Hayricks* (de la Faille 1427), *Sea with Sailing Boats* (de la Faille 1433), *View in the Park* (de la Faille 1449), *A Garden* (de la Faille 1454), *The Postman Roulin* (de la Faille 1458), *Harvest in Provence* (de la Faille 1486), *Sheaves* (de la Faille 1489), *Arles: View from the Wheatfields* (de la Faille 1490), *Mousmé* (de la Faille 1503), *Sailing Boats Coming Ashore* (cat. no. 21; de la Faille 1430a), *The Zouave* (cat. no. 23; de la Faille 1482a), and *The Road to Tarascon* (cat. no. 22; de la Faille 1502a). The last three drawings are in the Thannhauser Collection at the Guggenheim.

Boats at Saintes-Maries was done after the painting *Seascape at Saintes-Maries* (de la Faille 417; 17¼ x 20¾ in., 44 x 53 cm., Pushkin Museum, Moscow; P. Cabanne, *Van Gogh*, trans. M. Martin, Englewood Cliffs, 1963, p. 88, color repr.). Mark Roskill emphasizes that van Gogh's drawings were made after paintings and not from other drawings ("Van Gogh's Blue Cart," *Oud Holland*, Jg. LXXXI, no. 1, 1966, p. 13, fn. 32). In addition, there are two very similar reed pen drawings: *Sailing Boats Coming Ashore* (de la Faille 1430b; 9½ x 12½ in., 24 x 31.5 cm., Musée d'Art Moderne, Brussels), which van Gogh sent to Theo, and *Sailing Boats Coming Ashore* (de la Faille 1430; 9½ x 12½ in., 24 x 32 cm., Nationale-Galerie, East Berlin), which he sent to Bernard. A related drawing with color notes was enclosed in a letter which van Gogh wrote Bernard after his return from Saintes-Maries (*CLVG*, III, p. 489, repr.).

Van Gogh had written earlier about his intention and eagerness to go to Saintes-Maries (Letters 492, 494, and 495) but it appears that the trip took place only during the third week in June (C. W. Millard, "A Chronology of Van Gogh's Drawings of 1888," *Master Drawings*, vol. 12, summer 1974, pp. 159 and 163, fn. 33). Letter 499, written to Theo from Saintes-Maries, is dated c. June 22 by Hulsker (p. 334). Saintes-Maries de-la-Mer is a fishing village on the Mediterranean. A stagecoach left daily to travel the twenty-four miles from Arles to Saintes-Maries across the Camargue, the peninsula at the delta of the Rhône River (*CLVG*, II, Letter 498, p. 584, and *CLVG*, III, Letter B6, p. 490).

The strokes made with reed pens of varying widths in the Saintes-Maries drawings closely resemble the corresponding brushstrokes in the painting. However, in the Thannhauser drawing, the sky is indicated by dotting. Vincent first used reed pens at Arles, apparently because of his wish to produce works close to Japanese art. The combination of dots, commas, short lines, and hatching is used consistently in the drawings sent to John Russell.

EXHIBITIONS:

Adelaide, The National Art Gallery, *Exhibition of French and British Contemporary Art,* opened Aug. 21, 1939, no. 138, traveled to Melbourne, Town Hall, opened Oct. 16, and Sydney, David Jones, opened Nov. 20 (correspondence with R. Appleyard, Nov. 1973 and June 1975 and A. Dixon, Nov. 1973).

REFERENCES:

H. Thannhauser, "Documents inédits: Vincent van Gogh et John Russell," *L'Amour de l'Art,* XIXᵉ année, Sept. 1938, pp. 283, repr., and 284 (ex. coll. J. Russell); H. Thannhauser, "Van

Gogh and John Russell: Some Unknown Letters and Drawings," *The Burlington Magazine,* vol. LXXIII, Sept. 1938, pp. 99, pl. IIA, and 104 (private coll., France); Rewald, 1962, p. 227, repr. (June 1888); J. Leymarie, *Who Was van Gogh?,* trans. J. Emmons, Geneva, 1968, p. 95, repr.; H. Keller, *Vincent van Gogh: The Final Years,* New York, 1969, p. 26, repr.; de la Faille, 1970, pp. 503, repr., and 662, no. 1430a (*Sailing Boats Coming Ashore,* June 1888); *Masterpieces,* 1972, p. 31, repr.

---

22   The Road to Tarascon.
     End of July-early August 1888

Pencil and ink on wove paper, 9⅛ x 12⁹⁄₁₆ (23.2 x 31.9)

No watermark.

Signed l.r.: *Vincent*   Not dated.

PROVENANCE:
Received from the artist by John Peter Russell (d. 1931), 1888; inherited from Russell by his daughter, Jeanne Jouve, Paris, prob-

ably 1931-32; acquired from Jouve by J. K. Thannhauser, Paris, probably 1938-39 (notes Dec. 1972).

CONDITION:
Small tears at bottom margin and top center margin. Deacidified and rehinged by C. Gaehde (June 1973).

Tarascon is on the left bank of the Rhône River not far north of Arles. Vincent reports to Theo in Letter 496 (dated July 12 by Jan Hulsker, "Van Gogh's Extatische Maanden in Arles," *Maatstaf,* Jg. 8, Aug.-Sept. 1960, p. 334) that "one day I went to Tarascon, but unfortunately there was such a blazing sun and so much dust that day that I came back with an empty bag" (*CLVG,* II, p. 582). In Letter 499 he expresses a wish to go there again. However, no evidence indicates that he did.

In Letter 524 (dated c. August 14 by Hulsker) van Gogh describes "a rough sketch I made of myself laden with boxes, props, and canvas on the sunny road to Tarascon" (*CLVG,* III, p. 14). By this time the painting, *The Painter on the Road to Tarascon* (de la Faille 448; 19 x 17¼ in., 48 x 44 cm., now destroyed, formerly Kaiser Museum, Magdeburg; L. Goldscheider and W. Uhde, *Vincent van Gogh,* Oxford, 1941, color pl. 69), was completed and was included in a roll of thirty-five works that Second Lieutenant Milliet was soon to deliver to Theo in Paris (*CLVG,* III, Letter 524, p. 14).

The present drawing closely resembles the painting in the general disposition of road, trees, and field. However, the figure is omitted and the blazing sun is made explicit by the circle in the sky in the drawing. Sunlight is represented in the painting by golds and yellows and by the prominent foreground shadow. These differences between the painting and the present drawing, which was sent to Russell by August 3 (Letter 517), suggest that van Gogh may have worked more on the canvas and completed it after August 3 but before August 14. (See also cat. no. 21.)

Drawings of the road to Tarascon include *The Road to Tarascon with Figure* (de la Faille 1502; 9¾ x 13½ in., 25 x 34 cm., dated August 1888 in de la Faille, Kunst-

haus Zürich) and *Three Trees, Route de Tarascon* (de la Faille 1518; 10 x 13¾ in., 25.5 x 35 cm., dated summer 1888 in de la Faille, present whereabouts unknown). Both drawings as well as others that refer to the Tarascon road are placed in July 1888 by Charles W. Millard ("A Chronology for Van Gogh's Drawings of 1888," *Master Drawings,* vol. 12, summer 1974, p. 159).

Van Gogh represented the sun as a circle prominent in the sky in several drawings of the period (de la Faille 1439, 1441, 1442, 1472a, 1506, and 1514).

EXHIBITIONS:

Adelaide, The National Art Gallery, *Exhibition of French and British Contemporary Art,* opened Aug. 21, 1939, no. 139, traveled to Melbourne, Town Hall, opened Oct. 16, and Sydney, David Jones, opened Nov. 20 (correspondence with R. Appleyard, Nov. 1973 and June 1975 and A. Dixon, Nov. 1973).

REFERENCES:

H. Thannhauser, "Documents inédits: Vincent van Gogh et John Russell," *L'Amour de l'Art,* XIXᵉ année, Sept. 1938, pp. 284 and 285, repr.; H. Thannhauser, "Van Gogh and John Russell: Some Unknown Letters and Drawings," *The Burlington Magazine,* vol. LXXIII, Sept. 1938, pp. 99, pl. 11c, and 104 (private coll., France); H. Graber, ed., *Vincent Van Gogh: Briefe an Emile Bernard, Paul Gauguin, John Russell, Paul Signac und Andere,* Basel, 1941, repr. opp. p. 68 *(Landschaft bei Arles);* F. Elgar, *Van Gogh,* trans. J. Cleugh, New York, 1958, p. 167, repr.; de la Faille, 1970, pp. 522, 523, repr., and 665, no. 1502a *(The Road to Tarascon: Sky with Sun,* Arles, Aug. 1888); *Masterpieces,* 1972, p. 33, repr. *(The Road from Tarascon);* R. Pickvance, "The new De La Faille," *The Burlington Magazine,* vol. CXV, Mar. 1973, p. 179 (corrects omission of signature); B. Petrie, *Van Gogh,* London, 1974, pl. 77.

23   The Zouave.
      End of July-early August 1888

Ink on wove paper, 12⅝₆ x 9⅝₆
(31.9 x 24.3)

No watermark.

Signed l.l.: *Vincent*   Not dated.

PROVENANCE:
Received from the artist by John Peter Russell (d. 1931), 1888; inherited from Russell

by his daughter, Jeanne Jouve, Paris, probably 1931-32; acquired from Jouve by J. K. Thannhauser, Paris, probably 1938-39 (notes Dec. 1972).

CONDITION:
Deacidified and rehinged by C. Gaehde (June 1973).

Vincent wrote to his brother Theo (*CLVG*, II, Letter 501, p. 591; dated June 29-30 by Jan Hulsker, "Van Gogh's Extatische Maanden in Arles," *Maatstaf*, Jg. 8, Aug.-Sept. 1960, p. 334): "I have a model at last— a Zouave— a boy with a small face, a bull neck, and the eye of a tiger, and I began with one portrait, and began again with another, the half-length I did of him was horribly harsh, in a blue uniform, the blue of enamel saucepans, with braids of a faded reddish-orange, and two stars on his breast, an ordinary blue, and very hard to do. That bronzed, feline head of his with the reddish cap, against a green door and the orange bricks of a wall." The painting referred to is *A Bugler of the Zouave Regiment* (de la Faille 423; 25½ x 21¼ in., 65 x 54 cm., Rijksmuseum, Amsterdam; *Vincent van Gogh Paintings and Drawings: A Choice from the Collection of the Vincent van Gogh Foundation*, Amsterdam, 1968, p. 74, color repr.). The present drawing is a copy of the painting. (See cat. no. 21.)

A Zouave is a member of "a body of light infantry in the French army, originally recruited from the Algerian Kabyle tribe of Zouaoua, but afterwards composed of French soldiers distinguished for their physique and dash, and formerly retaining the original Oriental uniform" (*Oxford English Dictionary*, Oxford, 1933, vol. XII, p. 103).

The Zouave described in Letters 501, 502, B8, and W5 has been confused with the Second Lieutenant of the Zouave Regiment named Milliet, who was a friend of van Gogh (Letters 506, 541, 541a, 553b, and B16). Douglas Cooper (*The Burlington Magazine*, 1938, p. 227) was the first to distinguish between the two people and identify van Gogh's representations of each. The physiognomies and uniforms in *A Bugler of the Zouave Regiment* and *The Zouave* (de la Faille 424) differ from those in *Portrait of Milliet* (de la Faille 473).

In addition to the present drawing, which was sent to Russell, van Gogh executed a drawing in pen, brown ink, blue crayon, and watercolor and inscribed it *"A mon cher copain Emile Bernard"* (de la Faille 1482; 12 x 9 in., 30.5 x 22.9 cm., The Metropolitan Museum of Art, New York). The copy sent to Bernard follows the painting less closely than the present drawing since the distinction between the background areas and any indication of the bricks have been omitted and slightly more of the figure's sash and jacket is visible. In the Thannhauser drawing, the stocky figure with bull neck and intense eyes is described with attention to such details as the roughness of his beard and complexion.

In Letter 502 van Gogh wrote to Theo: "Anyway, I shall send you a drawing of the Zouave today" (*CLVG*, II, p. 595). This probably refers to the full-length view, *The Zouave Seated* (de la Faille 1443; 20½ x 26 in., 52 x 66 cm., Collection John Nicholas Brown, Providence, R.I., ex. coll. J. van Gogh-Bonger).

EXHIBITIONS:

Adelaide, The National Art Gallery, *Exhibition of French and British Contemporary Art,* opened Aug. 21, 1939, no. 137, traveled to Melbourne, Town Hall, opened Oct. 16, and Sydney, David Jones, opened Nov. 20; Minneapolis, University Gallery, University of Minnesota, *The Nineteenth Century: One Hundred Twenty-five Master Drawings,* Mar. 26-Apr. 23, 1962, no. 119, traveled to The Solomon R. Guggenheim Museum, May 15-June 28.

REFERENCES:

H. Thannhauser, "Documents inédits: Vincent van Gogh et John Russell," *L'Amour de l'Art,* XIXᵉ année, Sept. 1938, pp. 281, repr., and 284 (*Le Zouave Milliet,* ex. coll. John Russell); H. Thannhauser, "Van Gogh and John Russell: Some Unknown Letters and Drawings," *The Burlington Magazine,* vol. LXXIII, Sept. 1938, pp. 94, repr., and 104 (private coll., France); D. Lord (pseud. for D. Cooper), "Letter: Van Gogh and John Russell," *The Burlington Magazine,* vol. LXXIII, Nov. 1938, p. 227 (correcting identification of the Zouave); H. Graber, ed., *Vincent Van Gogh: Briefe an Emile Bernard, Paul Gauguin, John Russell, Paul Signac und Andere,* Basel, 1941, repr. opp. p. 44; K. Berger, *Französische Meisterzeichnungen des Neunzehnten Jahrhunderts,* Basel, 1949, pp. 30 and 88, repr., no. 54; P. J. Sachs, *Modern Prints and Drawings,* New York, 1954, p. 50, pl. 41; F. Elgar, *Van Gogh,* trans. J. Cleugh, New York, 1958, pp. 154, repr., and 183; Rewald, 1962, p. 262, repr. *(Portrait of a Zouave Bugler);* J. Leymarie, *Who Was van Gogh?,* trans. J. Emmons, Geneva, 1968, p. 107, repr.; N. Wadley, *The Drawings of van Gogh,* London, 1969, p. 37 and pl. 92 *(The Zouave Milliet);* de la Faille, 1970, pp. 516, repr., and 665, no. 1482a *(The Zouave: Head and Shoulders,* June 1888); J. Hulsker, ed., *Van Gogh's "Diary": The Artist's Life in His Own Words and Art,* New York, 1971, pp. 112, repr., and 168 *(The Zouave); Masterpieces,* 1972, p. 34, repr.

24 **Mountains at Saint-Rémy.**

July 1889

*(Montagnes à Saint-Rémy; The Alpilles
with Dark Hut; Hills at Saint-Rémy;
Collines à Arles; Berglandschaft)*

Oil on canvas, 28¼ x 35¾ (71.8 x 90.8)

Not signed or dated.

PROVENANCE:

Sent by the artist to Theo van Gogh, Sept.
1889 (Letter 607); acquired in exchange by
Eugène Boch,[1] Monthyon (Seine-et-Marne),
June 1890 and still in his possession in 1908;
Galerie E. Druet, Paris, by 1912;[2] Walther
Halvorsen,[3] Paris, from 1918; Trygve
Sagen, Oslo;[4] Galerien Thannhauser, Berlin,
by 1927.

CONDITION:

Lined at an earlier unrecorded date before
1965. Flattening of pigment resulted. Scattered loss of paint in the sky and localized
cleavage in the trees at the center. A three-
inch vertical repair at the upper right was
referred to as old damage in 1939 (Registrar's files, The Museum of Modern Art,
New York, 39.351). At the lower right, a
seven and five-eighths-inch vertical tear and
a four and one-quarter-inch horizontal tear
were repaired at an undetermined date before 1965 (Jan. 1975).

References in the artist's letters to the present painting provide information about its
provenance, date, and subject matter. It is first mentioned in Letter 600 (dated c. July
9, 1889, by Jan Hulsker, "Van Gogh's Bedreigde Leven in St. Rémy en Auvers,"
Maatstaf, Jg. 8, Jan. 1961, p. 663): "The last canvas I have done is a view of mountains with a dark hut at the bottom among some olive trees" (*CLVG,* III, p. 193).
Van Gogh painted it at Saint-Rémy while a patient at the Hospital of Saint-Paul-de-
Mausole. He used an empty cell on the ground floor as a studio and was allowed
freedom to paint outside the hospital. The Alpilles range is visible from the hospital,
and the view from in front bears a striking resemblance to the present picture (fig. a).

After receiving news from his brother that they were expecting a child and shortly
after writing Letter 600, van Gogh had another mental seizure while painting in the
fields, and he remained in his room for the next six weeks (Rewald, 1962, p. 545).

1. Theo arranged the exchange with Boch, a Belgian painter (1885-1944), and told Vincent
about it in a letter dated June 23, 1890 (*CLVG,* III, Letter T38, p. 573). In exchange Vincent received Boch's *La Mine de l'Agrappe* (Amsterdam, Stedelijk Museum, *Collectie
Theo van Gogh,* exh. cat., 1960, no. 16). In Sept. 1888 Vincent met Boch, who was staying
with Dodge MacKnight at Fontvieille (Letter 531). At that time Boch was thirty-three years
old and had already been working in Paris for ten years (M. E. Tralbaut, *Vincent van
Gogh,* New York, 1969, p. 253). Van Gogh's *Portrait of Eugène Boch* dates from Sept.
1888 (de la Faille 462; 23⅝ x 17¾ in., 60 x 45 cm., Musée du Louvre, Galerie du Jeu de
Paume, Paris; de la Faille, 1970, p. 287, color repr.). His sister, the painter Anna Boch,
purchased van Gogh's painting *The Red Vineyard* (de la Faille 495; Nov. 1888) at the exhibition of the XX in Brussels in Feb. 1890 (Rewald, 1962, p. 374).
2. De la Faille, 1928, vol. I, p. 175. According to de la Faille the present picture is Druet photo
nos. 2896 and 61103.
3. According to his widow, Halvorsen destroyed all his correspondence before his death in
1972. She remembers that her husband sold the remainder of his collection to Flechtheim in
Berlin before leaving Paris in 1920 (correspondence with Anita Halvorsen, Nov. 1976).
4. Notes made by J. K. Thannhauser in Dec. 1972 and by D. C. Rich in Mar. 1975 indicate
that it belonged to Sagen after Halvorsen and before Thannhauser.

When his correspondence with Theo was resumed in August, van Gogh refers again to the present picture (Letters 601, 602, and 607), and he now associates it with a passage in a book by Edouard Rod. The book in question, *Le Sens de la vie*, had been sent to him late in June by his sister, Wil (see Letters 596 and W13).

In Letter 607 (dated Sept. 20 by Hulsker), the artist writes about the "Mountain": "But after all it seemed to me it expressed the passage in Rod's book—one of the very rare passages of his in which I found something good—about a desolate country of somber mountains, among which are some dark goatherds' huts where sunflowers are blooming" (*CLVG*, III, p. 217). In Book III of *Le Sens de la vie*, which is entitled "Altruisme," chapters IV and V are about a mountain. Rod writes of the *montagnards: "Ils semblent indifférent au bien-être: leurs chalets de bois sont petits et noirs, . . . ils mangent les légumes qu'ils ont fait pousser dans leurs jardinets où se balancent de rares tournesols, . . .* (p. 223). ("They seem indifferent to life's comforts: their wooden huts are small and black, . . . they eat the vegetables which they have grown in their little gardens where an occasional sunflower sways, . . .") Rod also refers to goats. (The passage was brought to my attention by Audrey Helfand.)

It must be kept in mind that the association with Rod's book arises at least a month after Vincent first mentioned the painting and probably after he completed work on the canvas.

There are other compositions close in subject and in date to the Thannhauser painting (de la Faille 611, 615, 618, 619, and 635).

EXHIBITIONS:[5]
Paris, Galerie E. Druet, *Vincent van Gogh,* Jan. 6-18, 1908, no. 3 (*Collines à Arles,* lent by E. Boch);[6] New York, Armory of the Sixty-ninth Infantry, *International Exhibition of Modern Art,* Feb. 15-Mar. 15, 1913, no. 424 (*Collines à Arles,* lent by E. Druet), traveled to The Art Institute of Chicago, Mar. 24-Apr. 16, no. 408, repr., Boston, Copley Hall, Apr. 28-May 19, no. 213, repr.; Prague, Spolku Výtvarných Umělcu Mánes, *Exhibition of French Art,* Dec. 1923-Jan. 1924 (?),[7] no. 55 (*Landscape of Arles,* oil, 93 x 73 cm.); Berlin, Künstlerhaus (organized by the Galerien Thannhauser), *Erste Sonderausstellung in Berlin,* Jan. 9-Feb. 15, 1927, no. 117, repr. *(Berglandschaft);* New York, The Museum of Modern Art, *Art in Our Time,* May 10-Sept. 30, 1939, no. 70, repr. *(Hills at Saint-Rémy);* on loan to The Museum of Modern Art until Apr. 1941 (MOMA Registrar's Files 39.351); Cincinnati Modern Art Society,

5. Since J. K. Thannhauser (notes, Dec. 1972) remembered that the painting was exhibited by Heinrich Thannhauser in 1908 and since his father was an associate of F. J. Brakl in Munich, it is possible that the present picture was included in the van Gogh exhibition held in Mar. 1908 (listed in de la Faille, 1970, p. 691) or in Oct.-Dec. 1909 at the Moderne Kunsthandlung (F. J. Brakl), perhaps as nos. 39 or 45 (Gordon, 1974, vol. II, pp. 343-44). There were also paintings by van Gogh exhibited in Mar.-Apr. 1909 in Munich at the Kunstsalon W. Zimmerman (Gordon, 1974, vol. II, p. 249).

6. Information from Gordon, 1974, vol. II, pp. 244-45.

7. The present picture corresponds with no. 55 (*Landscape of Arles,* oil, 93 x 73 cm.) in the Dec. 1923 exhibition of French art although it is not reproduced in the catalogue nor is the lender's name given (correspondence with J. Kotalík, Jan. 1974). De la Faille (1928 and 1970) identifies the present picture as the single work exhibited at an unspecified location in Prague in Jan. 1924. J. K. Thannhauser also stated that it was exhibited in Prague in Jan. 1924 (notes made by D. C. Rich, Mar. 1975). Kotalík concurs that the picture probably remained in Prague in the first month of 1924 (correspondence, Jan. 1974).

fig. a.
The Alpilles from the Hospital of Saint-Paul-de-Mausole, Saint-Rémy.

Paintings of School of Paris, Apr. 12-May 12, 1940 (no cat.; correspondence with S. C. Johnson, Jan. 1974); San Francisco, Palace of Fine Arts, *Golden Gate International Exposition,* May 25-Sept. 29, 1940, no. 272, repr.; The Detroit Institute of Arts, *Modern Paintings from the Museum of Modern Art,* Jan. 3-Feb. 2, 1941 (no cat.; correspondence with C. Elam, Sept. 1976); The Baltimore Museum of Art, *Paintings by van Gogh,* Sept. 18-Oct. 18, 1942, no. 18, traveled to Worcester Art Museum, Oct. 28-Nov. 28; Pittsburgh, Carnegie Institute Museum of Art, *Modern Dutch Art,* Feb. 5-Mar. 1, 1943,[8] no. 24G *(Hills at Saint-Rémy);* The Cleveland Museum of Art, *Work by Vincent van Gogh,* Nov. 3-Dec. 12, 1948, no. 20, repr.; The Art Institute of Chicago, May-Aug. 1955 (correspondence with W. D. Bradway, Dec. 1973); New York, The Solomon R. Guggenheim Museum, *Van Gogh and Expressionism,* July 1-Sept. 13, 1964 *(Mountains at Saint-Rémy).*

REFERENCES:

G. Coquiot, *Vincent van Gogh,* Paris, 1923, p. 317 *(Vue de montagnes, avec une cabane noirâtre, dans les oliviers);* H. Hildebrandt, *Die Kunst des 19. und 20. Jahrhunderts,* Potsdam, 1924, pl. xiv *(Arlesische Landschaft,* Galerie Thannhauser); M. Osborn, "Klassiker der Französischen Moderne," *Deutsche Kunst und Dekoration,* vol. 59, Mar. 1927, p. 338, repr.; de la Faille, 1928, vol. I, p. 175 and vol. II, pl. clxxii *(Collines à Saint-Rémy,* July 1889); W. Scherjon, *Catalogue des tableaux par Vincent van Gogh décrits dans ses lettres,* Utrecht, 1932, p. 25, repr., no. 14 *(La Montagne* [Livre de Rod *Le Sens de la vie]);* V. Lamberto, *Vincent van Gogh,* Milan, 1936, pl. xx; W. Scherjon and J. de Gruyter, *Vincent van Gogh's Great Period: Arles, St. Rémy and Auvers sur Oise,* Amsterdam, 1937, pp. 215, repr., and 217, no. 14; de la Faille, 1939, p. 427, repr., no. 619 *(Collines à St.-Rémy);* C. Nordenfalk, "Van Gogh and Literature," *Journal of the Warburg and Courtauld Institutes,* vol. X, 1947, p. 145 and pl. 38e; J. Seznec, "Literary Inspiration in Van Gogh," *Magazine of Art,* vol. 43, Dec. 1950, p. 286; *CLVG,* 1958, vol. III, pp. 193, 195-96, 216-17, and 573; A. Kuhn-Foelix, *Vincent van Gogh,* Bergen, 1958, p. 200 and pl. 46 *(Hügellandschaft bei St. Rémy);* F. Elgar, *Van Gogh,* trans. J. Cleugh, New York, 1958, pp. 168-69, repr., and 222; Rewald, 1962, p. 359, color repr. *(Mountains at Saint-Rémy);* M. W. Brown, *The Story of the Armory Show,* Greenwich, 1963, p. 246, no. 424; F. Daulte, "Une Donation sans précédent: la collection Thannhauser," *Connaissance des Arts,* no. 171, May 1966, p. 64, repr. (erroneously states that it was the only painting van Gogh sold during his life); de la Faille, 1970, pp. 248, repr., 249, and 635, no. 622 *(The Alpilles with Dark Hut,* July 1889); *Masterpieces,* 1972, p. 35, repr.; R. Treble, *Van Gogh and His Art,* London, 1975, p. 104, pl. 84.

8. The painting was not included in the exhibition when it opened in Albany in Jan. 1943 and it did not travel (correspondence with L. A. Arkus, Feb. 1974).

25 Letter to John Peter Russell.

Late January 1890

Ink on laid paper, 7 x 8⅞ (17.8 x 22.5)

Watermark of a shield (2¼ x 1¾ in.)
with the word "UNIVERSAL" below

Not dated.

PROVENANCE:

Received from the artist by John Peter
Russell (d. 1931), 1890; inherited from Russell by his daughter, Jeanne Jouve, Paris,
probably 1931-32; acquired from Jouve by
J. K. Thannhauser, Paris, probably 1938-39
(notes Dec. 1972).

My dear friend Russell,[1]

Today I am sending you a little roll of photographs of pictures by Millet, which you may not know.[2]

However this may be, the purpose is to remind you of myself and my brother.

Do you know that my brother has got married in the meantime, and that he is now expecting his first child?[3] Let's hope all goes well— he has a very nice Dutch wife.

How much it pleases me to write you after such a long silence! Do you remember when we met our friend Gauguin[4] almost at the same time— I think you were the first, and I the second?

He is still struggling on—alone, or nearly alone, like the brave fellow he is. I feel sure you have not forgotten him.

1. The translation is from *The Complete Letters of Vincent van Gogh*, III, pp. 249-50, courtesy of The New York Graphic Society. The letter (623a) was translated by C. de Dood, who completed the work of J. van Gogh-Bonger who, at the time of her death in 1925, had reached Letter 526 (*CLVG*, I, pp. xii and lxvii).

2. Vincent had just received the photographs in question from Theo (*CLVG*, III, Letter 625, p. 252, where it is dated Feb. 1). Van Gogh was interested in "translating" works by Millet. However, as he wrote in Letter 625 (dated Feb. 2 by J. Hulsker, "Van Gogh's Bedreigde Leven in St. Rémy en Auvers," *Maatstaf*, Jg. 8, Jan. 1961, p. 664): "I have scruples of conscience about doing the things by Millet which you sent me, for instance, and which seemed to me perfectly chosen, and I took the pile of photographs and unhesitantly sent them to Russell, so that I shall not see them again until I have made up my mind" (p. 252).

   According to R. L. Herbert, there were many Millet photographs available at that time so that it is difficult to know which ones Theo sent. Adolphe Braun was the most important early source for photographs of Millet's work: the appendix to A. Sensier, *La Vie et l'oeuvre de J.-F. Millet*, Paris, 1881 [pp. 403-4], includes a list of photographic reproductions of forty-seven paintings, pastels, and drawings which could be purchased from Braun. In addition, several dealers had Millet photographs including Durand-Ruel and, significantly, Boussod et Valadon. Since Theo worked for the latter, their photographs would have been readily accessible to him (correspondence with R. L. Herbert, Aug. 1976).

3. His nephew and namesake, Vincent W. van Gogh, was born on Jan. 31, 1890.

4. According to Rewald (1962, pp. 41, 540-41), van Gogh met Gauguin in Nov. 1886 after Gauguin's return from Pont-Aven to Paris. B. Welsh-Ovcharov points out that there is actually no concrete evidence for a close personal relationship between the two artists until very late 1887 (pp. 24-25). Citing the reference in the present letter she finds it possible that van Gogh and Gauguin met through an intermediary such as A. S. Hartrick (1864-1950; p. 56, fn. 28).

Mon cher ami Russell

Je vous envoie aujourd'hui
un petit rouleau de photographies
d'après Millet que peut-être
vous ne connaissez pas.
Quoi qu'il en soit c'est pour
vous rappeler mon frère et
moi à votre bon souvenir. –
Savez vous que mon frère s'est
marié depuis et que juste de
ces jours ci il attend son premier né
Puisse cela aller bien – il a une
bien brave femme hollandaise
Que cela me fait plaisir de vous
écrire après un long silence

Vous souvenez vous du temps que
simultanément presque que vous
je crois le premier et moi après
rencontrâmes l'ami Gauguin
Il lutte toujours – et seul ou
presque seul en brave qu'il
est. Suis sûr que vous ne
l'oubliez pas pourtant
Nous sommes lui et moi encore
toujours amis je vous l'assure
mais peut être vous n'ignorez pas
que moi je suis malade et
ai en plus d'une fois des crues
nerveuses graves et du délire
Cela a été cause qu'ayant dû
aller dans un asile d'aliénés
nous nous sommes séparés
lui et moi. Mais que de
fois avons nous auparavant
causé de vous ensemble
Gauguin est actuellement encore
avec un de mes compatriotes

nommé de Haan et de Haan le
loue beaucoup et s'en trouve
pas mal d'être avec lui
Vous trouverez article sur des
toiles de moi aux vingtistes je
vous assure que moi je dois
beaucoup à des choses que Gauguin
me disait pour le dessin et
tiens en haute très haute estime
sa façon d'aimer la nature
Car à mon avis il vaut encore
mieux comme homme que
comme artiste. Est ce que cela
va bien chez vous! et travaillez
vous toujours beaucoup!
Quoique ce ne soit pas une
cause de joie d'être malade
pourtant je n'ai pas le droit de
m'en plaindre car il me semble
que la nature fait que la maladie
est un moyen de nous redresser de
nous guérir plutôt qu'un mal
absolu.
Si jamais vous venez à Paris

prenez si vous voulez une
toile de moi chez mon frère
si vous conservez l'idée de fonder
un jour une collection pour votre
patrie. Vous vous rappelez
que je vous en ai déjà parlé
que c'était mon grand désir
de vous en donner une dans
ce but. Comment va
l'ami Mac Knight. S'il
est encore avec vous ou
s'il y a avec vous
d'autres que j'ai eu le
plaisir de rencontrer dites
leur bien le bonjour pour moi
Veuillez surtout me rappeler
au bon souvenir de
Mme Russell et croyez
moi avec poignée de main
en pensée.   bien à vous
           Vincent van Gogh
c/o Docteur Peyron
St Rémy en Provence

I assure you that he and I are still friends, but perhaps you are not unaware that I am ill, and that I have had serious nervous crises and delirium more than once. This was the cause of our parting company, he and I, for I had to go into a lunatic asylum.[5] But, before that, how many times we spoke of you!

At the moment Gauguin is still with one of my fellow countrymen by the name of De Haan,[6] and De Haan praises him highly, and does not think it at all bad to be with him.

You will find [an] article about some canvases I have at the exhibition of the *Vingtistes*.[7] I assure you that I owe much to the things Gauguin told me on the subject of drawing, and I have the highest respect for the way he loves nature.[8] For in my opinion he is worth even more as a man than as an artist.

And is everything going well with you? And are you still working hard?

Though it is not pleasant to be ill, yet I have no right to complain, for it seems to me that nature sees to it that disease is a means of putting us on our legs again and of healing us, rather than an absolute evil.

If you should go to Paris, please go and take a canvas of mine at my brother's, if you still stick to the idea of someday getting together a collection for your native country.[9]

You will remember that I have already told you it is my great desire to give you one for this purpose. How is our friend MacKnight? If he is still with you, and if there are others with you whom I have had the pleasure of meeting, please remember me to them.

Above all give my kind regards to Mrs. Russell, and believe me, with a handshake in thought,

Sincerely yours, Vincent van Gogh

5. Vincent's breakdown occurred on Dec. 23, 1888, and Gauguin left Arles a day or two after Christmas (M. Roskill, *Van Gogh, Gauguin and the Impressionist Circle*, Greenwich, 1970, p. 270).

6. The Dutchman is Jacob Meyer de Haan (1852-1895). In 1888 he went to Paris, met Gauguin, and stayed with Theo, who sent de Haan's drawings to Vincent (*CLVG*, III, Letters T1 and T2, pp. 530-31). (See W. Jaworska, *Gauguin and the Pont-Aven School*, trans. P. Evans, Greenwich, c. 1972, pp. 95-106.)

   During the winter of 1889-90, Gauguin stayed with de Haan at Le Pouldu in Brittany. On Jan. 3, 1890, Theo wrote to Vincent: "I have had no news from Gauguin. He is very happy because De Haan is with him, for the latter pays for his whole maintenance and for his paints" (*CLVG*, III, Letter T23, p. 560). On Feb. 9, 1890, Theo wrote that "Gauguin arrived in Paris yesterday" (*CLVG*, III, Letter T28, p. 564).

7. The article is G.-Albert Aurier's "Les Isolés: Vincent van Gogh," *Mercure de France*, vol. I, no. 1, Jan. 1890, pp. 24-29. The exhibition of the XX opened in Brussels on Jan. 18, 1890 (Rewald, 1962, pp. 367-73). Like the Millet photographs mentioned above, Theo had recently sent the article to his brother (*CLVG*, III, Letter 625, p. 251).

8. Likewise, in his letter to Aurier, van Gogh states: "I owe much to Paul Gauguin" (*CLVG*, III, Letter 626a, p. 256).

9. Russell's plan was never realized. Before returning to Australia in 1921, he sold his collection in Paris at the Hôtel Drouot, Mar. 31, 1920.

This letter was written late in January 1890, before van Gogh learned of the birth of his nephew (which occurred on Jan. 31) and after Theo had sent him Aurier's article, which appeared in the first issue of *Mercure de France*.

Unlike the earlier letters in English, van Gogh wrote to Russell in French. The existing correspondence contains no mention of Russell for a considerable period of time before January 1890. However, Letter 625 (dated February 2 by Jan Hulsker), which sheds light on several aspects of the present letter, does mention Russell's name several times. Vincent writes of having "written a note to Russell once more, to remind him a little of Gauguin, for I know that Russell as a man has much gravity and strength" (*CLVG*, III, p. 252). In addition, van Gogh thought of Russell with regard to Millet: "If for my part I wanted to go on—let's call it *translating* certain pages of Millet, then, to prevent anyone from being able, not to criticize me, which wouldn't matter, but to make it awkward for me or hinder me by pretending that it is just copying—then I need someone among the artists like Russell or Gauguin to carry this thing through and make a serious job of it. . . . And not now, but in a few months' time, I shall try to get a candid opinion from Russell himself on the usefulness of the thing" (Letter 625, pp. 252-53).

Russell's reply to the present letter is mentioned in Letter 628 (*CLVG*, III, p. 260).

EXHIBITION:

New York, Wildenstein and Co., *Van Gogh,* Mar. 24-Apr. 30, 1955, no. 110.

REFERENCES:

H. Thannhauser, "Documents inédits: Vincent van Gogh et John Russell," *L'Amour de l'Art,* XIXe année, Sept. 1938, p. 286 (end of Jan. 1890); H. Thannhauser, "Van Gogh and John Russell: Some Unknown Letters and Drawings," *The Burlington Magazine,* vol. LXXIII, Sept. 1938, p. 103; H. Graber, ed., *Vincent Van Gogh: Briefe an Emile Bernard, Paul Gauguin, John Russell, Paul Signac und Andere,* Basel, 1941, pp. 124-26 (German trans.); *CLVG,* 1958, vol. III, Letter 623a, pp. 249-50 (end of Jan. 1890); J. Hulsker, "Van Gogh's Bedreigde Leven in St. Rémy en Auvers," *Maatstaf,* Jg. 8, Jan. 1961, p. 664 (end of Jan.); *Masterpieces,* 1972, p. 30, repr.; A. Galbally, "Amitie: Russell and Van Gogh," *Art Bulletin of Victoria,* 1976, pp. 36-37; B. Welsh-Ovcharov, *Vincent van Gogh: His Paris Period 1886-88,* Utrecht and The Hague, 1976, p. 56, fn. 28.

Aristide Maillol

Born December 1861, Banyuls-sur-Mer
Died September 1944, Banyuls-sur-Mer

26 Woman with Crab. c. 1902(?)-1905
   (*La Femme au crabe; Frau mit Krebs*)

Bronze, 6 x 5¾ x 4¾ (15.2 x 14.6 x 12.1)

Signed with the artist's monogram "AM" in a circle on the base between the crab and the figure's left foot.   Not dated.

PROVENANCE:

Acquired from the artist by Alfred Wolff, Munich, by 1917;[1] acquired from Wolff by J. K. Thannhauser.

1. According to notes made by J. K. Thannhauser (Dec. 1972), Wolff was a director of the Deutsche Bank. The archives of the Bank confirm that Wolff was director of the Munich branch from 1905 until 1909 and from 1911 until 1917 (correspondence with W. Kohl, Feb. 1977). Thus, it appears likely that Wolff acquired the sculpture before 1917 although no documentary evidence exists.

Woman with Crab is one of the bronzes cast by Ambroise Vollard. About 1900 Vuillard introduced Maillol to Vollard, who bought some terra-cottas and had them cast in bronze (Johnson, pp. 39-40, and New York, Paul Rosenberg and Co., *Aristide Maillol*, exh. cat., 1958, p. 10). According to Una Johnson, Vollard's edition of *Woman with Crab* was first issued about 1903 (p. 102, no. 97, and p. 195). It has not been possible to locate a catalogue of the Maillol exhibition which took place at the Galerie Vollard from June 15-30, 1902 (conversation with L. Konheim and correspondence with Johnson, Nov. 1976). Consequently, a precise date for *Woman with Crab* cannot be determined. The artist certainly had conceived of the image by April 1905 when Octave Mirbeau, writing about the women in Maillol's sculpture, specifically mentions "qu'elle joue enfantinement, sur la sable, avec un crabe" ("Aristide Maillol," *La Revue*, XVIe année, vol. LV, Apr. 1905, p. 328).

Dina Vierny dates *Woman with Crab* 1930, citing the fact that Maillol listed it in *L'Inventaire de l'oeuvre sculptée* under that year (correspondence, Feb. 1976). However, a bronze of the same subject was reproduced as early as 1922 (B. Ternovets, "French Sculpture in Moscow," *Sredi Kollektsionerov*, no. 10, Oct. 1922, p. 3) and appeared also in Germany in the 1920s (C. Einstein, *Die Kunst des 20. Jahrhunderts*, Berlin, 1926, p. 514, repr. [Silberberg collection, Breslau] and Düsseldorf, Galerie Flechtheim, *Lebende Ausländische Kunst aus Rheinischem Privatbesitz*, exh. cat., Oct. 1928, no. 90).

Linda Konheim notes (Jan. 1978) that although the 1902-5 date attributed to this work is very plausible, it is not possible to document a date earlier than 1917 for this piece. (The 1917 date has been clearly established on the basis of the provenance of this bronze). She feels that since there is no illustration of the woman with crab mentioned by Mirbeau in 1905, it cannot be determined if he is referring to the same piece or a different version of the same subject until further evidence is obtained. Maillol frequently reworked his own motifs, and two versions of *Woman with Crab* already exist.

An apparently identical cast of *Woman with Crab* is in The Art Institute of Chicago and another is in the collection of Dr. Ruth M. Bakwin, New York. A bronze with two artist's monograms is in the Dial Collection, on loan to the Worcester Art Museum. The first-edition cast by Vollard bears Rudier's foundry mark (conversation with A. Rosenberg, Feb. 1977); an example was included in an exhibition at The National Museum of Western Art, Tokyo (*Maillol*, 1963, no. 46). Later, Maillol executed terra-cottas of the same subject which differ slightly from the bronze: one is dated c. 1930 by John Rewald (*Maillol*, London, 1939, pp. 108-9, repr., and 166); another, in which the position of the hands varies, has two artist's monograms (New York, Sotheby Parke Bernet, *Important Impressionist and Modern Paintings and Sculpture*, May 26, 1976, no. 22, repr., dated 1920, Collection John Rewald). Vierny knows of only one drawing of a similar subject, which depicts a crouching woman without the crab (pencil and ink on gray paper, 7¾ x 8½ in., 19.5 x 21.5 cm., Collection D. Vierny, New York, The Solomon R. Guggenheim Museum, *Aristide Maillol*, exh. cat., 1975-76, no. 144, repr.).

REFERENCES: (not specifically to the Thannhauser cast):
U. E. Johnson, *Ambroise Vollard Editeur*, New York, 1944, pp. 40, 102, and 195, no. 97;
M. Bouvier, *Aristide Maillol*, Lausanne, 1945, pp. 118-19, repr.; *Masterpieces*, 1972, p. 36, repr. (c. 1900-1905).

Edouard Manet

Born January 1832, Paris
Died April 1883, Rueil

27   Before the Mirror. 1876
(Devant la glace; Devant la psyché;
Frau vor dem Spiegel)

Oil on canvas, 36¼ x 28⅛ (92.1 x 71.4)

Signed l.r.: *Manet*   Not dated.

PROVENANCE:

Inventory of the contents of Manet's studio on Dec. 28, 1883, no. 20;[1] Paris, Hôtel Drouot, *Vente Manet,* Feb. 4-5, 1884, no. 43 *(Devant la glace);* acquired at sale by Dr. Albert Robin;[2] purchased from Robin, Feb. 1901, by Bernheim-Jeune; sold jointly to Durand-Ruel and Cassirer, Mar. 1901[3] (correspondence with G. Gruet, Nov. 1976); purchased from Cassirer by Durand-Ruel, Paris, Dec. 1902; sold to Durand-Ruel, New York, Jan. 1903; bought back by Durand-Ruel, Paris, Jan. 1910; acquired again by Durand-Ruel, New York, Aug. 1916; sold to Flanagan, Apr. 1917 (above from correspondence with C. Durand-Ruel, Nov. 1976); included in New York, American Art Association, *Catalogue of Highly Important Old and Modern Paintings belonging to . . . Mr. Joseph F. Flanagan, Boston,* Jan. 14-15, 1920, no. 65, repr. *(Devant la psyché);* purchased by American Art Association, Feb. 1920; sent to Carl O. Nielsen,[4] Feb. 1923 (correspondence with C. Durand-Ruel, Nov. 1976); belonged to J. K. Thannhauser by 1927.

CONDITION:

Lined at an unrecorded date prior to 1965 (Dec. 1974).

The theme of a woman before a mirror appears in the late 1870s not only in the present picture but also in Manet's *Nana* (60⅝ x 45¼ in., 150 x 116 cm., Kunsthalle, Hamburg; Hofmann, color repr. as frontispiece) and in Berthe Morisot's work (M.-L. Bataille and G. Wildenstein, *Berthe Morisot,* Paris, 1961, nos. 64 and 84). As Werner Hofmann indicates, the theme has its origins earlier (pp. 69-88).

Daniel Catton Rich (conversations, autumn 1973 and Apr. 1975) found no direct relationship between *Nana* and *Before the Mirror.* The backgrounds and mirrors are different, and the Thannhauser painting does not have the complexity of meaning implicit in the presence of the gentleman. Rich agreed with Hofmann's placing the Thannhauser picture before *Nana,* which must have been begun in the autumn of 1876 (pp. 17-18).

EXHIBITIONS:

Paris, Galerie de la Vie Moderne, *Exposition des oeuvres nouvelles d'Edouard Manet,* Apr. 10-30, 1880, no. 8 *(Devant la glace);* Vienna, Galerie Miethke, *Manet-Monet,* May 1910, no. 6, repr. *(Vor dem Spiegel);* New York, Durand-Ruel, *Exhibition of Paintings and Pastels by Edouard Manet and Edgar Degas,* Apr. 5-29, 1916, no. 2; New York, Durand-Ruel, *Exhibi-*

1. See Jamot and Wildenstein, vol. I, p. 107. Fernand Lochard photographed all the paintings and drawings in Manet's studio at his death. Of these photographs the present picture is no. 246.
2. Dr. Robin of Paris acquired at the Manet sale nos. 11, 43, 48, 57, 66, 73, and 100, which included not only *Before the Mirror* but also *Nana* (no. 11). He bequeathed no. 73 to the Musée de Dijon in 1920.
3. Rouart-Wildenstein lists "Gerard, Paris 1901" after Bernheim-Jeune and before Cassirer. Not mentioned by Bernheim-Jeune or Durand-Ruel.
4. Nielsen's name is omitted by Rouart-Wildenstein. Nielsen, from Oslo, lent three paintings to the Manet exhibition at the Ny Carlsberg Glyptotek, Copenhagen, from Jan. 27-Feb. 17, 1922; none is the present picture.

tion of Paintings by Modern French Masters, Apr. 18-24, 1920, no. 7 *(Devant la psyché);* Berlin, Künstlerhaus (organized by the Galerien Thannhauser), *Erste Sonderausstellung in Berlin,* Jan. 9-Feb. 15, 1927, no. 146, repr. *(Vor dem Spiegel);* San Antonio, The Marion Koogler McNay Art Institute, *A Summer Exhibition,* June-Aug. 1961, no. iii, repr.

REFERENCES:

T. Duret, *Edouard Manet et son oeuvre,* Paris, 1902, p. 246, no. 213 *(La Toilette devant la glace,* 1875-77); J. Meier-Graefe, *Entwickelungsgeschichte der Modernen Kunst,* Stuttgart, 1904, vol. III, p. 56, repr. *(Devant la psyché,* 1876); E. Moreau-Nélaton, "Catalogue général: peintures et pastels," manuscript on deposit in the Cabinet des Estampes, Bibliothèque Nationale, Paris [1906], no. 216 *(Devant la glace,* D.213); V. Fleischer, "Ausstellungen," *Der Cicerone,* Jg. II, 1910, p. 369 *(Vor dem Spiegel);* J. Meier-Graefe, *Edouard Manet,* Munich, 1912, p. 321 and pl. 187; T. Duret, *Manet and the French Impressionists,* trans. J. E. C. Flitch, London, 1912, p. 238, no. 213; F. Burger, *Einführung in die Moderne Kunst,* Berlin, 1917, vol. I, p. 96, repr.; E. Moreau-Nélaton, *Manet raconté par lui-même,* Paris, 1926, vol. II, pp. 43, 66-67, 141, and fig. 222 *(Devant la glace,* c. 1877); T. Duret, *Histoire de Manet et de son oeuvre,* Paris, 1926, p. 266, no. 213; J. Meier-Graefe, "Die Franzosen in Berlin," *Der Cicerone,* Jg. XIX, Jan. 1927, p. 50, repr.; M. Osborn, "Klassiker der Französischen Moderne," *Deutsche Kunst und Dekoration,* vol. 59, Mar. 1927, p. 343, repr. *(Vor dem Spiegel);* B. E. Werner, "Französische Malerei in Berlin," *Die Kunst für Alle,* Jg. 42, Apr. 1927, p. 224, repr.; A. Tabarant, *Manet: Histoire catalographique,* Paris, 1931, pp. 298-99 and 582, no. 246 *(Devant la glace,* 1876); P. Jamot and G. Wildenstein, *Manet,* Paris, 1932, vol. I, pp. 107 and 154, no. 278 and vol. II, fig. 85 *(Devant la glace,* c. 1877); C. Zervos, "Manet et la femme," *Cahiers d'Art,* 7ᵉ année, nos. 8-10, 1932, p. 331, repr.; A. Tabarant, *Manet et ses oeuvres,* Paris, 1947, pp. 290-91, 540, and 611, pl. 255; F. Daulte, "Une Donation sans précédent: la collection Thannhauser," *Connaissance des Arts,* no. 171, May 1966, pp. 62-63, repr. (statements made without proof); C. Gottlieb, "Picasso's *Girl Before a Mirror,*" *Journal of Aesthetics and Art Criticism,* vol. XXIV, summer 1966, p. 517, fn. 15; M. Venturi and S. Orienti, *L'opera pittorica di Edouard Manet,* Milan, 1967, no. 216; P. Schneider, *The World of Manet 1832-1883,* New York, 1968, pp. 7-9, 10-11, repr., and 142; M. Bodelsen, "Early Impressionist Sales 1874-94," *The Burlington Magazine,* vol. CX, June 1968, p. 342; *Masterpieces,* 1972, p. 11, repr.; W. Hofmann, *Nana: Mythos und Wirklichkeit,* Cologne, 1973, pp. 18, 89, 177, and pl. 25 *(Frau vor dem Spiegel,* 1876); D. Rouart and D. Wildenstein, *Edouard Manet,* Lausanne and Paris, 1975, vol. I, pp. 212 and 213, repr., no. 264 *(Devant la glace,* 1877); A. C. Hanson, *Manet and the Modern Tradition,* New Haven and London, 1977, p. 101, fn. 213.

28   Woman in Evening Dress. 1877-80
*(Femme en robe de soirée; Femme en robe
du bal; Jeune femme à l'écran; Portrait
de Mlle S. Reichenberg)*

Oil on canvas, 68⅝ x 32⅞ (174.3 x 83.5)

Signed at center left edge, not by the artist:[1]
Ed Manet   Not dated.

PROVENANCE:
Probably retained by the artist's widow;[2]
Cognacq, Paris, by 1902;[3] purchased from
Monteux by Bernheim-Jeune, Paris, Jan. 6,
1903[4] (stock book no. 12898, *Femme en*
robe du bal, 175 x 85 cm.); Carl Reininghaus, Vienna;[5] J. K. Thannhauser by 1931.

CONDITION:
Lined at an unknown date before 1965 in
such a manner that margins were trimmed
on all sides. Thinly painted with some abrasion at lower right and center left edges
(Dec. 1974).

Some time after its completion, Manet considered reducing the size and thus the composition of the present painting. In a photograph taken in 1883 by Fernand Lochard
in Manet's atelier after his death, a white line clearly defines a rectangle indicating the
proposed dimensions. The artist considered cutting down the canvas by 45.5 cm. at
the bottom, 5 cm. at the top, 20 cm. at the left, and 5 cm. on the right (Tabarant,
1931, p. 323) so as to eliminate the table, fan, and lower portion of the dress below
the model's gloved hands. However, the proposed changes were not carried out, and
any trace of the line has disappeared.

Although *Woman in Evening Dress* was found in the atelier after the artist's death,
it was neither included in the inventory of the contents of Manet's studio nor in
the Manet sale at the Hôtel Drouot on February 4-5, 1884. In the photographs annotated by Etienne Moreau-Nélaton (Cabinet des Estampes, Bibliothèque Nationale,
Paris, DC.300g, vol. III), the present picture is among those marked "Réserve" rather
than numbered according to the Manet sale (see PROVENANCE).

The sitter has occasionally been identified as Suzanne Reichenberg: first, when the
painting was lent by Bernheim-Jeune to an exhibition in 1904 at La Libre Esthétique
in Brussels and later by Adolphe Tabarant in 1931 (p. 323) and 1947 (p. 322). However, Théodore Duret, Moreau-Nélaton, and Paul Jamot and Georges Wildenstein

1. D. Wildenstein (correspondence, May 1977) thinks that the signature was added later by
   Mme Manet or some other member of the family. However, A. C. Hanson (correspondence,
   Nov. 1976) states that the signature is not by Mme Manet.
2. Tabarant, 1947, p. 322. It is not known when the picture left the family.
3. Although the indexes in Jamot and Wildenstein and Rouart and Wildenstein list Gabriel
   Cognacq (d. 1952), the reference is probably to Ernest Cognacq (1839-1928). Study of
   Gabriel Cognacq's sale catalogue (Paris, Galerie Charpentier, May 14, 1952) indicates that
   Ernest purchased works c. 1901. Gabriel inherited part of his uncle's collection. However,
   no Cognacq archives remain (correspondence with T. Burollet, Nov. 1976).
4. Bernheim-Jeune still owned the picture in Mar. 1904. Unfortunately the gallery records do
   not indicate when or to whom it was sold. Tabarant (1947, p. 322) lists Jos. Hessel after
   Bernheim-Jeune and before Reininghaus. Rouart and Wildenstein make no mention of
   either Bernheim-Jeune or Hessel. Hessel's records do not exist (conversation with G. Gruet,
   May 1977).
5. It is not known when and from whom Reininghaus obtained the picture. No work by
   Manet was included in the Ausstellung Preis-Konkurrenz at the Kunstsalon G. Pisko,
   Vienna, Jan.-Feb. 1914. Carl Reininghaus' collection was dispersed soon after World War
   I (correspondence with E. Marik, Dec. 1976).

do not mention the identity of the sitter. Daniel Wildenstein knows of no documentary evidence to connect the painting and the person (correspondence, May 1977). No painting by Manet is known to represent Reichenberg and her descendants are not aware of the existence of a portrait by Manet of their distant relative (correspondence with Baron Philippe de Bourgoing, Nov. 1976).

Suzanne Angélique Charlotte Reichenberg (1853-1924) was an actress who appeared regularly with the Comédie Française from 1868 until 1898. Upon her marriage in 1900, she became the Baronne de Bourgoing (H. Lyonnet, *Dictionnaire des comédiens français,* Geneva, 1912, vol. II, p. 593). Reichenberg had blonde hair, blue eyes, and retained her youthful looks (Château de Versailles, *La Comédie Française 1680-1962,* exh. cat., 1962, p. 130). Comparison of the present picture with portraits of the actress does not provide conclusive proof but makes it unlikely that Manet's *Woman in Evening Dress* represents Suzanne Reichenberg (A. Houssaye, *La Comédie Française 1680-1880,* Paris, 1880, n.p.; *Paris illustré,* no. 66, Apr. 6, 1889 [p. 1]; *The Cosmopolitan,* vol. XI, Oct. 1891, p. 642).

The present picture has been dated 1875-77 by Duret, 1878 by Tabarant, 1879 by Jamot and Wildenstein, and 1880 by Denis Rouart and Daniel Wildenstein. Anne Coffin Hanson finds relatively little change in style between 1877 and 1880 and prefers a broader range in date (correspondence, Nov. 1976).

According to Tabarant (1947, no. 341), *Panier fleuri* (25⅝ x 32¼ in., 65 x 82 cm., private collection, New York; Rouart and Wildenstein, p. 263, repr., no. 342) is a sketch of the basket of flowers on the table in the present picture.

EXHIBITIONS:

Brussels, La Libre Esthétique, *Exposition des peintres Impressionistes,* Feb. 25-Mar. 29, 1904, no. 84 *(Portrait de Mlle S. Reichenberg);*[6] Kansas City, William Rockhill Nelson Gallery of Art, *Summer Exhibition,* 1955 *(Lady in a Striped Dress,* lent by J. K. Thannhauser).

REFERENCES:

T. Duret, *Edouard Manet et son oeuvre,* Paris, 1902, p. 250, no. 231 *(Femme en robe de soirée,* 1875-77, coll. Cognacq, Paris); E. Moreau-Nélaton, "Catalogue général: peintures et pastels," manuscript on deposit in the Cabinet des Estampes, Bibliothèque Nationale, Paris [1906], no. 257 ("Jeune femme à l'écran, 180 x 85 cm., D. 231"); T. Duret, *Manet and the French Impressionists,* trans. J. E. C. Flitch, London, 1912, p. 239, no. 231 *(Woman in Evening Dress,* 1875-77, coll. Cognacq, Paris); T. Duret, *Histoire de Manet et de son oeuvre,* Paris, 1926, p. 269, no. 231 *(Femme en robe de soirée,* 1875-77); A. Tabarant, *Manet: Histoire catalographique,* Paris, 1931, pp. 322, 323, and 583, no. 272 *(Femme en robe de soirée,* 1878, Galerie Thannhauser, Berlin-Lucerne); C. Zervos, "Manet et la femme," *Cahiers d'Art,* 7ᵉ année, nos. 8-10, 1932, p. 331, repr. *(Femme en robe de soirée);* P. Jamot and G. Wildenstein, *Manet,* Paris, 1932, vol. I, p. 161, no. 331, and vol. II, fig. 138 *(Femme en robe de soirée,* 1879, Galerie Thannhauser); P. Colin, *Edouard Manet,* Paris, 1932, p. 180, pl. lxv; M. Florisoone, *Manet,* Monaco, 1947, p. 79, repr. *(Femme en robe de soirée [Suzanne Reichenberg],* 1879); A. Tabarant, *Manet et ses oeuvres,* Paris, 1947, pp. 322, 323, 541, and 612, pl. 288 *(Une femme en robe de soirée,* 1878); M. Venturi and S. Orienti, *L'opera pittorica di Edouard Manet,* Milan, 1967, p. 108, repr., no. 246 (1878); *Masterpieces,* 1972, p. 12, repr. (1878); D. Rouart and D. Wildenstein, *Edouard Manet,* Lausanne and Paris, 1975, vol. I, pp. 262 and 263, repr., no. 341 *(Femme en robe de soirée [Suzanne Reichenberg?],* 1880).

6. In addition, two Bernheim-Jeune lists preserved in the archives of Octave Maus in the Département d'Art Moderne at the Musées Royaux des Beaux-Arts, Brussels, mention "12898, Manet, Reichenberg" (M. Colin kindly provided the above information in correspondence, Dec. 1976).

Henri Matisse

Born December 1869, Le Cateau-Cambrésis
Died November 1954, Nice

29   Male Model. c. 1900
      (Homme nu debout; Male Nude; Aktstudie)

India ink on wove paper, 12⁵/₁₆ x 10⁷/₁₆   PROVENANCE:
(31.3 x 26.5)   Presumably acquired from the artist by
Watermark upside down at bottom edge: Heinz Braune;[1] acquired from Braune by
ADALON-LES-ANNONAY B CRAYON   J. K. Thannhauser, Oct. 1929.

Signed l.r.: *Henri-Matisse*   Not dated.

1. Braune, who knew Matisse, was Director of the Breslau Museum and, later, Director of the
   Stuttgart Museum. J. K. Thannhauser acquired several works by Matisse from him. Braune
   knew Hans Purrmann since their student years in Munich, and on at least one occasion
   Purrmann bought a work from Matisse for Braune (B. and E. Göpel, *Leben und Meinun-
   gen des Malers Hans Purrmann*, Wiesbaden, 1961, pp. 230 and 250).

The model is Bevilaqua, an Italian who posed for Matisse's first major bronze, *Le Serf*. It is recorded that he posed hundreds of times while Matisse was working on the sculpture from about 1900 to 1903 (Barr, pp. 48 and 530, fn. 1).

Bevilaqua was an Abruzzi peasant (originally named Pignatelli) who posed for Auguste Rodin as early as 1877-78. He was the model for the legs of Rodin's *Walking Man* and *Saint John the Baptist* (Elsen, p. 28). Not surprisingly, both works are cited as sources for *Le Serf*. According to Albert E. Elsen (p. 29), Matisse was well aware of Bevilaqua's association with Rodin and discussed the latter's working methods with his model. Earlier, perhaps in 1898 or 1899, Matisse had taken some of his drawings to Rodin but was discouraged by his lack of interest (Elsen, p. 16, and Geldzahler, p. 500).

The Thannhauser drawing belongs with a group of works done in the first years of the century which culminated in *Le Serf*. This group includes a drawing of two male nudes and a head titled *Savages* (black ink applied with pen and brush on white paper, 12½ x 9½ in., 33 x 24 cm., Isabella Stewart Gardner Museum, Boston; Hadley, p. 60, no. 30, repr.) and a bust-length drawing of Bevilaqua (pencil, 12 x 9 in., 30.5 x 23 cm., Musée Matisse, Nice-Cimiez, kindly brought to my attention by Victor Carlson in correspondence, Oct. 1976). In addition, two paintings, the *Male Nude* (39¾ x 28⅜ in., 100 x 72 cm., c. 1900, The Museum of Modern Art, New York; J. Jacobus, *Henri Matisse*, New York, 1972, p. 95, color repr.) and *Académie d'homme* (25⅝ x 18⅛ in., 65 x 46 cm., Statens Museum for Kunst, Copenhagen; G. Diehl, *Henri Matisse*, Paris, 1954, pl. 13), have the subject, date, and overall composition in common with the present drawing.

Elsen (p. 27) and Carlson (correspondence, Oct. 1976) consider the Thannhauser drawing to be more closely related to Matisse's paintings than to his sculpture. The horizontal molding or articulation of the background wall is found in the present drawing and in the painting at The Museum of Modern Art. Elsen (p. 27) cites the way the arms project out from the body in the drawing to relate it to the paintings. Indeed, the raised arm appears in the Copenhagen *Académie* and in an *Academic Study* published by Elsen (19 x 13 in., 48.3 x 33 cm., Collection Dr. Maurice Galanté, San Francisco; fig. 36).

Le Serf itself differs from the Thannhauser drawing in the downward angle of the head, the striding pose of the legs, and the absence of the lower arms (height 36¼ in., 92 cm.; casts are in The Museum of Modern Art, New York; The Cone Collection, The Baltimore Museum of Art; The Art Institute of Chicago; and The Fogg Art Museum, Harvard University, Cambridge, Mass.). The sculpture was originally designed with arms which, either by the artist's intention or perhaps by accident, no longer existed when the plaster was cast in bronze (see Geldzahler, p. 499, and Elsen, pp. 29-30). A photograph taken by Hans Purrman showing Matisse in his studio at 19, quai St. Michel depicts *Le Serf* with the arms and with clenched fists at his thighs (Elsen, p. 30, and J. Russell, *The World of Matisse*, New York, 1969, p. 33).

EXHIBITION:

Berlin, Galerien Thannhauser, *Henri Matisse*, Feb.-Mar. 1930, probably no. 113.[2]

2. In the exhibition, no. 113 was *Das Modell*; no. 109, *Männlicher Akt*; and no. 105, *Stehender Akt*. J. K. Thannhauser remembered that the present drawing was included (notes, Dec. 1972).

REFERENCES:

R. Schacht, *Henri Matisse*, Dresden, 1922, p. 64, repr. (*Aktstudie*, private coll., Breslau); A. H. Barr, Jr., *Matisse: His Art and His Public*, New York, 1951, pp. 44, repr., 48, 49, and 531 (*Male Model*, c. 1900); H. Geldzahler, "Two Early Matisse Drawings," *Gazette des Beaux-Arts*, vol. LX, Nov. 1962, pp. 497-502 and p. 498, repr. (*Male Nude*, 1900-1901); J. Selz, *Matisse*, trans. A. P. H. Hamilton, New York, 1964, p. 8, repr. (*Model*, c. 1900); R.vN. Hadley, ed., *Drawings*, Isabella Stewart Gardner Museum, Boston, 1968, p. 59 (in comparison with *Savages*); The Baltimore Museum of Art, *Matisse as a Draughtsman*, exh. cat., 1971, pp. 14 and 26; J. Jacobus, *Henri Matisse*, New York, 1972, p. 64, fig. 80 (*Male Model*, c. 1900); A. E. Elsen, *The Sculpture of Henri Matisse*, New York, 1972, p. 27, fig. 30 (*Male Model*, c. 1900); *Masterpieces*, 1972, p. 40, repr.; Paris, Musée National d'Art Moderne, *Henri Matisse: Dessins et sculpture*, exh. cat., 1975, p. 64 (*Homme nu debout*).

---

30   Woman Before Mirror. November 1939
(Jeune femme devant un miroir)

India ink on wove paper, 15 x 11⅛ (38.1 x 28.3)

No watermark.

Signed and dated l.l.: *Henri Matisse   nov. 39*

PROVENANCE:

Purchased from Mrs. Cramer, Paris, by H. C. Goldsmith, 1951; purchased from Goldsmith by J. K. Thannhauser, 1952 (correspondence with H. C. Goldsmith, Apr. 1977).

This drawing, which is dated November 1939, was executed at the Hôtel Régina in Cimiez, near Nice, where Matisse returned around mid-October 1939, having stayed there the previous year. A photograph of the *camera lucida* in Matisse's quarters at the hotel includes the same mirror, door, and iron grillwork of the balcony as in the drawing (L. Aragon, *Henri Matisse, A Novel*, trans. J. Stewart, New York, 1971, vol. I, p. 59, fig. 23).

Matisse represented the motif of a woman reflected in a mirror frequently in drawings from 1936-37 (see, for example, *Cahiers d'Art*, 11ᵉ année, nos. 3-5, 1936, pp. 101, 103, and 105; R. J. Moulin, *Henri Matisse: Drawings and Paper Cut-Outs*, New York, 1969, pls. 22 and 23; and Paris, Musée National d'Art Moderne, *Henri Matisse: Dessins et sculpture*, exh. cat., 1975, sculpture nos. 93 and 97).

The motif of a woman looking in a mirror with her arms raised over her head appeared as early as 1901 in *La Coiffure* (36⅝ x 27½ in., 93 x 69.9 cm., Philadelphia Museum of Art; A. H. Barr, Jr., *Matisse: His Art and His Public*, New York, 1951, p. 306, repr.). Likewise, the pose of the model can be traced back to a 1906 sculpture, *Standing Nude with Arms Raised over Her Head* (A. E. Elsen, *The Sculpture of Henri Matisse*, New York, 1972, p. 68, fig. 82).

EXHIBITION:

Kansas City, William Rockhill Nelson Gallery of Art, *Summer Exhibition*, 1955 (label on reverse reads: *Woman Before a Mirror;* incorrectly dated 1954, lent by J. K. Thannhauser).

REFERENCES:

M. Malingue, *Matisse: Dessins*, Paris, 1949, pp. 14 and 18, repr. (*Dessin à l'encre de chine*); *Masterpieces*, 1972, p. 41, repr.

Amedeo Modigliani

Born July 1884, Leghorn
Died January 1920, Paris

31 **Young Girl Seated.** 1918-19
(Jeune fille sur une chaise; Fillette; Bimba seduta)

Oil on canvas, 35⅞ x 20⅞ (91.1 x 53)

Signed u.r.: *modigliani*   Not dated.

PROVENANCE:
Purchased from Antoine Villard[1] by Bernheim-Jeune, Paris, June 1928; sold to Georges Bernheim, Oct. 1928 (correspondence with G. Gruet, Nov. 1976); remained with G. Bernheim at least until Feb. 1934; possibly acquired from Bernheim by Renou et Colle, Paris (correspondence with M. Covo, July 1977); purchased from Renou et Colle by Charles Boyer, Dec. 1937 (correspondence, Feb. 1977); purchased from Boyer by M. Knoedler and Co., New York, Oct. 1949; purchased from Knoedler by Henry Pearlman, Feb. 1950 (correspondence with R. Finnegan, Sept. 1974); acquired by J. K. Thannhauser some time in the mid-1950s, after Feb. 1954 (correspondence with H. Pearlman, Nov. 1973).

CONDITION:
Abrasion at edges, and corners worn and punctured by nails. Chip on sitter's left side of jaw (Apr. 1968 and Jan. 1975).

Modigliani is known to have painted a few landscapes during his stay in the south of France, which lasted from March or April 1918 until May 31, 1919. A letter written by the artist to his dealer, Leopold Zborowski, would place the landscapes within the first months of 1919 (P. Sichel, *Modigliani,* New York, 1967, p. 430, and Modigliani, p. 110). Modigliani also included a landscape background with trees in *La Belle epicière* (39⅜ x 25⁹⁄₁₆ in., 100 x 65 cm., private collection, Paris; C. Roy, *Modigliani,* Geneva, 1958, p. 62, color repr.) and in several portrait drawings (G. Jedlicka, *Modigliani,* Zürich, 1953, pl. 40, and A. Ceroni, *Amedeo Modigliani,* Milan, 1958, p. 31).

The present picture has not previously been grouped with Modigliani's representations of landscape. However, the green area of the ground can only be interpreted as grass, and the dark, slightly tilted vertical is a tree trunk. The sitter's head is seen against a wall not unlike that in *Landscape in the Midi* (21⅝ x 18⅛ in., 55 x 46 cm.; Pfannstiel, 1956, no. 245 [1918]; Ceroni, 1958, no. 99 [1917-18]; Lanthemann, p. 132, no. 366 [1919]; and A. Werner, *Amedeo Modigliani,* New York, 1966, p. 129, color repr.).

Young Girl Seated must have been painted during Modigliani's stay in the south of France in 1918-19. The artist lived at a variety of addresses in Nice including 13, rue de France and at the Hôtel Tarelli, and he stayed, probably for a few months, with Anders and Rachèle Osterlind at a villa adjacent to Renoir's in Cagnes.

Just as it is almost impossible to determine precise dates that Modigliani lived at a given address, it is very difficult to assign secure dates to his work. The present picture has been dated 1917 by Arthur Pfannstiel, 1918 by Ambrogio Ceroni and J. Lanthemann, and 1919 when lent to exhibitions by Henry Pearlman. Likewise, Modigliani's painting *La Belle epicière,* with which it shares many similarities, has been dated 1917 (Pfannstiel, 1956, no. 191), 1918 (Ceroni, 1958, no. 102), and 1919 (Lanthemann, no. 365).

1. Probably the artist (1867-1934) who exhibited his own work at the Galerie Bernheim-Jeune, Paris, from Mar. 21-Apr. 5, 1921, and who had a collection as well.

The sitter for the *Young Girl Seated* has neither been identified nor found in any other work by Modigliani, and no preparatory drawing for the Thannhauser painting has been located. Since it was the artist's custom to paint each canvas in a single sitting, the presence of pencil lines in the girl's face and hands may indicate that Modigliani worked directly on the canvas without a prior sketch.

EXHIBITIONS:

Venice, XVII Esposizione Biennale Internazionale d'Arte, *Mostra individuale di Amedeo Modigliani,* 2nd ed., 1930, no. 32 (*Ragazza,* coll. Georges Bernheim, Paris); Basel, Kunsthalle, *Modigliani,* Jan. 7-Feb. 4, 1934, no. 55 (*La Fillette assise,* 1918, 91 x 53 cm., lent by Georges Bernheim); Dallas, Museum of Fine Arts, *Some Businessmen Collect Contemporary Art,* Apr. 6-27, 1952, no. 37 (*Seated Girl in Landscape,* 1919, lent by H. Pearlman); Palm Beach, The Society of the Four Arts, *Amedeo Modigliani,* Jan. 8-31, 1954, no. 25, repr. (c. 1919, lent by H. Pearlman), traveled to Miami, The Lowe Gallery, Feb. 11-28.

REFERENCES:

A. Pfannstiel, *Modigliani,* Paris, 1929, p. 35 (listed in *catalogue présumé* under 1917, *Jeune fille sur une chaise,* ex. coll. Bernheim-Jeune, Paris); P. Descargues, *Amedeo Modigliani,* Paris, 1951, pl. 56 (*Fillette*); *Art Digest,* vol. 26, Apr. 1, 1952, p. 9, repr.; N. Ponente, "Modigliani," *Commentari,* vol. III, Apr.-June 1952, pl. xlv, fig. 6 (*Bimba seduta,* 1918, coll. H. Pearlman); A. Pfannstiel, *Modigliani et son oeuvre,* Paris, 1956, pp. 123-24, no. 212 (1917); J. Modigliani, *Modigliani: Man and Myth,* trans. E. R. Clifford, New York, 1958, p. x, pl. 46 (1917-18); A. Ceroni, *Amedeo Modigliani: Dessins et sculptures,* Milan, 1965, p. 45 and pl. 194 (c. 1918); A. Ceroni, *I dipinti di Modigliani,* Milan, 1970, p. 101, no. 254 (*Giovane seduta,* 1918); J. Lanthemann, *Modigliani: Catalogue raisonné,* Barcelona, 1970, pp. 128 and 242, repr., no. 312 (*Fillette assise,* 1918); *Masterpieces,* 1972, p. 81, repr. (1917-18).

After Amedeo Modigliani

32   Caryatid
      (*Cariatide*)

Oil on canvas, 39¼ x 29 (99.8 x 73.7)

Inauthentic signature u.r.: *Modigliani*
Not dated.

PROVENANCE:

Purchased from Monsieur Mantaux, a Belgian collector, by Paul Haim, Paris, 1956-57 (letter from Haim to T. M. Messer, June 3, 1977); purchased from Haim by J. K. Thannhauser, c. 1956-57 (conversation with Haim, Mar. 1, 1977, and May 24, 1977).

CONDITION:

Unlined. Not varnished. Inpainting in scattered areas of figure's right leg at an unknown date prior to 1965. Dented puncture at lower right (Apr. 1968). Evidence that the canvas has been stretched at least three times prior to 1965. Ground cracks throughout. On reverse, evidence of soil and approximately twenty patches with wax resin (Jan. 1975 and Apr. 1977).

The present canvas is quite evenly painted so as to produce a mat surface effect without much variation in brushwork and without a sense of how the figure was realized in paint. In contrast, when observed closely, Modigliani's paintings dating from 1910-15 display varied and often agitated brushwork: areas where paint has been rubbed thin with the brush, touches of considerable impasto, and even places where the support has remained bare. Above all, in the present picture, the stylized and faceless head of the model, the manner of highlighting, and the smoothly continuous outline of the figure are emphatically unlike Modigliani's work. The artist always indicated faces, even in summary sketches.

From 1909 through 1914 Modigliani concentrated on sculpture and carved directly in stone. A *Caryatid* executed in limestone is in The Museum of Modern Art, New York (height 36¼ in., 92 cm., Gift of Mrs. Simon Guggenheim; A. Werner, *Modigliani the Sculptor*, New York, 1962, pls. 14-17). From the same years there are many works on paper depicting caryatids in pastel, watercolor, gouache, or pencil: J. Lanthemann catalogues seventy-five; Marcel Rötlisberger ("Les Cariatides de Modigliani: Notice critique," *Critica d'arte*, vol. 7, no. 38, 1960, pp. 98-112) lists forty-nine; and Ambrogio Ceroni (*Amedeo Modigliani: Dessins et sculptures,* Milan, 1965) includes twenty.

Oil paintings of caryatids with arms raised so as to support weight above are much rarer. Ceroni lists three (*I dipinti di Modigliani,* Milan, 1970) while Rötlisberger and Lanthemann include another version as well (nos. 2 and 527 respectively). The Thannhauser *Caryatid* is omitted from publications by Arthur Pfannstiel (*Modigliani*, Paris, 1929, and *Modigliani et son oeuvre,* Paris, 1956), Franco Russoli (*Modigliani*, London, 1959), Ceroni (1965, 1970, and *Amedeo Modigliani,* Milan, 1958), and Rötlisberger.

The *Caryatid* in the Kunstsammlung Nordrhein-Westfalen in Düsseldorf (28¾ x 19¾ in., 73 x 50 cm.; C. Roy, *Modigliani,* Lausanne, 1958, p. 48, color repr.) belonged until the mid-1960s to Dr. Paul Alexandre, who acquired works from Modigliani before World War I exclusively. Among the few canvases of caryatids Modigliani painted, it is by far the closest in composition to the Thannhauser painting. However, comparison of details reveals differences. The head of the Düsseldorf caryatid not only has detailed features but wavy hair, forehead curls, and a necklace while the present work lacks any details. Furthermore, the right arm of the caryatid in the present picture has been moved so as to partially obscure the face and neck. As a result, the sense of anatomy and structure, so strong in Modigliani's work is destroyed.

EXHIBITION:

Paris, Galerie Charpentier, *Cent Tableaux de Modigliani,* Apr. 16-June 18, 1958, no. 14 (1912-13, private coll.).[1]

REFERENCES:

J. Lanthemann, *Modigliani: Catalogue raisonné,* Barcelona, 1970, pp. 139 and 296, repr., no. 531 (1911-12); *Masterpieces,* 1972, p. 80, repr. (c. 1914).

1. According to R. Nacenta (correspondence, Feb. 1977), the picture was not lent by Thannhauser but by an unidentified collector.

Pablo Ruiz Picasso

Born October 1881, Malaga
Died April 1973, Mougins

33

33   The End of the Road. 1898-99
      (Au Bout de la route; Redemption;
      Le Double cortège)

Oil wash (?) and conté crayon on paper,
18⁹⁄₁₆ x 12⅛ (47.1 x 30.8)

Watermark of a crown above a shield upon
which appears diagonally: JOHANNOT[1]

Signed l.r.: *P. Ruiz Picasso*   Not dated.

PROVENANCE:
Unidentified private collection, Barcelona;
J. K. Thannhauser by 1957.

CONDITION:
The support is worn at corners. Removed
from cardboard mount, tear at upper right
repaired, and work deacidified by C.
Gaehde (Aug. 1976).

The signature, which includes the names of both his father (Ruiz) and mother
(Picasso), belongs to an early form used by the artist primarily before 1900 and
occasionally through 1901.

     John Richardson thinks that the watercolor was done in 1898 either in Barcelona
or Horta de Ebro after Picasso had been ill with scarlet fever in Madrid (p. 16). Pierre
Daix places it in Barcelona and allows for a date of 1898-99 (Daix and Boudaille,
p. 107, and correspondence, June 1975).

     According to Jaime Sabartés, who met the artist in Barcelona after his return from
Horta de Ebro in 1899, Picasso went to Horta de Ebro in the mountainous country-
side of Tarragona for seven or eight months after a short stay in Barcelona in late
June 1898 (*Picasso: An Intimate Portrait*, trans. A. Flores, New York, 1948, p. 42).
Juan-Eduardo Cirlot (1972, p. 174) specifies June 24 as the date Picasso accom-
panied his friend Pallarés to Horta de Ebro, where he remained until February 1899.

fig. a.
Picasso, *Entierro en el Campo (Burial in the Country)*,
pastel on paper, 9½ x 12 in., 24.1 x 30.6 cm., Museo
Picasso, Barcelona (MAB 110.233). © S.P.A.D.E.M.,
1978.

1. The paper is manufactured in France and was often used by Picasso: for example in Z. I.
   12 (discussed in text) and XXI. 66, 67, 115, and 117.

fig. b.
Picasso, *La Llamada de la Muerte (The Call of Death)*,
ink on paper, 9³⁄₁₆ x 13³⁄₈ in., 23.4 x 34 cm. Museo
Picasso, Barcelona (MAB 110.780). © S.P.A.D.E.M.,
1978.

fig. c.
Picasso, *La Llamada de la Muerte (The Call of Death)*,
ink on paper, 9⁷⁄₁₆ x 13³⁄₈ in., 24 x 34 cm., Museo
Picasso, Barcelona (MAB 110.688). © S.P.A.D.E.M.,
1978.

Later, in the summer of 1909, Picasso returned to the same village which, since 1919, is called Horta de San Juan.

In the early 1960s, when Richardson showed Picasso a photograph of this work, the artist said: "Death waits for all at the end of the road, even though the rich go there in carriages and the poor on foot" (p. 16, and correspondence with D. C. Rich, Nov. 1973). In the background a row of carriages proceeds to the right while a line of people follows a curving road from the foreground to the same point in the upper right. There, awaiting them, is a winged figure of Death who carries a scythe and whose facial features suggest a skeleton. Beyond are cypress trees and the walls of a cemetery.

The same figures of a woman holding a child by the hand are found in a crayon drawing (Z. I.12, 1898) formerly in the collection of Josef Stransky (crayon on paper, 19 x 10 in., 48.2 x 25.4 cm., ex. coll. Gargalo, Madrid; *French Masters of the XIX and XX Century: The Private Collection of Josef Stransky,* New York, c. 1935, n.p.).

The theme of death, the overall composition, the walled cemetery, and the procession of figures seen in back view all occur in a pastel in the Museo Picasso in Barcelona (fig. a; first brought to my attention by Marilyn McCully). The pastel, *Entierro en el Campo (Burial in the Country),* has predominantly dark green and dark purple tones accented by white and touches of red. In the work in the Museo Picasso, the artist shows a funeral procession with a priest and men bearing a coffin along the road to the cemetery. However, in the work in the Thannhauser Collection, Picasso presents an allegorical view of death.

There are also two pen-and-ink drawings in the Museo Picasso related to the present work. *La Llamada de la Muerte (The Call of Death)* (fig. b) includes male figures walking with crutches and a figure carrying another, as does *The End of the Road*. Although the figures are seen frontally moving from right to left, their poses generally correspond to those seen in back view in the Thannhauser work. Certain figures also appear in *La Llamada de la Muerte (The Call of Death)* (fig. c), where the man with a cane corresponds to the man with a crutch, and the adult figure carrying another recurs. However, here, at the left stands a figure of Death. (I am grateful to Rosa Maria Subirana for advice, information, and permission to reproduce the three works in the Museo Picasso which will be published in her catalogue of the Barcelona collection.)

A winged figure of Death with a scythe appears in two conté crayon drawings, *The Kiss of Death,* both in the Museo Picasso (MAB 110.750 and 110.778R; Cirlot, 1972, p. 118, repr., no. 199 and p. 234, repr., no. 664, respectively, where they are dated Barcelona 1899-1900).

Anthony Blunt and Phoebe Pool found *The End of the Road* close to the work of Isidro Nonell (1873-1911) both in style and in the representation of a line of peasants (pl. 65). In addition, Nonell's drawings of single figures which were published before 1898 resemble individual figures in the Picasso (see E. Jardi, *Nonell,* New York, 1970, pls. 8, 30, 202, and 212). McCully (conversation, Dec. 1977) thinks that the present work reflects Nonell's *Annunciation in the Slums* (Jardi, pl. 9).

EXHIBITIONS:

New York, The Museum of Modern Art, *Picasso: 75th Anniversary Exhibition,* May 22-Sept. 8, 1957, p. 14, repr. *(Redemption),* traveled to The Art Institute of Chicago, Oct. 29-Dec. 8; Philadelphia Museum of Art, *Picasso,* Jan. 8-Feb. 23, 1958, no. 1, repr.; New York, The Museum of Modern Art, *Art Nouveau: Art and Design at the Turn of the Century,* June 6-Sept. 6, 1960, no. 222, repr. *(The End of the Road),* traveled to Pittsburgh, Carnegie Institute Museum of Art, Oct. 13-Dec. 12, Los Angeles County Museum, Jan. 17-Mar. 5, 1961, and The Baltimore Museum of Art, Apr. 1-May 15.

REFERENCES:

H. Seling, ed., *Jugendstil: Der Weg ins 20. Jahrhundert,* Munich, 1959, pp. 29 and 113, and pl. 24 (c. 1898); Blunt and Pool, 1962, p. 30 and pl. 64 *(The End of the Road, 1898);* J. Richardson, *Pablo Picasso: Watercolours and Gouaches,* London, 1964, pp. 16 and 17, pl. 1 (1898); Daix and Boudaille, 1967, no. I.2, pp. 22 and 107, repr. (1898-99); H. H. Arnason, *History of Modern Art,* New York, 1968, pp. 117 and 118, fig. 187; Zervos, 1969, vol. XXI, no. 79 and pl. 35 *(Le Double Cortège,* 1898); *Masterpieces,* 1972, p. 44, repr. (c. 1898); Daix, 1977, pp. 29 and 33, fn. 6.

34   Le Moulin de la Galette.   Autumn 1900

Oil on canvas, 34¾ x 45½ (88.2 x 115.5)
Signed l.r.: *P. R. Picasso*   Not dated.

PROVENANCE:
Purchased from Galerie Berthe Weill, Paris, by M. Huc,[1] c. 1900; Moderne Galerie (Heinrich Thannhauser), Munich, c. 1909; purchased from Moderne Galerie by Paul von Mendelssohn Bartholdy, Berlin, c. 1910;[2] repurchased from Bartholdy by J. K. Thannhauser, c. 1935.

CONDITION:
Glue lined prior to 1965. Scattered areas of inpainting along right edge (May 1975).

Picasso confirmed to Pierre Daix that *Le Moulin de la Galette* was the first painting he did after arriving in Paris in October 1900 (correspondence, June 1975). Alfred Barr was the first to propose that this was so *(Picasso: Forty Years of His Art,* exh. cat., 1939, p. 24).

Evidently the World's Fair had attracted the young artist and several of his Spanish friends to Paris (Blunt and Pool, 1962, p. 12). They had originally intended to go to London, a destination they never reached (Penrose, p. 62). Picasso lived in the studio Isidro Nonell had used at 49, rue Gabrielle in Montmartre with Carlos Casegemas and Manuel Pallarés. He was back in Barcelona for Christmas (J. Sabartés, *Picasso: An Intimate Portrait,* trans. A. Flores, New York, 1948, pp. 43, 47, 223). It was during this stay in Paris that he adopted the signature P. R. Picasso.

The Moulin de la Galette was a dancing spot at the site of a mill atop Montmartre. Long a favorite of artists, Renoir, van Gogh, Toulouse-Lautrec, Steinlen, van Dongen, Dufy, and Utrillo painted there. A photograph showing Toulouse-Lautrec seated at a white rectangular table is reproduced in P. Huisman and M. G. Dortu, *Lautrec by Lautrec,* New York, 1964, p. 75. Other photos of the Moulin appear on p. 79 of the same book and in M. Pianzola, *Théophile-Alexandre Steinlen,* Lausanne, 1971, p. 47.

Ramón Casas (1866-1932) lived in the apartment which Santiago Rusiñol had leased in the Moulin de la Galette (M. McCully, *Els Quatre Gats and Modernista Painting in Catalonia in the 1890's,* Ph.D. dissertation, Yale University, 1975, p. 25). Casas painted the subject several times in the 1890s: for example, *Baile en el "Moulin de la Galette"* (Museo del Cau Ferrat, Sitges). His plein-air painting of the Moulin de la Galette was undoubtedly known to Picasso before he went to Paris since it had been in the Museo de Bellas Artes in Barcelona from 1891 (J. F. Ráfols, *Ramón Casas,* Barcelona, c. 1949, pl. 10). The art editor of *Pèl & Ploma,* Casas drew the portrait of Picasso with Montmartre and the Moulin de la Galette in the background that appeared in the June 1901 issue of the magazine (vol. III, no. 77, p. 14).

1. Weill (p. 67) specified: *"à M. Huc, une peinture importante: Le Moulin de la Galette vendue, (eh! eh!) 250 francs . . ."* The reference is to Arthur Huc, manager of *La Dépêche de Toulouse,* who commissioned two posters from Toulouse-Lautrec (J. Adhémar, *Toulouse-Lautrec: His Complete Lithographs and Drypoints,* New York, 1965, nos. 4 [L.D. 340] and 74 [L.D. 67]) and owned two paintings by Lautrec (M. G. Dortu, *Toulouse-Lautrec et son oeuvre,* New York, 1971, vol. I, nos. 243, 264). Years later, in 1941, Matisse remembered that Huc of *La Dépêche de Toulouse* bought one of his works from Weill (J. D. Flam, *Matisse on Art,* London, 1973, p. 87).

2. J. K. Thannhauser notes, Dec. 1972. Bartholdy also owned Z. I. 274, 351, and 206 (*Head of a Woman,* see cat. no. 39). The family is that of the composer Felix Mendelssohn (M. F. Schneider, *Mendelssohn oder Bartholdy?,* Basel, 1962).

fig. a.
Steinlen's cover for *Gil Blas illustré,* 10ᵉ
année, no. 28, July 13, 1900.

Picasso's painting has frequently been compared to the work of Toulouse-Lautrec. His debt to Lautrec was acknowledged by critics at the time of Picasso's 1901 Vollard exhibition (Blunt and Pool, p. 13) and later by the artist himself (D. Ashton, *Picasso on Art: A Selection of Views,* New York, 1972, p. 51). Closest among Lautrec's works to the Thannhauser picture is *Au Moulin Rouge,* 1892 (48½ x 55⅜ in., 122.5 x 139.7 cm., The Art Institute of Chicago; see D. C. Rich, *Toulouse-Lautrec: Au Moulin Rouge,* London, c. 1949, p. 10 and fig. 10). The Lautrec would appear to be the source for the cut-off figure in the foreground, the strong diagonal at the left, and for the figures grouped around the table; however, it lacks the dancing figures, the night setting, and the emphasis on black of Picasso's palette. M. G. Dortu lists the work as belonging to the Galerie Manzi-Joyant by 1902 (*Toulouse-Lautrec et son oeuvre,* New York, 1971, vol. II, p. 258, no. 427). Dortu does not know if *Au Moulin Rouge* was in the possession of Manzi-Joyant in 1900 and has not found it exhibited in that year (correspondence, Feb. 1976).

For Picasso, an accessible source reflecting Lautrec's painting could have been the cover of *Gil Blas illustré* for the July 13, 1900, issue by Théophile-Alexandre Steinlen (1859-1923) which appeared under the caption *"Au bal du 14 juillet, par Jacques Crépet"* (fig. a). A night scene with lights and dancing couples, it includes female figures in the left foreground and even the two with their heads close together that appear in Picasso's painting. In both, the colors are predominantly black with red, yellow, and white. Picasso's knowledge of *Gil Blas* before the Paris visit is well-documented (Vallentin, p. 30; P. Pool, "Sources and Backgrounds of Picasso's Art," *The Burlington Magazine,* vol. CI, May 1959, p. 179).

Michel Hoog (*Impressionism,* exh. cat., 1974, p. 186) emphasized Picasso's indebtedness to Renoir's *Dancing at the Moulin de la Galette,* 1876 (51½ x 68⅞ in., 130.8

x 174.6 cm., Musée du Louvre, Galerie du Jeu de Paume, Paris), which was painted at the site. Although Picasso could have seen the Renoir at the Luxembourg in Paris in 1900, the pictures do not seem related in style, color, and light, or in the appearance of the figures.

The woman dancer at the far right in the Thannhauser picture clearly refers to the work of Toulouse-Lautrec. It is probably closest to a lithograph of Marcel Lender, the actress (L. Delteil, *Le Peintre graveur illustré,* Paris, 1920, vol. X, no. 102), of which a special third state was published in *Pan* (vol. I, no. 3, 1895, p. 197).

The same woman seated at the left, whose gaze boldly confronts the spectator, may appear at the far right in Picasso's drawing *Le Retour de l'exposition* (not in Z.; $18\frac{1}{2}$ x $24\frac{3}{8}$ in., 47 x 62 cm., private collection; Daix, 1977, pp. 36-37, pl. 4; kindly brought to my attention by Marilyn McCully). In addition, Picasso's sketch of two women seated at a table (Z.XXI. 255; conté crayon, 21 x 13 cm., 1901) captures the spirit and contains the profile of the woman at the left at the table in his *Le Moulin de la Galette* so as to suggest a contemporary date. Unlike the Toulouse-Lautrec and the Renoir, Picasso's *Moulin de la Galette* is strikingly dominated by women. Their white faces, red mouths, and fashionable hats stand out in a night illuminated by electric lights.

EXHIBITIONS:

New York, The Museum of Modern Art, *Picasso: Forty Years of His Art,* Nov. 15, 1939-Jan. 7, 1940, no. 5, repr., traveled to The Art Institute of Chicago, Feb. 1-Mar. 3, Boston, Institute of Modern Art, Apr. 27-May 26; New York, The Museum of Modern Art, *Masterpieces of Picasso,* July 15-Sept. 7, 1941, no. 5; New York, M. Knoedler and Co., *Picasso Before 1907,* Oct. 15-Nov. 8, 1947, no. 3; New York, The Museum of Modern Art, *Picasso: 75th Anniversary Exhibition,* May 22-Sept. 8, 1957, p. 15, repr., traveled to The Art Institute of Chicago, Oct. 29-Dec. 8; Philadelphia Museum of Art, *Picasso,* Jan. 8-Feb. 23, 1958, no. 4, repr.; London, Tate Gallery (organized by the Arts Council of Great Britain), *Picasso,* July 6-Sept. 18, 1960, no. 4, pl. Ib; Paris, Grand Palais, *Hommage à Pablo Picasso,* Nov. 1966-Feb. 1967, no. 3, repr.

REFERENCES:

Zervos, 1932, vol. I, no. 41, pl. 20; B. Weill, *Pan! dans l'Oeil!,* Paris, 1933, p. 67; A. M. Frankfurter, "Picasso in Retrospect: 1939-1900," *Art News,* vol. 38, Nov. 18, 1939, p. 11, repr.: H.F. Mackenzie, *Understanding Picasso,* Chicago, 1940, pl. l; J. Cassou, *Picasso,* Paris, 1940, p. 36, repr.; A. H. Barr, Jr., *Picasso: Fifty Years of His Art,* New York, 1946, pp. 18, repr., 19, and 253; Cirici Pellicer, 1946, p. 64 and no. 20, repr.; J. Merli, *Picasso, el artista y la obra de nuestro tiempo,* rev. ed., Buenos Aires, 1948, pl. 24; Cirici Pellicer, 1950, no. 18, repr.; W. S. Lieberman, *Pablo Picasso: Blue and Rose Periods,* New York, 1954, pl. 12; W. Boeck and J. Sabartés, *Picasso,* New York, 1955, p. 117; Paris, Musée des Arts Décoratifs, *Picasso,* exh. cat., 1955, definitive ed., p. 20; J. C. Aznar, *Picasso y el cubismo,* Madrid, 1956, p. 319, fig. 214; A. Vallentin, *Pablo Picasso,* Paris, 1957, p. 48; Penrose, 1958, no. 8, pl. l; P. de Champris, *Picasso: ombre et soleil,* Paris, 1960, pl. 3; H. L. C. Jaffé, *Picasso,* New York, 1964, p. 15; Daix, 1965, p. 28; F. Daulte, "Une Donation sans précédent: la collection Thannhauser," *Connaissance des Arts,* no. 171, May 1966, p. 68, repr.; T. Reff, review of A. Blunt and P. Pool, *Picasso: The Formative Years, The Art Bulletin,* vol. XLVIII, June 1966, p. 267; Daix and Boudaille, 1967, no. II. 10, pp. 28, 29, repr.,33, 122; A. Fermigier, ed., *Picasso,* Paris, 1967, p. 41, repr.; L. Wertenbaker, *The World of Picasso,* New York, 1967, pp. 21, repr., and 31; H. H. Arnason, *History of Modern Art,* New York, 1968, pp. 117, 118, repr.; D. Cooper, *Picasso Theatre,* New York, 1968, p. 341 and pl. 25; S. Finkelstein, *Der junge Picasso,* Dresden, 1970, pp. 44, 45, 162, and pl. 54; N. F. Broude, "Picasso's Drawing, *Woman with a Fan:* The Role of Degas in Picasso's Transition to his 'First Classical Period,' " *Oberlin College*

Bulletin, vol. 29, winter 1972, p. 87, fn. 9; J. Warnod, *Washboat Days,* trans. C. Green, New York, 1972, pp. 61, 65; J.-L. Daval, "Guidelines," in J. Leymarie, *Picasso: The Artist of the Century,* New York, 1972, pp. 203, repr., and 291; F. Elgar and R. Maillard, *Picasso,* rev. ed., New York, 1972, p. 182; *Masterpieces,* 1972, p. 45, repr.; H. Kramer, "Picasso's Very First Painting in Paris," *The New York Times,* July 28, 1974, Section D, p. 17, repr.; D. Porzio and M. Valsecchi, *Understanding Picasso,* New York, 1974, color pl. 2; E. Quinn and P. Descargues, *Picasso,* Paris, 1974, p. 206, repr.; New York, The Metropolitan Museum of Art, *Impressionism,* exh. cat., 1974, p. 186; Daix, 1977, p. 37.

---

35   Au Café. 1901
       (Le Comptoir; The Counter)

Charcoal on paper, 8 7/16 x 10 1/16 (21.4 x 25.6)

Signed l.l.: *P. R. Picasso*   Not dated.

PROVENANCE:

J. K. Thannhauser by 1932.[1]

CONDITION:

Flattened and creases at top and bottom retouched by C. Gaehde (June 1973).

1. J. K. Thannhauser (notes, Dec. 1972) stated that he acquired the present drawing and cat. nos. 37 and 38 from Santiago Laporta in Barcelona. No collector by this name is known.

Alejandro Cirici Pellicer states that this drawing was published in *Arte Joven,* the small magazine for which Picasso was art editor and Francisco de Asis Soler literary editor in Madrid in 1901. According to Joseph Phillip Cervera, it is reproduced in *Arte Joven,* no. 3, May 3, 1901, n.p., without title or caption, and, although it appears on the same page as Soler's short story "La última sensación," it is not an illustration for the story (correspondence, Dec. 1975).

In the Café (Z. VI. 373; D-B. d. III; 11⅞ x 16½ in., 30 x 42 cm., Collection Masoliver, Barcelona), which was also published in *Arte Joven,* includes figures which appear to be the same as the man with the hat standing at the left and the man at the far right in the Thannhauser drawing. Another related drawing shows Picasso and a group of artists in Madrid. These are from left to right: an unknown man, the poet Cornuti, Soler, Picasso, and Alberto Lozano (Z. I. 36; D-B. d.III. 5; 9¼ x 12 in., 23.5 x 30.5 cm., Collection Mr. and Mrs. Walter Bick, Canada). Pierre Daix dates both Madrid, early in 1901. In the signatures for each of these related works the artist reverts to an early form, *P. Ruiz Picasso,* whereas the Thannhauser drawing is signed *P. R. Picasso* (see cat. no. 34).

EXHIBITIONS:

Kunsthaus Zürich, *Picasso,* Sept. 11 - Oct. 30, 1932, no. 252 (label on reverse of frame reads: *Café,* 1900); Buenos Aires, Galería Müller,[2] *Picasso,* Oct. 1934, no. 28 (label on reverse of frame reads: *Café,* Madrid 1900).

REFERENCES:

Zervos, 1932, vol. I, no. 37, pl. 18 (*The Counter,* Madrid, 1900); Cirici Pellicer, 1946, no. 37, repr. (*El Mostrador,* 1900); Cirici Pellicer, 1950, no. 33, repr. (*Le Comptoir,* 1901); *Masterpieces,* 1972, p. 46, repr.

2. J. K. Thannhauser arranged for the exhibition and lent many of the works (conversation with D. C. Rich, Mar. 1975). No catalogue has been located although the bibliography in J. Merli, *Picasso, el artista y la obra de nuestro tiempo,* Buenos Aires, 1942, p. 305, states that the preface was by Frederico C. Müller. The exhibition numbers are derived from a printed label on the reverse of each work.

36 · The Fourteenth of July. 1901
(Le Quatorze juillet)

Oil on cardboard mounted on canvas, 18⅞ x 24¾ (48 x 62.8)

Signed u.r.: *Picasso*   Not dated.

PROVENANCE:
Purchased by J. K. Thannhauser, Paris, 1936-39 (conversation with D. C. Rich, Mar. 1975); Gift of Justin K. Thannhauser, 1964 (64.1707).

CONDITION:
Entire painted surface quite heavily varnished. Brown color of support visible in places (May 1975).

In the preface to the catalogue of the April 1-15, 1902, exhibition at the Galerie Berthe Weill, Adrien Farge describes the Thannhauser picture in these terms: "a brilliant 14th of July brings together in the most glittering colors all the surging movement and intense life of a popular holiday" (trans. J. Emmons in Leymarie).

July 14, 1901, was the first time Picasso experienced Bastille Day. Fernande Olivier, whom he met in 1904, recalled that "only the popular festivals and carnivals interested him in France. He always enjoyed being a spectator at the July Fourteenth celebrations, but he never felt involved in them emotionally" (*Picasso and His Friends*, trans. J. Miller, New York, 1965, p. 126; first published 1931).

The precise date of Picasso's arrival in Paris in 1901 for a second visit is not known. Pierre Daix believes it was May at the latest (1967, p. 33). Jaime Sabartés (*Picasso: Documents iconographiques,* Geneva, 1954, p. 309) and Maurice Jardot (Paris, Musée des Arts Décoratifs, *Picasso,* exh. cat., 1955, definitive ed., p. 20) have specified the end of March. A drawing by Picasso dated 1901 represents the artist arriving in Paris with Jaume André Bonsons (Z. VI. 342; D-B. d. IV. 12). Picasso's patron Mañach provided a studio at 130ter, boulevard de Clichy where they lived. Picasso remained in Paris until the end of the year. It was during this stay in Paris that he began to use only his mother's name as a signature. All sources date the Thannhauser painting from this time.

Early in June Picasso was introduced to Ambroise Vollard (J. Sabartés, *Picasso: An Intimate Portrait,* New York, 1948, p. 51). Subsequently an exhibition of paintings by Francisco de Iturrino (1864-1924) and Picasso took place at the Galerie Vollard in rue Laffitte from June 25 until July 14.

In 1901 the most accessible representations of the Fourteenth of July appear to have been by two non-French artists, van Gogh and Steinlen. Van Gogh's *Impression de 14 juillet,* 1886, was exhibited in Paris at his important retrospective at Bernheim-Jeune from March 15-31, 1901, as no. 22. At that time the picture belonged to Joseph Hessel, Paris (de la Faille, 1970, F222, p. 118; 17¼ x 15¼ in., 44 x 39 cm., Collection Mrs. L. Jäggli-Hahnloser, Winterthur, Switzerland; Gordon, 1974, vol. II, p. 27; J. Leymarie, *Fauvism,* Lausanne, 1959, p. 20, color repr.). The most striking similarity between the two pictures is the boldly expressive red, white, and blue brushwork representing flags and bunting. While the possibility that Picasso saw the van Gogh is remote, it seems certain that he would have known about the Bernheim-Jeune exhibition, which was an important impetus to the Fauves. Antonina Vallentin relates that "asked later what had been the predominant influence on him during the early days in Paris, he unhesitatingly replies: 'Van Gogh!' " (p. 32).

PICASSO   *The Fourteenth of July*

Théophile-Alexandre Steinlen (1859-1923) did many versions of the subject, including one in the July 11, 1901, issue of *L'Assiette au Beurre* (vol. I, no. 15, pp. 3-4), the cover of the July 13, 1900, *Gil Blas illustré* (10ᵉ année), and an 1895 oil of *Le 14 Juillet* (Musée Petit Palais, Geneva; M. Pianzola, *Théophile-Alexandre Steinlen*, Lausanne, 1971, cover, color repr.). Picasso's painting does not bear a significant resemblance to Steinlen's representations, which are night scenes with hanging lanterns (see cat. no. 34).

Picasso's *The Fourteenth of July* resembles his *On the Upper Deck* (Z. XXI. 168; D-B. V. 61; 19⅜ x 25¼ in., 49.2 x 64.2 cm., The Art Institute of Chicago) and *The Flower Seller* (Z. XXI. 207; D-B. V. 65; 13½ x 20½ in., 33.7 x 52.1 cm., Glasgow Art Gallery and Museum) in the use of light-colored background buildings to limit depth and in the cutting off of the scene represented. All three are close in style, painted on cardboard, signed in a similar manner, and date from 1901.

EXHIBITIONS:

Paris, Galerie Berthe Weill, *Tableaux et pastels de Louis Bernard-Lemaire et de Picasso*, Apr. 1-15, 1902, no. 5;[1] Mexico City, Sociedad de Arte Moderno (organized by The Museum of Modern Art, New York), *Picasso*, June 1944, p. 41, and Added Corrections List; Santa Barbara Museum of Art, *Fiesta Exhibition 1953: Picasso, Gris, Miró, and Dali*, Aug. 4-30, 1953, no. 2.

REFERENCES:

Zervos, 1932, vol. I, pp. xxvi-xxvii; Cirici Pellicer, 1946, pp. 95, 168, 170; C. Zervos, "Oeuvres et images inédites de la jeunesse de Picasso," *Cahiers d'Art*, 25ᵉ année, no. II, 1950, p. 314, repr.; Cirici Pellicer, 1950, pp. 100, 172, 174; Zervos, 1954, vol. VI, no. 334 and pl. 41; A. Vallentin, *Picasso*, Eng. ed. edited by K. Woods, Garden City, 1963, p. 46; Daix and Boudaille, 1967, no. V. 70, pp. 42, 43, 45, and 187, repr.; H. H. Arnason, *History of Modern Art*, New York, 1968, p. 90, repr.; *Masterpieces*, 1972, p. 47, repr.; J. Leymarie, *Picasso: The Artist of the Century*, New York, 1972, p. 207; Daix, 1977, pp. 44 and 49, fn. 19.

1. According to Daix and Boudaille (p. 52), when Picasso returned to Barcelona in Jan. 1902, Pedro Mañach kept some of his work, which was shown at Berthe Weill's gallery at 25, rue Victor-Massé in Apr. This exhibition was organized by Mañach and included fifteen paintings by Picasso. According to Vallentin none was sold. Picasso was exhibited there again from June 2-15 (jointly with Matisse) and Nov. 15-Dec. 15, 1902. Sabartés mentions that Picasso first met Mañach at Berthe Weill's gallery in 1900 (*Picasso: An Intimate Portrait*, p. 48).

37   Woman and Child. 1903
      (Femme et enfant; Deux enfants; Two
      Children; Frau mit Kind
      nach Carrière)

Conté crayon on wove paper, 13¼ x 9⅛
(33.7 x 23.2)

Watermark: VILASECA

Signed l.r.: *Picasso;* inscribed l.r., not by the
artist: *D'Eugéne Carriére;* inscribed, not by
the artist, on reverse: *10 centimetro*   Not
dated.

PROVENANCE:

J. K. Thannhauser by 1932.[1]

CONDITION:

Same manufacture of paper and same
watermark as *Man with Pack* (see cat. no.
38). Likewise, similar horizontal grid patterns on the reverse of both drawings (May
1973).

1. J. K. Thannhauser (notes, Dec. 1972) stated that he acquired the present drawing and cat.
   nos. 35 and 38 from Santiago Laporta in Barcelona. No collector by this name is known.

fig. a.
Front page of *El Liberal,* Año III, num. 848, August 10, 1903.

fig. b.
Carrière, *The Artist with His Wife and Their Son,* 1895-96, 94½ x 49 in., 240 x 124.5 cm., The National Gallery of Canada, Ottawa.

According to J. K. Thannhauser (notes, Dec. 1972), Picasso remembered having made the present drawing for a Barcelona newspaper in connection with an article on contemporary art. The *Woman and Child* does appear in slightly modified form on the front page of *El Liberal* in Barcelona on Monday, August 10, 1903 (fig. a). The newspaper reproduction has translated the solid black areas of conté crayon into linear patterns of parallel lines and crosshatching, undoubtedly so that it would reproduce better. Under the newspaper reproduction of the present drawing is printed "Eugenio Carrière." The present work and two other drawings are identified at the end of the article (p. 2) as the work of Pablo Ruiz Picasso. The other drawings represent a figure from Puvis de Chavannes (cat. no. 38) and Auguste Rodin's sculpture of Jules Dalou. All three illustrate an article, "Las Crónicas de Arte: La Pintura y La Escultura allende los Pirineos," written by Carlos Juñer Vidal, brother of Sebastian Juñer and a friend of Picasso.

Other illustrations by Picasso appear in *El Liberal* during 1902: a drawing of a woman, dated Paris 1902 (Z. VI. 444), accompanies an article by Carlos Juñer Vidal (Año II, num. 353, Apr. 6, 1902 [p. 7]); a large drawing of the festival of the Merced published by Alejandro Cirici Pellicer, 1950, under "Documents" (Año II, num. 540, Oct. 5, 1902, p. 1); and a drawing of Sebastian Juñer-Vidal (Año II, num. 551, Oct. 16, 1902, p. 1).

The exact source for *Woman and Child* is a painting by Eugène Carrière entitled *The Artist with His Wife and Their Son* (fig. b). It represents Carrière (1849-1906) with his wife, Sophie Demousseaux, born 1855, and youngest son, Jean-René, born 1888. Neither Picasso's conté crayon drawing nor the illustration in *El Liberal* included the figure of the artist in the background.

The question of how Picasso knew the Carrière painting remains unanswered. The picture is not mentioned in the Carrière bibliography, it is not included in exhibitions, and reproductions of it have not been found in magazines Picasso is known to have seen regularly. The provenance of the large canvas has not been traced farther back than the mid-1960s.

Carrière's painting is not dated but a date can be arrived at on the basis of the age of Jean-René. Myron Laskin (correspondence, Jan. 1974) suggests 1895-96. His argument is reinforced by the great similarity between Jean-René in the Ottawa painting and in an oil sketch of the boy's head which has been dated 1895 (J.-P. Dubray, *Eugène Carrière*, Paris, 1931, repr. opp. p. 25). Robert J. Bantens prefers a date of 1897-1900 (correspondence, Nov. 1975).

It is entirely possible that Picasso saw Carrière's painting during a visit to Paris. From 1900 Carrière's atelier was in the Villa des Arts, 15, rue Hégésippe-Moreau (J.-R. Carrière, *De la vie d'Eugène Carrière: Souvenirs, lettres, pensées,* Toulouse, 1966, p. 24). From at least June through December 1901, Picasso lived a few blocks away at 130ter, boulevard de Clichy. In 1902 Hermen Anglada Camarasa's address is listed as 9, rue Hégésippe-Moreau (Brussels, La Libre Esthétique, *Neuvième Exposition,* exh. cat., 1902, p. 9). Among Picasso's Catalan friends, Ramón Casas, Santiago Rusiñol, Miguel Utrillo, Sebastian Juñer, and Hermen Anglada Camarasa had contact with Carrière's work (conversation with M. McCully, Oct. 1976).

Picasso was in Paris from October 1902 until the beginning of January 1903, although he did not live near Carrière's studio at the time. Before the 1903 newspaper came to light, Pierre Daix (correspondence, Mar. 1976) dated the Thannhauser drawing from the winter of 1902-3 during Picasso's sojourn in Paris.

Since the Thannhauser drawing relies so essentially on Carrière's painting, it has to be assumed that Picasso saw either the original or a reproduction of it. Rosa Maria Subirana finds Picasso's copy uncharacteristically close to the Carrière and she questions its authorship (conversation, May 1977) whereas Marilyn McCully accepts the present drawing as by Picasso (conversations, Oct. 1976 and Dec. 1977).

The article for which Picasso contributed the three illustrations is a review of a book by Manuel Rodriquez Códola, *La pintura en la Exposición Universal de Paris de 1900,* which was published in Barcelona in May 1903. The book itself contains no illustrations. The works by Carrière and Puvis de Chavannes which Picasso used to illustrate the article were not exhibited at the World's Fair, which he surely visited. The third drawing is of a sculpture by Rodin, *Jules Dalou* (1883), which was on view at the fair (*Catalogue officiel illustré de l'art français de 1800 à 1889,* no. 1794). However, this drawing is not included in the Picasso literature if, in fact, it survives.

The inauthentic inscription on the present drawing was added by the same person who wrote "D'August Rodin" under the third drawing in *El Liberal.* Daix (correspondence, Mar. 1976) considers the signature authentic, dating it from 1903-4.

EXHIBITION:
Kunsthaus Zürich, *Picasso,* Sept. 11-Oct. 30, 1932, no. 258 (*Frau mit Kind nach Carrière,* 1902).

REFERENCES:

Zervos, 1932, vol. I, no. 134 and pl. 66 (*Two Children, 1902*); Cirici Pellicer, 1946, pl. 143 (*Dos Niños, 1902*); Cirici Pellicer, 1950, pl. 136 (*Deux Enfants, 1902*); Blunt and Pool, 1962, pp. 10, 31, and pl. 93; T. Reff, review of A. Blunt and P. Pool, *Picasso: The Formative Years, The Art Bulletin,* vol. XLVIII, June 1966, p. 267 (first identifies source); *Masterpieces,* 1972, p. 48, repr. (c. 1902); R. J. Bantens, *Eugène Carrière—His Work and His Influence,* Ph.D. dissertation, Pennsylvania State University, 1975, pp. 260-63 and 745, repr.

---

38   Man with Pack. 1903
      (*Homme au sac; Homme à la besace;* [1]*Man
      with a Wallet; Lastträger*)

Conté crayon on wove paper, 13⁹⁄₁₆ x 9⅛ (33.8 x 23.2)

Watermark: JOSE

Inauthentic signature l.l.:[2] *Picasso;* inscribed, not by the artist, on reverse: *12 centimet[res]*[3]   Not dated.

PROVENANCE:
J. K. Thannhauser by 1932.[4]

CONDITION:
Discolored lead white upper right. Old repair of small tear at upper left. Same manufacture of paper[5] and same watermark as cat. no. 37 (May 1973).

The present work is a copy of a drawing in the Museo Picasso, Barcelona (fig. a; Cirlot, 1972, no. 229). The outline of the figure in the drawing in the Museo Picasso and that in the Thannhauser version coincide perfectly. Yet the Barcelona drawing lacks the entire pack, has more detail and modeling and none of the emphasis on very simplified lines of the present one.

The drawing in the Thannhauser Collection is reproduced line for line on the front page of the Barcelona newspaper *El Liberal* for Monday, August 10, 1903 (Año III, num. 848, p. 1), and the following page states: "Reproducciones de Pablo Ruiz Picasso" (see cat. no. 37). Next to the newspaper reproduction of the present drawing is the caption "De Puvis de Chavannes." The illustration lacks the false signature at the lower left and the discoloration now present at the upper right in the Thannhauser drawing.

1. Daix points out that it is not a "besace" but a "sac" (correspondence, June 1975).
2. Indicated in the third edition (1957) of Zervos, I, 190. An inauthentic signature is found also in vol. I, nos. 47, 114, 124-27, 129, 138-40, 143-54, 156, 157, 159, 170, 171, 173, and 178, which are all ex. coll. Juñer, Barcelona. The signature appears also in D-B.d. IX. 10 now in the Museo Picasso, Barcelona.
3. In *El Liberal* the illustration of *Man with Pack* takes up exactly 12 cm. of column space (measured vertically as the arrow on reverse of present drawing indicates).
4. J. K. Thannhauser (notes, Dec. 1972) stated that he acquired the present drawing and cat. nos. 35 and 37 from Santiago Laporta in Barcelona. No collector by this name is known.
5. According to Oriol Vals, Conservator of Paper, Museo de Arte Moderno, Barcelona, paper with the JOSE VILASECA watermark was manufactured near Barcelona at the beginning of the twentieth century and still is (conversation, May 1977).

Richard J. Wattenmaker (p. 170) has pointed out that the *Man with Pack* is derived from Puvis de Chavannes (1824-1898; specifically, the right section of *Sainte Geneviève ravitaillant Paris* in the Pantheon, Paris, which he completed in 1897 (Paris, Grand Palais, *Puvis de Chavannes*, exh. cat., 1977, no. 217 and *Art et Décoration*, vol. XXV, Jan.-June 1909, opp. p. 136, color repr.). Picasso has retained the pose of the man at the extreme left unloading the ship but he has altered slightly the position of the arms, changed the jug into a pack, transformed Puvis' clothed figure into a nude, and completed the man's face, which is cut off in the Pantheon mural.

Wattenmaker (p. 169) proves that Picasso knew Puvis' mural by interpreting his notes on an ink drawing of *Three Figures* in the Museo Picasso, Barcelona (MAB 110. 468; 5¾ x 7¼ in., 14.6 x 18.1 cm.; Cirlot, p. 269 repr., no. 957). Not only does *Three Figures* copy a detail from the left section of *Sainte Geneviève ravitaillant Paris* but Picasso's annotation reads: "De Puvis en el Panteon / el cuadro de la hambre" ("From Puvis in the Pantheon / a picture of the famine").

Picasso could have worked from reproductions of the Pantheon murals or preparatory drawings for them. Jacques Foucart (correspondence, June 1977) states that reproductions of Puvis' work were commonly found in magazines and newspapers. In addition, Picasso's friend, Mécislas Golberg (1868-1907) had published a book on Puvis in 1901 (P. Pool, "Picasso's Neo-Classicism: First Period, 1905-6," *Apollo*, vol. LXXXI, Feb. 1965, p. 124. A copy of the book has not been located).

Picasso stayed in Paris from October 1902 to January 1903 when he returned to Barcelona, where he remained for all of 1903. Earlier he had visited Paris in 1900 and 1901 (see cat. nos. 34 and 36).

The drawing in the Museo Picasso bears an inscription at the upper right, "DOZ," which means December 1902 according to Rosa Maria Subirana (correspondence, July 1976). She has not yet been able to determine conclusively who wrote the date (conversation, May 1977). The inscription appears on several drawings in the Museo Picasso which are related to their *Man Carrying a Sack* (MAB 110.437, 110.447, 110.462, 110.464, 110.490, 110.491, 110.498, and 110.529).

Picasso is known to have made more than one drawing of the same image in Barcelona in 1902. For *The Two Sisters* (D-B. VII. 22) nearly identical figures are repeated and simplified to accentuate contour in D-B. d. VII.4 and 6 and Addenda 14. In the latter, the lines have been greatly simplified and all details eliminated but the drawing's authenticity is unquestionable since it remained in Picasso's collection.

The Thannhauser drawing dates from between December 1902 and August 10, 1903. It is not certain that Picasso himself made the copy in the Thannhauser Collection but it is clear that the drawing is the one which appeared in *El Liberal*. Subirana thinks that the Thannhauser drawing is not by Picasso (conversation, May 1977). Marilyn McCully is of the opinion that it was done by another hand after the Barcelona drawing for reproduction (conversation, Dec. 1977). The appearance of the *Man with Pack* in *El Liberal* together with *Woman and Child* (cat. no. 37) combined with the fact that both drawings are executed on Spanish paper of the same manufacture (but never known by Subirana and Vals to have been used by Picasso) make it necessary to consider cat. nos. 37 and 38 together.

There is no reason to doubt the August 1903 newspaper credit to Picasso for the illustrations to an article on French art around 1900. The present drawing and cat. no. 37 were intended to reproduce works by artists widely admired at the turn of the century. At that time Picasso was a young artist whose work was not known outside

38

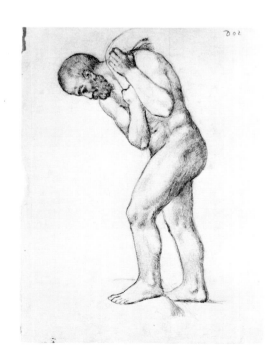

fig. a.
Picasso, *Hombre cargando un saco (Man Carrying a Sack),* conté crayon on paper, 12¼ x 9¼ in., 31.2 x 23.5 cm., Museo Picasso, Barcelona (MAB 110.531).
© S.P.A.D.E.M., 1978.

the circle of *Els Quatre Gats* in Barcelona. He probably welcomed whatever fees he received for illustrations that were published.

Picasso's illustrations appeared elsewhere in *El Liberal* (see cat. no. 37) and in the five issues of *Arte Joven* (1901), of which he was art editor. In addition, his work was accepted for publication in *Joventut, Catalunya Artística, Pèl & Ploma* in Spain, and *Gil Blas illustré* in Paris (12ᵉ année, no. 30, July 25, 1902, p. 4). A complete list follows for these Spanish periodicals (except for *Arte Joven)* where Picasso's illustrations were published. *Joventut:* Añy I, no. 22, July 12, 1900, p. 345; no. 27, Aug. 16, 1900, p. 424; Añy V, no. 204, Jan. 7, 1904, pp. 8 and 13; *Catalunya Artística:* Añy I, no. 13, Sept. 6, 1900, p. 208; no. 17, Oct. 4, 1900, p. 268; Añy II, no. 38, Feb. 1901, p. 104; *Pèl & Ploma:* Añy I, no. 65, Dec. 1, 1900, p. 4; Añy III, no. 77, June 1901, pp. 15, 16, 17, 18; no. 80, Sept. 1901, p. 110, and Añy IV, no. 100, Dec. 1903, p. 368.

EXHIBITIONS:

Kunsthaus Zürich, *Picasso,* Sept. 11 - Oct. 30, 1932, no. 271 (label on reverse of frame reads: *Lastträger,* 1903); Buenos Aires, Galería Müller, *Picasso,* Oct. 1934, no. 35[6] (label on reverse of frame reads: *Cargadores,* 1903).

REFERENCES:

Zervos, 1932, vol. I, no. 190 and pl. 88 (*Man with a Wallet,* Barcelona, 1903); Cirici Pellicer, 1946, p. 161, repr.; Cirici Pellicer, 1950, p. 165, repr.; *Masterpieces,* 1972, p. 51, repr.; R. J. Wattenmaker, *Puvis de Chavannes and The Modern Tradition,* exh. cat., Art Gallery of Ontario, Toronto, 1975, p. 170, fig. 31 (1902).

6. See cat. no. 35, fn. 2.

---

39   Head of a Woman. 1903
      (*Tête de femme*)

Pastel on paper mounted on wove paper, 12³⁄₁₆ x 10⁷⁄₁₆ (31 x 26.5)

Signed u.r.: *Picasso*   Not dated.

PROVENANCE:

Paul von Mendelssohn Bartholdy, Berlin;[1] acquired from Bartholdy by J. K. Thannhauser by 1937.

CONDITION:

At an unknown date prior to 1965, repair made from left edge across woman's face and down to neck. Some inpainting. Stains and scattered spots (May 1973).

The sitter's identity is not known but her features are recognizable in other pastels executed in Barcelona in 1903: *Bust of a Woman* (Z. VI. 462; D-B. IX. 18; ex. coll. Sebastian Junyent, Barcelona) and especially *Mother and Child* (Z. I. 169; D-B. IX. 7; 8½ x 6⅛ in., 47.5 x 41 cm., signed and dated 1903, Museo Picasso, Barcelona). A drawing for the latter is dated January 1903 (Z. VI. 599). As Pierre Daix and Georges

1. See cat. no. 34, fn. 2.

Boudaille have observed (p. 58), in the work done after Picasso's return to Barcelona in January 1903, the sitters are no longer anonymous and their glances make contact with the viewer.

The signature resembles others of the period.

EXHIBITION:

Buenos Aires, Galería Müller, *Picasso,* Oct. 1934, no. 16.[2]

REFERENCES:

Zervos, 1932, vol. I, no. 206, pl. 92; Cirici Pellicer, 1946, no. 183, repr.; Cirici Pellicer, 1950, no. 175 (1903); D. Sutton, *Picasso: Peintures époques bleue et rose,* Paris, 1955, no. 29, repr.; Daix and Boudaille, 1967, no. IX. 8, repr. (Barcelona, 1903); *Masterpieces,* 1972, p. 50, repr.

2. According to J. K. Thannhauser, the picture was on consignment from Bartholdy (conversation with D. C. Rich, Mar. 1975). See also cat. no. 35, fn. 2.

40   El Loco. 1903-4
(Le Fou au chien; Fool with a Dog;
Madman with a Dog)

Watercolor on wove paper, 12¹³⁄₁₆ x 9⅛
(32.6 x 23.2)

Inscribed u.r.: *El loco*   Not signed or
dated.

PROVENANCE:
Ricardo Viñes, Paris;[1] A. Bellier, Paris,[2]
until 1935; acquired from Bellier by Alex
Reid and Lefevre, Ltd., London; purchased
from Reid and Lefevre, 1935, by R. J. L.
Griffin (correspondence with G. S. Corcoran of Reid and Lefevre, Dec. 1973); Mr.
and Mrs. Jonathan Griffin, London, by
1938-42 (correspondence with A. S. Mur-
ray, Feb. 1974, and L. Thomas, Nov. 1973);
purchased from Griffin by Theodore
Schempp, New York, 1942 (correspondence
with D. C. Rich, Oct. 1974); acquired from
Schempp by J. K. Thannhauser, New York,
c. 1943.

CONDITION:
Unidentified watermark center right. Small
tear lower right. Removed from mount and
rehinged by C. Gaehde (June 1973).

El loco means "the madman" in Spanish. The inscription is in Picasso's handwriting.
Caridad (Z. VI. 438; D-B. d. IX. 22; 10¼ x 14¼ in., 26 x 36 cm., Collection Marcel Mabille, Brussels) includes the madman with a dog from *El Loco*. There, the man
sits cross-legged with a hand outstretched to accept the coin offered him while the
dog cowers behind him. The dog appears again in two watercolors dated Barcelona
1903-4 (D-B. X.1 and X.3). A madman is also depicted in a large watercolor, which
is signed and dated 1904 and inscribed to Sebastian Junyent (*Madman*, Z. I. 232;
D-B. X.6; 33⅞ x 14³⁄₁₆ in., 86 x 36 cm., Museo Picasso, Barcelona).

Picasso had returned from Paris to Barcelona by mid-January of 1903 and remained
there into March 1904. He shared a studio with Angel de Soto at 17, Calle Riera de
San Juan until the beginning of 1904. At that time, Picasso rented a studio for himself at 28, Calle del Commercio. Pierre Daix and Georges Boudaille (p. 62) suggest a
date at the beginning of 1904 for the present work but indicate that Picasso's "last
works from Barcelona in the first months of 1904 could just as well have been from
1903" (p. 218).

EXHIBITIONS:
Boston, The Museum of Fine Arts, on loan from Mr. and Mrs. Jonathan Griffin, 1939-42;
Boston, The Museum of Fine Arts, *Drawings and Prints by Picasso,* Apr. 26-June 12, 1940
(correspondence with L. Thomas, Museum of Fine Arts, Nov. 1973).

REFERENCES:
Zervos, 1932, vol. I, no. 184 and pl. 86 (*Fool with a Dog,* 1903, coll. Viñes, Paris); Daix and
Boudaille, 1967, no. X. 5, pp. 62, 233, and 235, repr. (*El Loco [Madman with a Dog],* Barce-
lona, 1903-4); P. Lecaldano, *The Complete Paintings of Picasso: Blue and Rose Periods,* New
York, 1970, no. 103, pl. xx (*Beggar Man with Dog*); *Masterpieces,* 1972, p. 49, repr. (1903).

1. Viñes (1885-1943) was a Spanish pianist who lived in Paris. As early as 1904 he won a
   prize there in music (F. Michel et al., *Encyclopédie de la musique,* Paris, 1961, vol. III, p.
   861). His association with Picasso is attested to by a photograph of them together with
   Mme Picasso ("Spectacles espagnols à Paris," *Cahiers d' Art,* 3ᵉ année, no. 3, 1928, p. 142,
   repr.). Viñes owned another Barcelona 1903 watercolor (Z.I. 186; D-B. d. IX. 20).
2. Probably Alphonse Bellier, who once owned D-B. VI. 16.

41   Woman Ironing. 1904
      (La Repasseuse; Die Büglerin; Die Plätterin)

Oil on canvas, 45¾ x 28¾ (116.2 x 73)

Signed l.r.: *Picasso*   Not dated.

PROVENANCE:

Ambroise Vollard, Paris; Der Neuer Kunst-salon, Munich (?);[1] Moderne Galerie (Heinrich Thannhauser), Munich, c. 1913 (J. K. Thannhauser notes, Dec. 1972); Karl Adler, Berlin and Amsterdam, 1916; purchased

from Adler by J. K. Thannhauser, late 1930s.[2]

CONDITION:

Not lined. Repair of cut along right edge and right half of bottom edge in 1952. Abrasion on woman's raised shoulder prior to 1965 (May 1975).

Twice before, Picasso had treated the theme of a woman ironing: *Girl Ironing*, 1901 (not in Z; D-B. VI. 27; 19½ x 10⅛ in., 49.5 x 25.7 cm., The Metropolitan Museum of Art, New York) and *Woman Ironing*, 1904 (D-B. d.XI.ll; pastel, 15 x 21 in., 38.1 x 53.3 cm., ex. colls. Walter P. Chrysler and Mrs. Maurice Newton; New York, Sotheby Parke Bernet, *Important 19th and 20th Century Paintings and Sculpture*, Oct. 17, 1973, no. 54, color repr.). The earlier painting and the pastel are predominantly blue with white in the woman's bodice and white highlights on her face. In both the figure is represented virtually full-length and from the side. The shoulder is not raised, although the head leans forward and the outline of the front leg is slightly accentuated. The pastel includes an interior scene with bed, stove, lamp, and two chairs which support the ironing board.

The large painting in the Thannhauser Collection is far removed from these two versions. The figure is seen frontally and half-length. The blue tonality and specific details have disappeared to be replaced by neutral colors and a stark, anonymous figure and space.

The present composition reflects Degas' work, specifically *Les Repasseuses (Women Ironing)*, 1882 (fig. a; Lemoisne, 1946, vol.II, no. 686), which was in the Durand-Ruel collection in Paris from 1895 and *Women Ironing*, c. 1884 (30 x 32⅜ in., 76 x 82 cm.; Lemoisne, 1946, vol. III, p. 447, repr., no. 785). Because the latter belonged to Count Isaac de Camondo, Paris, from 1893 until 1908 when it went to the Louvre (G. Bazin, *Trésors de l'impressionnisme au Louvre*, Paris, 1958, p. 208), it seems improbable that Picasso saw it. It is possible but unlikely that Picasso saw the former in the Durand-Ruels' apartment in rue de Rome which was open to the public every Tuesday (correspondence with C. Durand-Ruel, Jan. 1976). Picasso was certainly aware of the firm, which figures in a humorous sketch (R. Penrose, *Portrait of Picasso*, rev. ed., New York, 1971, pl. 54).

In both pictures Degas uses a table with a bowl on it at the front of the composition to cut off the figures. Picasso was inspired by the woman on the right who presses down hard with both arms extended, both hands on the iron, and her head

1. According to *Die Kunst für Alle*, Jg. 28, May 1913, p. 383, Der Neuer Kunstsalon owned the present picture as well as Z.I. 79, 167, 302. J. K. Thannhauser told D. C. Rich that the picture did not belong to the Moderne Galerie at the time of the Feb. 1913 exhibition (conversation, Mar. 1975).

2. Correspondence with E. Adler, Oct. 1974, who gave 1939 as the date J. K. Thannhauser bought the painting, whereas Thannhauser mentioned 1937 (notes, Dec. 1972).

fig. a.
Degas, *Les Repasseuses (Women Ironing)*, 1882,
32 x 29⅝ in., 81.2 x 75.2 cm., Collection Durand-Ruel,
Paris.

bent forward. Common to all three paintings are the neutral mottled background and the textural quality of the painted surface. However, in Picasso's figure, the head leans far down to the left, accentuated by the raised shoulder.

When the Thannhauser painting was exhibited in Berlin in 1913, a critic in *Der Cicerone* compared the *Woman Ironing* to Degas' painting of the same subject then at Paul Cassirer's. It is not known which version was shown at the Cassirer exhibition, *Degas and Cézanne*, in November 1913, as no. 22, *Die Plätterin* (Gordon 1974, vol. II, p. 753). Degas' versions of the subject include Lemoisne 276, 277, 329, 356, 685-87, 785, and 786.

The same pose as in the Thannhauser painting appeared earlier in Picasso's *The Blue Room*, 1901 (Z.I. 103; D-B. VI.15; 20⅛ x 24⅝ in., 51 x 62.5 cm., The Phillips Collection, Washington, D.C.) in the form of a woman bathing (observed by Finkelstein, p. 35).

Picasso's *Old Guitarist* (oil on panel, 48⅛ x 32½ in., 122.3 x 82.5 cm., The Art Institute of Chicago; D-B. IX.34, p. 63, color repr.), which was painted in Barcelona in 1903, provides deeper insight into the *Woman Ironing*. The left shoulder of each figure is distorted so that it becomes the highest point from which the contour line of the body descends in a smooth movement to the horizontal of the neck and the curve of the lowered head. The facial features are viewed in profile. The woman's eye is not described: instead there is a dark area of shadow which must be interpreted as the equivalent of the old guitarist's sightless eye (see R. W. Johnson, "Picasso's 'Old Guitarist' and the Symbolist Sensibility," *Artforum*, vol. XIII, Dec. 1974, pp. 52-62; D-B., pp. 228-29; Finkelstein, p. 35). When the artist painted *Woman Ironing*, he must have had in mind the figure of the *Old Guitarist*, which he had finished about a year earlier. Like him, the woman ironing becomes an image of suffering and isolation. As Erich Steingräber has suggested (p. 52), it is a secular *imago pietatis*.

Picasso arrived in Paris in April 1904 with Sebastian Juñer. He lived at 13, rue Ravignan (place Emile-Goudeau) in the building which Max Jacob called the "Bateau-Lavoir," in the studio that his friend, Paco Durio (1875-1940), had used from 1901-4.

Pierre Daix and Georges Boudaille (p. 64) identify the sitter as Margot, the daughter of Frédé, who owned the café *Le Lapin Agile* in rue des Saules. She later married the writer Pierre Mac Orlan and lived until 1963. She is also recognizable in *Woman with a Crow* (Z. I. 240; D-B. XI.10) and *Woman with a Helmet of Hair* (Z.I.233; D-B. XI.7) both done in 1904. Daix and Boudaille (p. 65) place *Woman Ironing* slightly later in that year than these pictures because of its lack of color and greater degree of abstraction.

EXHIBITIONS:

Munich, Moderne Galerie (Heinrich Thannhauser), *Pablo Picasso,* Feb. 1913, no. 28 (1906); Stuttgart, Kgl. Kunstgebäude, *Grosse Kunstausstellung,* May-Oct. 1913, no. 420; Berlin, Ausstellungshaus am Kurfürstendamm, *Herbstausstellung,* autumn 1913, no. 171; Hamburg, Kunstverein, *Europäische Kunst der Gegenwart,* 1927;[3] Amsterdam, Stedelijk Museum, *Parijsche Schilders,* Feb. 25-Apr. 10, 1939, no. 85 (correspondence with J. M. Joosten, Dec. 1973); New York, The Museum of Modern Art, *Picasso: Forty Years of His Art,* Nov. 15, 1939-Jan. 7, 1940, no. 27, repr., traveled to The Art Institute of Chicago, Feb. 1-Mar. 3, Boston, Institute of Modern Art, Apr. 27-May 26; New York, The Museum of Modern Art, *Masterpieces of Picasso,* July 15-Sept. 7, 1941, no. 27; The Museum of Modern Art, *Art in Progress,* May 24-Oct. 15, 1944, p. 99, repr.; The Minneapolis Institute of Arts, *20th Century French Painters,* May 3-June 1, 1947 (correspondence with S. L'Heureux, Mar. 1974); New York, M. Knoedler and Co., *Picasso Before 1907,* Oct. 15-Nov. 8, 1947, no. 18; The Art Gallery of Toronto, *Picasso,* Apr. 1949, no. 2; Paris, Musée National d'Art Moderne, *L'Oeuvre du XXᵉ siècle,* May-June 1952, no. 85, repr.; New York, The Museum of Modern Art, *Picasso: 75th Anniversary Exhibition,* May 22-Sept. 8, 1957, p. 20, repr.

REFERENCES:

H. Hildebrandt, "Die Frühbilder Picassos," *Kunst und Künstler,* Jg. 11, Apr. 1913, p. 378, repr.; M. K. Rohe, "Pablo Picasso," *Die Kunst für Alle,* Jg. 28, May 15, 1913, p. 383, repr. (1906, lent by Neuer Kunstsalon, Munich); H. Friedeberger, "Die Berliner Herbstausstellung," *Der Cicerone,* Jg. V, Nov. 1913, p. 800; C. Einstein, *Die Kunst des 20. Jahrhunderts,* Berlin, 1926, vol. I, pl. vii (1903); *Cahiers d' Art,* 2ᵉ année, no. 6, 1927, supp. p. 7, repr. (installation view, Hamburg exhibition); A. Level, *Picasso,* Paris, 1928, p. 55 and pl. 9; Zervos, 1932, vol. I, no. 247, pl. 111 (1904, ex. coll. A. Vollard); J. Cassou, *Picasso,* Paris, 1940, p. 49, repr.; A. H. Barr, Jr., *Picasso: Fifty Years of His Art,* New York, 1946, p. 32, repr.; Cirici Pellicer, 1946, pp. 175, 179, pl. 188 (1904); J. Merli, *Picasso, el artista y la obra de nuestro tiempo,* rev. ed., Buenos Aires, 1948, pl. 106; Cirici Pellicer, 1950, pp. 179, 183, pl. 180; J. A. Gaya Nuño, *Picasso,* Barcelona, 1950, pl. 13; G. Lindahl, "Konstnären och Samhället," *Paletten,* vol. 12, no. 4, 1951, p. 98, repr.; W. S. Lieberman, *Pablo Picasso: Blue and Rose Periods,* New York, 1954, pl. 20; W. Boeck and J. Sabartés, *Picasso,* New York, 1955, pp. 38-39, 123; F. Elgar, *Picasso,* New York, 1956, p. 22 and n.p., repr.; A. Vallentin, *Pablo Picasso,* Paris, 1957, p. 90; Penrose, 1958, p. 106; P. de Champris, *Picasso: Ombre et soleil,* Paris, 1960, pp. 17, 287, pl. 7; Blunt and Pool, 1962, p. 21; H. L. C. Jaffé, *Picasso,* New York, 1964, pp. 19, 70, and 71, repr.; Daix, 1969, pp. 39, repr., 40-41, and 262; F. Daulte, "Une Donation sans précédent: la collection Thannhauser," *Connaissance des Arts,* no.

3. Known only from installation photographs in *Cahiers d'Art,* 2ᵉ année, no. 6, 1927, supp. p. 7. The Kunstverein has no records or catalogue of this exhibition (correspondence with C. Zinn, Apr. 1974).

171, May 1966, pp. 66, repr., and 67; Daix and Boudaille, 1967, no. XI. 6, pp. 56, 64, 65, and 240, repr.; A. Fermigier, ed., *Picasso,* Paris, 1967, p. 179, repr.; L. Wertenbaker, *The World of Picasso,* New York, 1967, pp. 44 and 45, repr.; H. H. Arnason, *History of Modern Art,* New York, 1968, pp. 95, 117, pl. 40; J-P. Crespelle, *Picasso and His Women,* New York, 1969, p. 49; P. Lecaldano, *The Complete Paintings of Picasso: Blue and Rose,* New York, 1970, p. 96, no. 125, and pl. xxiii; S. Finkelstein, *Der junge Picasso,* Dresden, 1970, pp. 35, 161, and pl. 25; N. F. Broude, "Picasso's Drawing, *Woman with a Fan:* The Role of Degas in Picasso's Transition to his 'First Classical Period,' " *Oberlin College Bulletin,* vol. 29, winter 1972, pp. 83 and 85, repr.; F. Elgar and R. Maillard, *Picasso,* rev. ed., New York, 1972, p. 186, repr.; Cirlot, 1972, p. 157 (1905); *Masterpieces,* 1972, p. 52, repr.; E. Steingräber, "La Repasseuse: zur frühesten Version des Themas von Edgar Degas," *Pantheon,* vol. XXXII, Jan.-Feb.-Mar. 1974, pp. 52 and 53, repr.

---

42 Young Acrobat and Child.

March 26, 1905

(Jeune acrobate et enfant; Two Harlequins; Saltimbanques et enfants; Harlequin and Boy; Two Boys)

Ink and gouache on gray cardboard, 12⁵⁄₁₆ x 9⅞ (31.3 x 25.1)

Signed and dated l.r.: *Picasso/Paris 26 Mars 05;* inscribed above signature: *A Mlle/A. Nachmann*

PROVENANCE:

Acquired through an unknown source from A. Nachmann, Cannes, by J. K. Thannhauser, Aug. 1939 (conversation with D. C. Rich, Mar. 1975).

CONDITION:

White pigment at bottom has oxidized (May 1973).

The present picture has previously been called *Two Harlequins* although it does not represent them (Daix and Boudaille). The young acrobat at the right is portrayed in similar attire in a drypoint dated March 1905 (B. Geiser, *Picasso: Peintre-Graveur,* Bern, 1933, vol. I, no. 6, repr. [*Les Deux Saltimbanques*]).

A considerably larger gouache shares with the Thannhauser version the same house and landscape as well as the two boys, although they appear somewhat younger in the present picture (*Two Acrobats with a Dog,* gouache on cardboard, 41½ x 29½ in., 105.4 x 74.9 cm., Collection Mr. and Mrs. William A. M. Burden, New York; Z. I. 300; D-B. XII.17; Rubin, p. 32, color repr.). The Burden gouache must have been completed by mid-April since it was published in the May 15 issue of *La Plume.* It seems to combine motifs from *Boy with a Dog* (Z.I. 306; D-B. XII. 16) and the present picture (Rubin).

Theodore Reff points out that at the end of 1904 Picasso again began to paint the harlequins and saltimbanques that had occupied him in 1901. He connects these harlequins and jesters with Picasso's idiots and madmen of 1902-4. Like them, clowns and acrobats were seen as symbols of human suffering ("Themes of Love and Death in Picasso's Early Work," in *Picasso in Retrospect,* New York, 1973, p. 29).

The warm brown and pink hues place the Thannhauser work, like others from 1905, within the Rose Period. Significantly, it is painted on gray board and includes various blues and grays as well as white.

During the Rose Period, Picasso's studio was near the Médrano circus. He later recalled: "I was really under the spell of the circus! Sometimes I came three or four nights in one week" (quoted in Brassaï, *Picasso and Company,* trans. F. Price, New York, 1966, p. 20, and confirmed by F. Olivier, *Picasso and His Friends,* trans. J. Miller, New York, 1965, pp. 51, 125-28). The rose tone that permeates Picasso's work of this time was the actual color of the interior of the Cirque Médrano (T. Reff, "Harlequins, Saltimbanques, Clowns, and Fools," *Artforum,* vol. X, Oct. 1971, p. 35).

The identity of the Mlle Nachmann referred to in the inscription remains unknown.

REFERENCES:

Picasso: Fifteen Drawings, New York, 1946, pl. 3; C. Zervos, "Oeuvres et images inédites de la jeunesse de Picasso," *Cahiers d'Art,* 25ᵉ année, no. 2, 1950, p. 328, repr.; Zervos, 1954, vol. VI, no. 718, pl. 87; H. Kay, *Picasso's World of Children,* Garden City, 1965, p. 64, repr.; Daix and Boudaille, 1967, no. XII. 15, repr. *(Young Acrobat and Child);* H. H. Arnason, *History of Modern Art,* New York, 1968, p. 119; P. Lecaldano, *The Complete Paintings of Picasso: Blue and Rose Periods,* New York, 1970, p. 99, no. 158, and color pl. xxx; W. Rubin, *Picasso in the Collection of The Museum of Modern Art,* New York, 1972, pp. 33 and 191 *(Young Acrobat and Child);* Cirlot, 1972, p. 157; *Masterpieces,* 1972, p. 53, repr. *(Two Harlequins).*

---

43   Vase of Flowers. 1905-6
(Vase de fleurs; Bouquet de fleurs)

India ink on wove paper, 10½ x 7¾ (26.7 x 19.7)

Signed: u.l.: *Picasso*   Not dated.

PROVENANCE:
J. K. Thannhauser before 1940.

CONDITION:
Support somewhat discolored. Deacidified, flattened, and rehinged by C. Gaehde (June 1973).

Pierre Daix (p. 245) places all still lifes of flowers in 1906, when Picasso went to Gosol in Spain (see cat. no. 44). However, this ink drawing resembles van Gogh's paintings of sunflowers so closely as to suggest van Gogh rather than Gosol as the point of departure. The van Gogh retrospective at the Salon des Artistes Indépendants in Paris from March 24 to April 30, 1905, included a painting of *Sunflowers* as no. 8 (de la Faille 455; 36¼ x 28½ in., 92 x 72.4 cm., Jan. 1889, Philadelphia Museum of Art). Picasso was in Paris at the time; reproductions would have been accessible if he did not see the exhibition.

Pierre de Champris (p. 211) points out the similarity between Picasso's drawing and another van Gogh, *Still Life: Fritillaries in a Copper Vase* (de la Faille 213; 29 x 23¾ in., 73.6 x 60.3 cm., summer 1887, Musée du Louvre, Galerie du Jeu de Paume, Paris) which has a spotted pattern in the background.

The signature is considerably later in date but had been added before 1940, when the work was published by Jean Cassou.

REFERENCES:

J. Cassou, *Picasso,* Paris, 1940, p. 149, repr. (*Bouquet de fleurs,* coll. Thannhauser); P. de Champris, *Picasso: Ombre et soleil,* Paris, 1960, pp. 211, 293, and pl. 251; Daix and Boudaille, 1967, no. d.XV. 41, repr. (*Vase of Flowers,* summer 1906); Zervos, 1970, vol. XXII, no. 339 and pl. 122 (*Vase de fleurs,* 1906); *Masterpieces,* 1972, p. 54, repr. (c. 1905).

44   Still Life: Flowers in a Vase. 1906
      (Nature morte: fleurs dans un vase)

Gouache on cardboard, 28⅜ x 22 (72.1 x 55.9)

Signed l.l.: *Picasso*   Not dated.

PROVENANCE:
Acquired from the artist by J. K. Thannhauser, Paris, 1937-39.

CONDITION:
The work was scratched by the artist with a sharp, pointed instrument and with a blunt one. Small nail punctures from the reverse at upper corners and near the two pieces of pottery (May 1975).

Still Life: Flowers in a Vase dates from the summer of 1906 when Picasso, accompanied by Fernande Olivier, went to Gosol in Spain. The chocolate pot is included in *Still Life with a Portrait* (Z. I. 342; D-B. XV. 14; 32¼ x 39½ in., 82 x 100.3 cm., The Phillips Collection, Washington, D.C.), which also depicts a Spanish wine vessel. Pierre Daix points out that Picasso did not paint still lifes of flowers in 1905 (p. 245), and that the earthenware he painted at Gosol drew him back to still life, a genre in which he had worked in 1901 in Paris (pp. 99 and 168-70; D-B. 292).

The roses and the blue flowers are reminiscent of the background flowers in *Boy with a Pipe* from the preceding year (Z. I. 274; D-B. XIII. 13; 39⅜ x 32 in., 100 x 81.3 cm., Collection Mr. and Mrs. John Hay Whitney, New York; W. Lieberman, *Pablo Picasso: Blue and Rose Periods,* New York, 1959, color pl. 31).

According to Christian Zervos, the painting was scratched with a penknife *(canif)* by the artist at the time it was painted *(Cahiers d'Art,* p. 324). When exhibited in 1932, the work was unsigned. J. K. Thannhauser remembered that Picasso signed it at the Thannhausers' home in Paris (notes, Dec. 1972).

EXHIBITION:
Paris, Galeries Georges Petit, *Picasso,* June 16 - July 30, 1932, no. 29 (*Nature morte au vase de fleurs,* 1905, 71 x 54 cm.).

REFERENCES:
C. Zervos, "Oeuvres et images inédites de la jeunesse de Picasso," *Cahiers d'Art,* 25ᵉ année, no. II, 1950, p. 324, repr. (*Fleurs,* 1905); Zervos, 1954, vol. VI, no. 889 and pl. 107 (1905); Daix and Boudaille, 1967, no. XV. 16, repr. (Gosol, summer 1906); P. Lecaldano, *The Complete Paintings of Picasso: Blue and Rose Periods,* New York, 1970, pp. 111, repr., and 112, no. 285 (*Pottery and Vase with Flowers,* 1906); *Masterpieces,* 1972, p. 56, repr. (1905-6).

45   Woman with Open Fan. 1906
(Femme à l'éventail; Portrait of a Lady)

Ink on wove paper, 6¾ x 4⁵⁄₁₆ (17.1 x 11)

No watermark.

Not signed or dated.

PROVENANCE:

Probably acquired from the artist by Arthur B. Davies, Nov. 1912;[1] purchased from Davies collection (New York, American Art Association, *The Arthur B. Davies Art Collection,* Apr. 16-17, 1929, no. 15, repr. *[Portrait of a Lady]*) by J. B. Neumann, New York; purchased from Neu-mann by Mr. and Mrs. Charles J. Liebman, New York, 1929;[2] purchased from Lieb-man collection (New York, Parke Bernet, *The Liebman Collection of Valuable Modern Paintings, Drawings and Sculptures,* Dec. 7, 1955, no. 27 *[Portrait of a Lady]*) by J. K. Thannhauser, New York.

CONDITION:

Horizontal tears repaired and loss at lower right replaced in 1971 by C. Gaehde (May 1973).

1. Ronnie Owen, the daughter of Davies, remembers that her father bought directly from Picasso. She thinks the drawing was most likely acquired in Nov. 1912, when her father was assembling works for the Armory Show and first met Picasso. Davies was also in Paris in 1924 and 1925. Since Miss Owen does not remember seeing the drawing brought home, the earlier date of 1912 is more likely. (I am indebted to Miss Owen for the above information from conversation, May 1975.) In addition, the fact that the drawing is not signed points to the earlier date. A pencil drawing of *Two Nudes* by Picasso (D-B. XVI. 18; Paris, autumn, 1906, The Art Institute of Chicago) also belonged to Davies. The Davies papers at the Archives of American Art, New York, do not mention the drawing.

2. Correspondence with C. J. Liebman, the collector's son, May 1977.

The woman's identity is not known. However, the line of her nose, the distinctive curls at the nape and forehead, and the pin at the neckline identify her as the model (shown half-length and without fan) in three other very similar drawings (Z. XXII. 451; Z. XXII. 452, D-B. d.XV. 37; and Z.XXII. 448, D-B. d.XV. 38). Less closely related but representing the same model are Z. VI. 762-64, 781, and 782.

An ink drawing, *Peasant Women of Andorra* (Z. VI. 780; 22 x 13¾ in., 55.9 x 35 cm., The Art Institute of Chicago), depicts two full-length female figures. Their features are similar to those of the sitter in the present work, and the woman at the left holds a fan. Pierre Daix assigns the Chicago drawing to the summer of 1906 at Gosol (p. 292), and Maurice Jardot states that it was drawn "from a photograph Picasso had found" *(Pablo Picasso Drawings,* New York, 1959, p. 153, no. 15). Both figures in the Chicago drawing are shown nude in Z. VI. 875, and the figure at the left holding a fan is portrayed with a man in D-B. d.XV. 28.

All the drawings referred to above were executed during Picasso's trip to Gosol in the summer of 1906. The model in the Thannhauser drawing is not represented in the *Carnet catalan,* Picasso's sketchbook of that summer. The year before, in Paris, Picasso had painted a large picture, *Woman with a Fan* (Z. I. 308; D-B. XIII. 14; The National Gallery of Art, Washington, D.C., Gift of W. Averell Harriman), but the model and composition bear little resemblance to those of the present drawing.

REFERENCES:

Zervos, 1954, vol. VI, no. 786, pl. 95 *(Dessin à la plume,* 1906, incorrect dimensions listed, coll. Mrs. Charles J. Liebman, New York); Daix and Boudaille, 1967, no. d.XV. 38 (mentioned as related version); *Masterpieces,* 1972, p. 57, repr.

---

46 Woman and Devil. 1906
(Femme et diable; Courtship)

India ink on laid paper, 12⅛ x 9⅛ (30.8 x 23.2)

Not signed or dated.

PROVENANCE:
Curt Valentin,[1] New York, by 1940; acquired from Valentin by J. K. Thannhauser.

CONDITION:
Removed from cardboard mount, cleaned, deacidified, and mat burn minimized by C. Gaehde (May 1973).

The drawing is related to *The Flower Girl* (Z. XXII. 346; D-B. XV. 58; pen and ink, 24⅞ x 19 in., 63.2 x 48.3 cm., 1906, The Museum of Modern Art, New York; confirmed by P. Daix in correspondence, June 1975). Both figures have in common the same facial features and the rope-like curly hair that encloses the body. However, the

1. Curt Valentin's records and correspondence do not indicate where he acquired the drawing. It did not come from Kahnweiler (correspondence with Galerie Louise Leiris, Paris, June 1975).

girl in The Museum of Modern Art drawing is clothed, holds a bouquet of flowers, and is disproportionately slim through the waist and hips. This drawing was probably done in Gosol during the summer of 1906 and is a study for the painting *The Peasants* (Z. I. 384; D-B. XV. 62; 85⅝ x 51 in., 218.5 x 129.5 cm., Paris, Aug. 1906, The Barnes Foundation, Merion, Pa.).

Christian Zervos places the Thannhauser drawing with one of a nude girl with a cupid on the right and a devil on the left (VI. 805) and another where a devil is on either side of the girl (803). These drawings lack the sexual overtones of the present work.

EXHIBITIONS:

New York, Buchholz Gallery (Curt Valentin), *Pablo Picasso: Drawings and Watercolors*, Mar. 5-30, 1940, no. 9 (*Woman and Devil*, 1906); New York, Buchholz Gallery, *Beaudin, Braque, Gris . . . and Picasso*, Apr. 7-26, 1941, no. 39 (*Woman and Devil*, 1906).

REFERENCES:

Zervos, 1954, vol. VI, no. 804 and pl. 97 (1905 or 1906); Curt Valentin Gallery, New York, *Picasso*, n.d., vol. II of unpublished "Black Albums" of photographs on deposit at The Museum of Modern Art, New York [pp. 29-30], repr. *(Woman and Devil); Masterpieces*, 1972, p. 55, repr. (*Courtship*, 1905-6).

47   Glass, Pipe and Packet of Tobacco. 1914
(Verre, pipe et paquet de tabac; Composition; Nature morte au paquet de tabac)

Gouache with pencil on wove paper, 7¹³⁄₁₆ x 11¹¹⁄₁₆ (19.8 x 29.7)

Signed on reverse: *Picasso*[1]   Not dated.

PROVENANCE:

Acquired from M. Perel, Paris, by Galerie Jeanne Bucher, Paris, 1947; purchased from Bucher by Paul Martin a few years later (correspondence with Galerie Jeanne Bucher, Sept. 1975); Robert Lebel, New York and Paris, until c. 1950;[2] purchased from Lebel by J. K. Thannhauser, New York.

CONDITION:

Removed from cardboard mount and re-hinged by C. Gaehde (June 1973).

Pierre Daix tentatively places the work with those executed in 1914 at Avignon (correspondence with J. Rosselet, Apr. 1977). The signature on the reverse is appropriate for the period. Both Picasso and Braque reintroduced strong and varied colors in their work during 1913-14. They employed the dotting technique of pointillism to animate the surface, suggest a play of light, and create a decorative effect.

1. Picasso rarely signed his paintings on the obverse between 1907-14 (see Brassaï, *Picasso and Company,* trans. F. Price, Garden City, 1966, p. 68, and Paris, Musée des Art Décoratifs, *Picasso,* exh. cat., 1955, definitive ed., p. 46).

2. Although Jeanne Bucher's records indicate otherwise, Lebel remembers purchasing the work before World War II and selling it to Thannhauser around 1950 (correspondence, Mar. 1974).

Evolving from the *papiers collés,* the colorful but not scientific technique of stippling appears in Picasso's paintings, watercolors, and gouaches. The confetti-like dots decorate the contemporary sculpture, *Glass of Absinth,* in which each of the five bronze casts is painted differently (Z. II. pt. 2, 581-84; see W. Rubin, *Picasso in the Collection of The Museum of Modern Art,* New York, 1972, p. 95, color repr.).

The same glass and background area but without the stippled effect are found in a 1914 painting (Z. XXIX. 38; 6⁵⁄₁₆ x 5⅛ in., 16 x 13 cm.; Duncan, 1961, p. 207, repr.). The pipe and glass also appear in another painting of 1914 (Z. XXIX. 33; 4⅞ x 7¹⁄₁₆ in., 12.5 x 18 cm.; Duncan, p. 207, repr.).

REFERENCES:

Masterpieces, 1972, p. 58, repr. (*Composition,* 1914-15); Zervos, 1975, vol. XXIX, no. 69 and pl. 28 (*Nature morte au paquet de tabac,* spring 1914).

---

48   Compotier and Musical Instruments. 1915
      (Compotier et instruments de musique;
      Instruments de musique; Musical
      Instruments)

Gouache and watercolor on laid paper, 8½ x 8⁷⁄₁₆ (21.6 x 21.4)

Signed u.l.: *Picasso;* signed on reverse l.l.: *Picasso.*   Not dated.

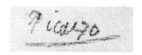

PROVENANCE:

Léonce Rosenberg, Paris;[1] M. Ader; purchased from Ader collection (Paris, Hôtel Drouot, *Tableaux modernes . . . ,* Nov. 29, 1950 [p. 2], repr. [*Nature morte*]) by D.-H. Kahnweiler; acquired from Kahnweiler by Curt Valentin, New York, Apr. 1951 (correspondence with Galerie Louise Leiris, Paris, June 1975); purchased from Valentin by J. K. Thannhauser, New York, by 1954.

CONDITION:

Old repair prior to 1965 of slight tear upper left (May 1973).

Compotier and Musical Instruments, which dates from the latter half of 1915, belongs with a group of like subject matter (Z. II. pt. 2, 544, 545, 548, VI. 1286, 1288, 1292, 1293, 1322, XXIX. 135, 138, 146-49, and New York, Sotheby Parke Bernet, *19th and 20th Century Paintings, Drawings, and Sculpture from the Collection of Norton Simon,* May 5, 1971, no. 73, color repr.). Of these VI. 1322, XXIX. 135 and 138 are closest to the present work, containing a stylized compotier at the top and

---

1. Léonce Rosenberg was Picasso's dealer during World War I, from the time D.-H. Kahnweiler was forced to leave France until Paul Rosenberg became his representative in 1918. A negative of the present work exists in the Léonce Rosenberg photo archive at the Service photographique, Caisse nationale des Monuments Historiques et des Sites (correspondence, Oct. 1974).

a woodwind instrument, zither, and guitar on a round table. Significantly, they were executed in watercolor and gouache. Picasso resumed use of these media in 1914 after a five-year intermission.

The strong vertical, the curve of the table, and the woodwind instrument in the Thannhauser drawing are found in *Musical Instruments* (Z. II. pt. 2, 853), a wood relief sculpture which Picasso constructed probably in 1913. An etching of the subject dates from 1914-15 (B. Geiser, *Picasso: Peintre-Graveur*, Bern, 1933, vol. I, no. 43).

The signature on the reverse appears to date from 1915 whereas that on the front was probably added in the early 1950s.

EXHIBITION:

New York, Curt Valentin Gallery, *Picasso*, Feb. 19-Mar. 15, 1952, no. 25 (*Musical Instruments*, 1915).

REFERENCES:

Bulletin de l'Effort Moderne, no. 35, May 1927, foll. p. 8 (*Instruments de musique*, 1915, not signed); Zervos, 1942, vol. II, pt. 2, no. 546 and pl. 253 (*Instruments de musique*, 1915, not signed); Curt Valentin Gallery, New York, *Picasso*, n.d., vol. II of unpublished "Black Albums" of photographs on deposit at The Museum of Modern Art, New York [p. 30], repr. (*Fruitbowl and Musical Instrument*, 1915); W. Boeck and J. Sabartés, *Picasso*, New York, 1955, p. 464, no. 74, repr.; A. Vallentin, *Pablo Picasso*, Paris, 1957, n.p., repr. under "Catalogue des oeuvres"; *Masterpieces*, 1972, p. 59, repr.

49   Three Bathers. August 1920
       (Trois baigneuses; Women by the Sea)

Pastel with oil and pencil on laid paper,
18¹³⁄₁₆ x 24³⁄₁₆ (47.8 x 61.4)

Watermark: CANSON & MONTGOLFIER
FRANCE

Signed l.r.: *Picasso;* dated u.r.: *19.8.20*

PROVENANCE:
Acquired from the artist by Galerie Simon
(D.-H. Kahnweiler), Paris; purchased from
Galerie Simon by G. F. Reber, Lugano,[1]
June 1924 (correspondence with Galerie

Louise Leiris, Paris, June 1975); probably
purchased from Valentine Gallery, New
York,[2] by Lee Ault soon after World War II
(correspondence with Ault, Feb. 1974); acquired from Ault shortly thereafter by J. K.
Thannhauser.

CONDITION:
Removed from cardboard mount, deacidified, and rehinged by C. Gaehde (Dec.
1976).

A pastel (Z. VI. 1404) identical in size and very close in composition to the *Three Bathers* (differing only in the lack of lateral rocks and background mountains) prob-ably precedes it as may a pencil drawing of *Six Bathers* (Z. IV. 166; 7⅞ x 8¼ in., 20 x 21 cm.) which includes the same three figures.

Individual figures in the Thannhauser pastel appear in other works from the sum-mer of 1920, which was the first Picasso spent at Juan-les-Pins. The reclining woman with a book is repeated in Z. IV. 163, 166, VI. 1387 and 1403. In Z. IV. 161, 166, and VI. 1387, a similar seated figure is placed at the right. The swimmer is identical to those in Z. IV. 166, VI. 1365 and 1387. She faces the opposite direction in a pastel (not in Z.; 20½ x 26 in., 52.1 x 66 cm., Collection Mr. and Mrs. Joseph H. Hazen, New York; *Picasso, An American Tribute: The Classic Phase,* exh. cat., 1962, no. 9, repr.) and rises further out of the water in another pastel (Z. IV. 173; 19½ x 25 in., 49.5 x 63.5 cm., Winterthur, Kunstmuseum, *Picasso: 90 Drawings and Works in Color,* exh. cat., 1971, no. 16, color repr.). In fact, the swimmer's arms and shoulders (all that is visible here) resemble the woman running in *By the Sea* (Z. IV. 169; oil on wood panel, 31½ x 39 in., 80 x 99 cm., erroneously dated 1923; New York, Sotheby Parke Bernet, *The Collection of . . . the Late G. David Thompson,* Mar. 24, 1966, no. 31, color repr.).

The enlargement of hands and feet seen in the present picture occurs as early as 1919 in *Sleeping Peasants* (Z. III. 371; tempera, 12¼ x 19¼ in., 31.1 x 48.9 cm., The Museum of Modern Art, New York). Interpretations of their distorted size are proposed by Roland Penrose (1958, p. 220) and Françoise Gilot (*Life with Picasso,* New York, 1964, p. 119).

The signature belongs to the period. Picasso first began the precise dating of his works in January 1920 (Z. IV. 15) and continued this practice frequently during that summer.

1. D. Cooper (correspondence with A. Rudenstine, Nov. 1975) remembers seeing the present picture at Reber's house but doubts that it was acquired directly from Reber by the Valen-tine Gallery. Reber died in 1959.

2. The catalogue of the Apr. 12-May 1, 1937, exhibition at the Valentine Gallery, New York, *Drawings, Gouaches and Pastels by Picasso,* lists five bathers (nos. 43-46 and 48). It is not possible to prove that the present picture was included although it seems likely. Nor has it been possible to determine when and from whom the Valentine Gallery might have ac-quired the work.

EXHIBITIONS:

Santa Barbara Museum of Art, *Fiesta Exhibition 1953: Picasso, Gris, Miró, and Dali*, Aug. 4-30, 1953, no. 15 (*Bathers*, 1920, incorrect dimensions listed); New York, Duveen Brothers, Inc., *Picasso, An American Tribute: The Classic Phase*, Apr. 25-May 12, 1962, no. 12, repr. (*Three Bathers*).

REFERENCES:

Zervos, 1951, vol. IV. no. 165 and pl. 52 (*Trois baigneuses*, pastel, 49 x 64 cm.); W. Boeck and J. Sabartés, *Picasso*, New York, 1955, p. 467, repr., no. 101; A. Vallentin, *Pablo Picasso*, Paris, 1957, n.p., repr. under "Catalogue des oeuvres"; Daix, 1965, pp. 120, repr., and 265 (*Women by the Sea*, pastel, 64 x 49 cm., coll. Reber, Lausanne); *Masterpieces*, 1972, p. 60, repr.

---

50   Dinard. Summer 1922
       (*Saint-Servan; Saint Servan, near Dinard*)

Pencil on wove paper, 16⅝ x 11⁹⁄₁₆
(42.2 x 29.4)

Signed l.l.: *Picasso*   Not dated.

PROVENANCE:

Acquired from the artist by Paul Rosenberg, Paris, in 1926 (correspondence with A. Rosenberg, Dec. 1974); purchased from Rosenberg by J. K. Thannhauser by 1932.

CONDITION:

Left edge of paper is serrated. Removed from mount, flattened, and deacidified by C. Gaehde (June 1973).

The drawing was done in Dinard and depicts Pointe Bric-à-Brac. Dinard, the fashionable seaside resort in Brittany, is on the left bank of the Rance River, near its mouth. At the time, villas and hotels were located at Pointe Bric-à-Brac near the Grande-Rue (now avenue George V).

The precise view that Picasso drew is found in a photograph of Dinard in which even such details as the dock and boat ramp in the foreground and the tree and archway at the lower left are shown from the same viewpoint (*Normandy and Brittany: Guide to the Seaside Resorts and Places of Interest*, London, 1930, p. 184, fig. 3). An earlier photograph is taken from the same angle but at a slightly greater distance so that it shows the vantage point from which the artist must have drawn it (N. H. Thomson, ed., *The Emerald Coast and Brittany: An English Guide to Brittany*, Dinard, 1913, p. 30, repr.).

The drawing must be dated 1922 since during that summer Picasso first went to Dinard, where he rented a villa for his wife and their young son (Penrose, 1958, p. 224).

The Thannhauser drawing is closely related to Z. XXX. 340, which represents the same view, and XXX. 327-30 as well as to Z. IV. 372-74 and 376. The present work is signed in a manner prevalent in the mid-1920s (see W. Boeck and J. Sabartés, *Picasso*, Paris, 1955, p. 485, for a typical signature of 1923).

EXHIBITIONS:

Paris, Paul Rosenberg, *Exposition de cent dessins par Picasso*, June-July 1927, probably no. 73 (*Vue de Saint-Servan*, 1921); Kunsthaus Zürich, *Picasso*, Sept. 11-Oct. 30, 1932, no. 319 (*Blick auf Saint-Servan*, c. 1921); Buenos Aires, Galería Müller, *Picasso*, Oct. 1934, no. 43[1] (label on reverse reads: *Vista de Servan*, 1921); New York, The Museum of Modern Art, *Picasso: 75th Anniversary Exhibition*, May 22-Sept. 8, 1957, p. 54, repr. (*St. Servan, near Dinard*, 1922), traveled to The Art Institute of Chicago, Oct. 29-Dec. 8; Philadelphia Museum of Art, *Picasso*, Jan. 8-Feb. 23, 1958, no. 105, repr. (*St. Servan, near Dinard*, 1922).

REFERENCES:

J. Cassou, *Picasso*, New York, 1940, p. 28, repr. *(View of St. Servan)*; S. Solmi, *Disegni di Picasso*, Milan, 1945, pl. xxii *(Veduta di St. Servan)*; Zervos, 1951, vol. IV, no. 375, pl. 153 *(Vue de Dinard*, 1922, incorrect medium listed); *Masterpieces*, 1972, p. 61, repr. *(Saint-Servan, near Dinard)*.

1. J. K. Thannhauser arranged for the exhibition and lent many of the works (conversation with D. C. Rich, Mar. 1975). No catalogue has been located although the bibliography in J. Merli, *Picasso, el artista y la obra de nuestro tiempo*, Buenos Aires, 1942, p. 305, states that the preface was written by Frederico C. Müller. The exhibition numbers are derived from a printed label on the reverse of each work.

51   Table Before the Window. 1922
      (Table devant la fenêtre)

Watercolor and pencil on laid paper, 5⁹⁄₁₆ x 4⁵⁄₁₆ (14.1 x 11)

Signed and dated u.r.: *Picasso/22*

PROVENANCE:

Purchased from the Galerie Simon (D.-H. Kahnweiler), Paris, by J. K. Thannhauser,

June 1929 (correspondence with Galerie Louise Leiris, Paris, June 1975).

CONDITION:

Top edge of paper is serrated. Removed from mount, flattened, deacidified, and re-hinged by C. Gaehde (June 1973).

Picasso frequently treated the theme of a still life on a table in front of a window between 1919 and 1925. This watercolor sketch has the same composition as other small works on paper (see Z. IV. 403, 405, and 406). The shape of the wine bottle first appears in 1922. The motif of fish on newspaper is found in Z. XXX. 395, Z. IV. 397, 404, 409-11, and 448. In discussing the latter work, *Still Life with Fish* (51³⁄₁₆ x 38³⁄₁₆ in., 130 x 97 cm., dated 1922-23, Collection Mrs. Albert D. Lasker, New York), Maurice Jardot indicates that such still lifes were done both at Dinard and later in Paris (Paris, Musée des Arts Décoratifs, *Picasso*, exh. cat., 1955, definitive ed., no. 58).

EXHIBITIONS:

Kunsthaus Zürich, *Picasso*, Sept. 11-Oct. 30, 1932, no. 323; Buenos Aires, Galería Müller, *Picasso*, Oct. 1934, no. 25 (J. K. Thannhauser notes, Dec. 1972); Adelaide, The National Art Gallery, *Exhibition of French and British Contemporary Art*, opened Aug. 21, 1939, no. 90, traveled to Melbourne, Town Hall, opened Oct. 16, and Sydney, David Jones, opened Nov. 20.

REFERENCES:

J. Cassou, *Picasso*, New York, 1940, pp. 116, repr., and 166; *Picasso: Fifteen Drawings*, New York, 1946, pl. 11; Zervos, 1951, vol. IV, no. 432 and pl. 179 (*Table devant la fenêtre*, incorrect medium listed); *Masterpieces*, 1972, p. 63, repr.

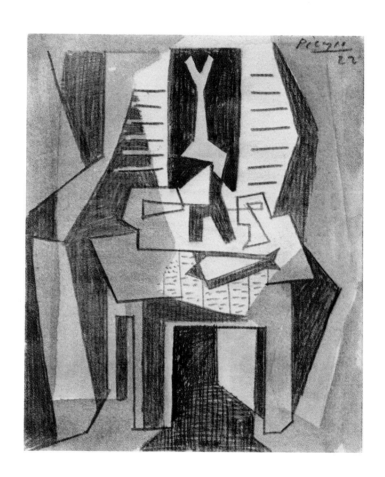

52   The Table. December 24, 1922
      *(Le Guéridon; Nature morte sur une table
      ronde)*

Watercolor and gouache on laid paper,
6⅞₁₆ x 4¹⁄₁₆ (16.3 x 10.3)

Signed l.r.: *Picasso*; dated on reverse: *24
Decembre/1922*

PROVENANCE:
Purchased from the artist by Galerie Louise
Leiris, Paris, 1952; purchased from Galerie
Leiris by Mrs. Jaray, London, Oct. 1953
(correspondence with Galerie Leiris, June
1975); Curt Valentin Gallery, New York;[1]
acquired from Valentin by J. K. Thannhauser.

A *guéridon* is a round table with a pedestal leg. The theme is virtually the same as
in cat. no. 51. Stylistically close to Z. IV.433 and Z. XXX. 420, 421, and 428 from
the same day and Z. IV. 431 of the following day, it remains remarkably similar to
a small gouache done three years earlier (Z. III. 442; *Nature morte devant une fenêtre,*
7⅞ x 5¼ in., 20 x 13.2 cm., dated 24 Decembre 1919).

   The Table is executed in watercolor and gouache, a technique Picasso favored from
1915 to 1922 more than at any other time. The manner of representing objects is
essentially that of Synthetic Cubism. Contrasting with the green tablecloth, the blue
provides open space and air around the table and window.

   The work was signed when purchased from the artist in 1952 (correspondence with
Galerie Leiris, June 1975); the style of the signature does indeed appear to date from
that time.

REFERENCES:

Masterpieces, 1972, p. 62, repr.; Zervos, 1975, vol. XXX, no. 425, pl. 135 *(Nature morte sur
une table ronde).*

1. According to J. K. Thannhauser (notes, Dec. 1972), the drawing came from Valentin. A
   label on the reverse, from Valentin's Gallery, bears the number L4193. The Gallery's
   unpublishd "Black Albums" of photographs on deposit at The Museum of Modern Art,
   New York, do not include *The Table,* but the work is in the "Green Albums" at the
   Modern of other photographs Valentin had (under *P,* vol. 6 [p. 8], repr. [*Round Table,*
   6½ x 4 in.]). Attempts to locate this work or any others from the Thannhauser Foundation in Valentin's records or correspondence have been unsuccessful. (I am indebted to
   Ralph Colin's generosity of time and advice and to the assistance of Pearl Moeller at The
   Museum of Modern Art.) Surely the work was at Curt Valentin's Gallery although it
   is not certain that he owned it. It is not known how long Mrs. Jaray owned the watercolor
   nor to whom it subsequently went.

53   Still Life with Apples. 1923
      *(Nature morte aux pommes; Trois pommes
      et verre)*

Enamel with sand on linen, 9½ x 13 (24.1 x 33)

Signed and dated u.l.: *Picasso/ 23*   Not dated.

PROVENANCE:

Acquired from the artist by Paul Rosenberg, Paris, 1925 (correspondence with A. Rosen-berg, Dec. 1974); probably acquired from Rosenberg by J. K. Thannhauser by 1932.

CONDITION:

Not varnished. Stress and traction cracks in painted areas. Cleavage at bottom center below knife. Trace of pencil outlining apples and knife (May 1975).

An area of sand in relief defines the plate and the glass. In addition, sand is mixed with the gray pigment, and grains are visible in the one-half-inch-wide blue border, which has been applied over the gray.

Closely related both in the use of sand and in the objects represented are Z. V. 60, 63, 65-68, 75-77, 80, 82, and 85-87. All date from 1923 and are small in size. Another version in the artist's collection was painted in May (Duncan, 1961, p. 209, repr.).

Picasso first included sand in such Cubist works as *Student with a Pipe* (Z. II. pt. 2, 444; oil, charcoal, pasted paper, and sand on canvas) and *Student with a Newspaper* (Z. II. pt. 2, 443; oil with sand on canvas), both done in the winter of 1913-14. According to Douglas Cooper, Braque added sand to paint by 1912 *(The Cubist Epoch,* New York, 1970, p. 57). Picasso resumed the technique from time to time, especially from 1923-24. It permitted variety in surface texture and gave the effect of the third dimension.

The shape of the glass reverts to other Cubist work (Z. II. pt. 2, 484, 485, 489, 516, 537, 572). Yet the black linear markings on the glass and the flat areas of color are characteristic of the works from the early 1920s.

EXHIBITIONS:

Paris, Paul Rosenberg, *Exposition d'oeuvres récentes de Picasso,* June-July 1926, probably no. 5[1] (*Verre, couteau et pommes,* 1923); Kunsthaus Zürich, *Picasso,* Sept. 11-Oct. 30, 1932, no. 131 (label on reverse reads: *Apfel,* 1923); Buenos Aires, Galería Müller, *Picasso,* Oct. 1934, no. 11[2] (label on reverse reads: *Naturalezza muerta con manzanas*); Adelaide, The National Art Gallery, *Exhibition of French and British Contemporary Art,* opened Aug. 21, 1939, no. 89 (*Nature morte,* 1923), traveled to Melbourne, Town Hall, opened Oct. 16, and Sydney, David Jones, opened Nov. 20.

REFERENCES:

C. Zervos, "De l'importance de l'objet dans la peinture d'aujourd'hui," *Cahiers d'Art,* 5ᵉ année, no. 6, 1930, p. 288, repr. (*Composition,* 1923); C. Zervos, *Pablo Picasso,* Milan, 1932, pl. xii (*Natura Morta,* 1923, Galerie Thannhauser, Berlin); C. Zervos, *Pablo Picasso,* Milan, 1937, pl. xii; Zervos, 1952, vol. V, no. 64 and pl. 36 (*Trois pommes et verre,* 1923); *Masterpieces,* 1972, p. 64, repr.

1. According to A. Rosenberg (correspondence, Dec. 1974) the present picture was certainly in the exhibition. Nos. 14, 16, 20, and 23 were all 1923 still lifes with apples.

2. See cat. no. 50, fn. 1.

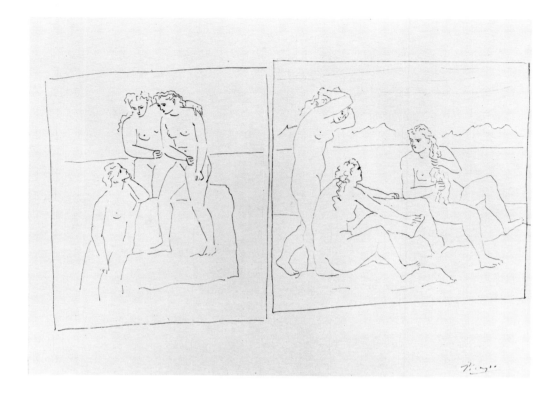

54   Two Groups of Bathers. 1923
(Deux groupes de baigneuses)

Ink on wove paper, 10³⁄₁₆ x 13⅞ (25.9
x 35.2)

Signed l.r.: *Picasso*   Not dated.

PROVENANCE:
Purchased from the artist by Paul Rosenberg, Paris, 1924 or 1925 (correspondence

with A. Rosenberg, Dec. 1974); probably
acquired from Rosenberg by J. K. Thannhauser by 1932.

During the summer of 1923 Picasso stayed at the Hôtel du Cap at Cap d'Antibes.
Douglas Cooper thinks that the drawing was probably done at that time (correspondence, July 1974).

Picasso often drew bathers during the early 1920s, combining them with classical
themes, beach scenes, and toilette subjects. Three women or three graces appear frequently among Picasso's etchings from 1922-23 (B. Geiser, *Picasso: Peintre-Graveur*,
Bern, 1933, vol. I, nos. 68, 102-8) and drawings from 1923 (Z. V. 98-104).

Related drawings of bathers that Picasso did in 1923 include Z. V. 19-21, 24-28,
31-36, 39-43, 46-51, 54-59, 105-6, and 136-39. The Thannhauser drawing was not
part of a sketchbook when acquired from the artist (correspondence with A. Rosenberg, Dec. 1974). It is closest to Z. V. 19, where two groups of bathers are separated
by an identical framing device and where the woman holding her hair to the side
with both hands is repeated. With this exception, the poses of the bathers in the
Thannhauser drawing are not found in the works listed above.

The gesture of a nude woman holding her hair to the side goes back to 1906, where it is found in a drawing, *Nude Combing Her Hair* (D-B. d. XVI. 6), and a painting of the same title (Z. I. 344; D-B. XVI. 9) which Daix relates to *The Harem* (Z. I. 321; D-B. XV. 40).

EXHIBITIONS:

Paris, Paul Rosenberg, *Exposition de cent dessins par Picasso,* June-July 1927, probably no. 61 (*Deux groupes de baigneuses,* 1923); Kunsthaus Zürich, *Picasso,* Sept. 11-Oct. 30, 1932, no. 343 (label on reverse reads: *Zwei Frauengruppen*).

REFERENCES:

Zervos, 1952, vol. V, no. 18, and pl. 12; *Masterpieces,* 1972, p. 65, repr.

---

55   Three Dancers. April 1925
      (Trois danseurs)

India ink on wove paper, 13⅜ x 9¾ (34 x 24.8)

Signed and dated u.r.: *Picasso/25*

PROVENANCE:

Purchased from the artist by Paul Rosenberg, Paris (conversation with A. Rosenberg, Feb. 1977); acquired from Rosenberg by G. F. Reber; acquired from Reber by Paul Adamidi Frascheri;[1] J. K. Thannhauser, New York.

CONDITION:

Collector's mark at lower right.[2] Tear at upper right. Slight stains from foxing. Removed from mount, flattened, and deacidified by C. Gaehde (June 1973).

The ballet played an important role in Picasso's life from 1917 through 1925. He designed the curtain, decor, and costumes for several productions in collaboration with Sergei Diaghilev's Russian Ballet. Picasso married a ballerina, Olga Koklova, from the Russian Ballet in 1918.

In April 1925, while on their way to Juan-les-Pins, Picasso and his family stopped at Monte Carlo, where Diaghilev's company was performing. It is possible to document his visit from April 12 at the latest through April 29. The ballet troupe left Monte Carlo at the end of the month (R. Alley, *Picasso: The Three Dancers,* Newcastle upon Tyne, 1967, p. 10).

1. D. Cooper (correspondence with A. Rudenstine, Nov. 1975) stated that the drawing went from Reber to Adamidi, perhaps c. 1931-32, and that the latter sold it in the 1940s. According to A. Rosenberg (conversation, Feb. 1977) Adamidi probably obtained the drawing from Reber.
2. Collector's mark not in F. Lugt, *Les Marques de collections de dessins et d'estampes ... Supplement,* The Hague, 1956. According to J. K. Thannhauser (notes, Dec. 1972) and D. Cooper, it is that of the Adamidi collection, Geneva.

Picasso sketched the boys from the corps de ballet practicing at the bar and, as
here, resting. Although they reappear in other Monte Carlo drawings, the figures
cannot be identified (correspondence with D. Cooper, July 1974). Jean Sutherland
Boggs observed that the artist was working from life in this group of drawings (The
Art Gallery of Toronto, *Picasso and Man,* exh. cat., 1964, p. 99).

When published in 1926 by Waldemar George in *Picasso Dessins* as "Album inédit
de l'artiste (1925)," none of the sketches was signed. Predominantly drawings of two,
three, or four dancers, the sketchbook included Z. V. 418, 422-25, 429, 431, 433,
435, 436, 455, and pls. 372, 374, and 375 in Cooper, *Picasso Theatre.* All have been
signed and dated since that time (see Paris, Musée des Arts Décoratifs, *Picasso,* exh.
cat., 1955, definitive ed., p. 47, for a discussion of the artist's signature in 1925).

REFERENCES:

W. George, *Picasso Dessins,* Paris, 1926, pl. 27 (not signed or dated; pls. 23-64 of "Album
inédit de l'artiste [1925]"); Zervos, 1952, vol. V, no. 431 and pl. 173 (*Trois danseurs,* signed
and dated 1925); D. Cooper, *Picasso Theatre,* New York, 1968, p. 353, and pl. 358 (*Three
Dancers Resting,* 1925, not signed or dated); A. Blunt, "Picasso's Classical Period (1917-25),"
The Burlington Magazine, vol. CX, Apr. 1968, p. 188; *Masterpieces,* 1972, p. 66, repr.

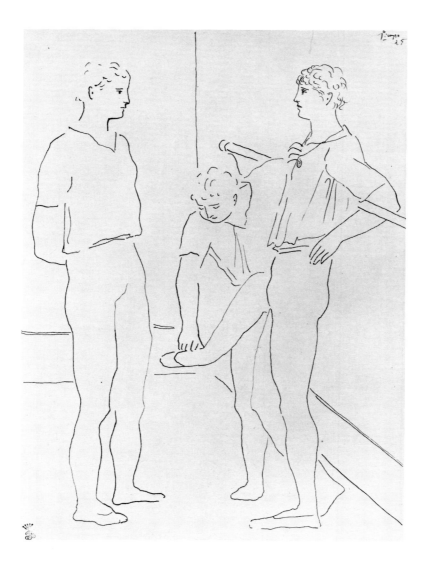

56   Woman Seated.   1926
      (Femme assise)

India ink on laid paper, 18¾ x 11¾ (47.6
x 29.9)

Signed and dated u.r.: *Picasso/26.*

PROVENANCE:
Purchased from the artist by D.-H. Kahnweiler, Paris, 1927; purchased from Kahnweiler by J. K. Thannhauser, 1929

(correspondence with Galerie Louise
Leiris, Paris, July 1975).

CONDITION:
Removed from mount, deacidified, upper
left corner repaired, and margins cleaned
by C. Gaehde (June 1973).

The possibilities of combining a frontal view with a profile to form a face were in-
vestigated by Picasso between 1925 and 1927. Here, the dark, right side of the face
can be read as a profile. Together with the white areas of forehead and chin on the
left side, it forms a complete head (see R. Melville, "The Evolution of the Double
Head in the Art of Picasso," *Horizon* [London], vol. VI, Nov. 1942, pp. 343-51).

The woman's head and striped dress are recognizable in at least three other drawings dated 1926 (Z. VII. 6, 7, and Paris, Galerie Vignon, *Collection de peintures de*

nos jours appartenant à Serge Lifar, exh. cat., 1929, no. 49, pl. V) and in a slightly earlier drawing (W. George, *Picasso Dessins,* Paris, 1926, pl. 61). The gesture of the hands, held in the lap and grasping each other, occurs earlier in an etching of 1922-23 (B. Geiser, *Picasso: Peintre-Graveur,* Bern, 1933, vol. I, no. 95) and in a drawing (George, pl. 56, upper right) in addition to three paintings (Z. VII. 60, 77, and 81).

Of these three paintings, the most clearly related to the Thannhauser drawing is *Seated Woman,* dated 1926-27 (Z. VII. 81; 51½ x 38½ in., 130.8 x 97.8 cm., The Art Gallery of Ontario, *Canadian Art,* vol. XXI, Sept.-Oct. 1964, p. 305, color repr.). Significantly, the painting is grisaille except for the red molding. The expressive distortions, the decorative patterns, and the interlocking shapes explored in the black-and-white drawings culminate in the Toronto picture, the colorful version in The Museum of Modern Art, New York, entitled *Seated Woman* (Z. VII. 77; oil on wood, 51⅛ x 38¼ in., 129.8 x 97.2 cm., 1927; W. Rubin, *Picasso in the Collection of The Museum of Modern Art,* New York, 1972, p. 125, color repr.), and in the grisaille *L'Atelier de la modiste* (Z. VII. 2; 68 x 101 in., 172.7 x 256.5 cm., 1926, Musée National d'Art Moderne, Paris; D. Porzio and M. Valsecchi, *Understanding Picasso,* New York, 1974, color pl. 85).

EXHIBITION:

Kunsthaus Zürich, *Picasso,* Sept. 11-Oct. 30, 1932, no. 338 (label on reverse of frame reads: *Sitzendes Mädchen,* 1926).

REFERENCES:

J. Bouret, *Picasso Dessins,* Paris, 1950, p. 61, repr.; Zervos, 1955, vol. VII, no. 24 and pl. 12 (*Femme assise); Masterpieces,* 1972, p. 67, repr.

---

57   Bird on a Tree.   August 1928
      *(L'Oiseau; Bird on a Branch; L'Oiseau sur
      la branche; Vogel auf Zweig)*

Oil on canvas, 13¾ x 9½ (34.9 x 24.1)

Signed and dated u.r.: *Picasso / 28*

PROVENANCE:

Acquired from the artist by J. K. Thann-hauser by 1930.

CONDITION:

Not varnished. Prior to 1965 minor repairs at lower left and lower right (May 1975).

Picasso told J. K. Thannhauser that during his sojourn in 1928 at Dinard "he was angry because this bird awakened him for quite a while unusually early every morning. Then suddenly one morning he jumped out of bed, looked out of his window, saw the bird in front of the rising sun, painted it, and from the following night on he slept through" (J. K. Thannhauser notes, Dec. 1972).

Christian Zervos specified August 13, 1928, as the date for *Bird on a Tree.* During that month Picasso painted at least twenty-five small canvases of bathers on the beach (Z. VII. 209-16, 218-27, 230, 232-36, and 239). Brilliantly colored, the work done at Dinard is characterized by vibrant stripes and flat patterns. Picasso was at Dinard by July 8 (Z. VII.199) and remained there until at least August 28 (Z. VII.239).

When first reproduced in 1929 the picture was neither signed nor dated. However, by the following year it was: undoubtedly Picasso added his signature and date at the time the painting went to Thannhauser.

The shape of the bird reappears in 1931 in *Deux hirondelles* (Z. VII.342).

EXHIBITIONS:

Kunsthaus Zürich, *Picasso,* Sept. 11-Oct. 30, 1932, no. 177; Buenos Aires, Galería Müller, *Picasso,* Oct. 1934, no. 15 (J. K. Thannhauser notes, Dec. 1972).

REFERENCES:

C. Zervos, "Picasso à Dinard été 1928," *Cahiers d'Art,* 4e année, no. 1, 1929, p. 7, repr. upside down (not signed or dated; caption reads: Dinard, 13 août 1928); *Documents,* vol. 2, no. 3, 1930, p. 126, repr. (signed and dated; Thannhauser, Berlin); *Cahiers d'Art,* 7e année, no. 3-5, 1932, p. 177, repr. (not signed or dated); C. Zervos, *Pablo Picasso,* Milan, 1932, pl. xxiv (signed and dated); C. Zervos, *Pablo Picasso,* Milan, 1937, pl. xxii; J. Cassou, *Picasso,* New York, 1940, pp. 134, repr., and 167; P. Eluard, *A Pablo Picasso,* Geneva and Paris, 1944, p. 112, repr.; P. Eluard, *Pablo Picasso,* New York, 1947, p. 112, repr.; Zervos, 1955, vol. VII, no. 217 and pl. 85 (*L'Oiseau,* Dinard, 13 août 1928); J. Runnqvist, *Minotauros,* Stockholm, 1959, pp. 90-91, pl. 99; Daix, 1965, pp. 138, 139, repr., and 266; F. Elgar and R. Maillard, *Picasso,* rev. ed., trans. F. Scarfe, New York, 1972, p. 212, repr.; *Masterpieces,* 1972, p. 68, repr.; G. Bernier, "Humorage à Picasso," *L'Oeil,* nos. 217-18, Aug.-Sept. 1973, p. 44, repr.

---

58   Reclining Nude. April 3, 1929
      (Nu couché)

Enamel on canvas, 7¼ x 12⅞ (18.4 x 32.7)

Signed and dated l.r.: *Picasso* / *3 Avril XX(IX)* (partially blurred by fingerprint)

PROVENANCE:

Acquired from the artist by Paul Rosenberg, Paris, 1929;[1] purchased from Stephen Hahn[2] by Niveau Gallery, New York, c. 1956; purchased soon thereafter from Niveau Gallery by J. K. Thannhauser (conversation with Margolies, May 1974).

CONDITION:

At an unrecorded date prior to 1965 glue lined and some inpainting in reclining figure's right arm and adjacent area of bed beneath (May 1975).

1. Correspondence with A. Rosenberg, Dec. 1974. The picture no longer belonged to Rosenberg in 1939. It is not known to whom it was sold or the exact date before 1939 that the transaction took place.
2. Correspondence with Hahn, Feb. 1974. Hahn cannot remember when and from whom he acquired the picture.

The reclining female nude, a traditional subject in art since antiquity, occurs throughout Picasso's work. Here, the model's legs and hips imply a supine pose, while the head encircled by raised arms suggests a prone position. (L. Steinberg analyzes Picasso's later explorations of such combined poses in *Other Criteria*, New York, 1972, chap. 6).

The dislocation of the breasts and buttocks and the distortion of the head and arms appeared during the summer of 1928 in figures playing and standing on the beach (Z. VII. 223, 225, 234). The reclining representations date from April 1929. Picasso kept in his collection another small oil painted, like the present picture, on April 3, 1929, where the triangular shapes of the breasts and the raised curves of the buttocks are retained but the legs are separated and seen frontally (not in Z.; 6¼ x 9½ in., 15.9 x 24.1 cm.; Duncan, 1961, p. 213, repr.). Both paintings include richly patterned backgrounds which Picasso was to develop further in the early 1930s. On April 4, 5, and 6 he painted Z. VII. 261, 270, and 240, respectively. Z. VII. 260 was done in the same month. The pose of the woman in the Thannhauser picture remains essentially unchanged in nos. 261 and 270.

Picasso painted a similarly distorted female nude in 1953 (Z. XVI. 100; 51¼ x 38¼ in., 130 x 97 cm.; Duncan, p. 182, color repr.). Both this painting and Z. XVI. 99 (where the decorative bed and sunlit interior resemble the present picture) were painted on December 29, 1953, and present the artist's remembrance of Françoise Gilot, who had left him the previous September.

REFERENCES:

C. Zervos, "Les Dernières oeuvres de Picasso," *Cahiers d'Art*, 4ᵉ année, no. 6, 1929, p. 238, pl. c; Zervos, 1955, vol. VII, no. 269 and pl. 110 *(Nu couché); Masterpieces*, 1972, p. 69, repr.

59   Woman with Yellow Hair.
December 1931
*(Femme aux cheveux jaunes; Woman with
Blond Hair; Woman Sleeping; Femme
endormie)*

Oil on canvas, 39⅜ x 31⅞ (100 x 81)

Signed l.l.: *Picasso;* dated on reverse of
stretcher: *27 Decembre/M.CM.XXXI.*

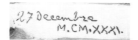

PROVENANCE:
Acquired from the artist by J. K. Thannhauser, Paris, 1937 (notes, Dec. 1972).

The sleeping woman with yellow hair is Marie-Thérèse Walter (1909-1977). Young and athletic, her striking looks intrigued Picasso. Here he has united forehead and nose in a single curve and has emphasized her full lips and prominent chin. (A photo-graph of her is included in P. Cabanne, "Picasso et les joies de la paternité," *L'Oeil,* no. 226, May 1974, p. 2, and another taken at a later date is in Porzio and Valsecchi, p. 41).

Upon meeting Marie-Thérèse years later, Françoise Gilot saw that "she was cer-tainly the woman who had inspired Pablo plastically more than any other . . . she had that high-color look of glowing good health one sees often in Swedish women. Her forms were handsomely sculptural, with a fullness of volume and purity of line that gave her body and her face an extraordinary perfection" (F. Gilot and C. Lake, *Life with Picasso,* New York, 1964, pp. 241-42).

It is generally agreed that Picasso met Marie-Thérèse when she was seventeen years old. A date of 1931 for this first meeting has been assumed. However, Marie-Thérèse and Picasso met by chance at six o'clock on Saturday, January 8, 1927, in front of the Galeries Lafayette in Paris (Daix, 1977, p. 213, fn. 2). Marie-Thérèse remembered that Picasso commented on her interesting face and expressed the wish to do her portrait (Cabanne, p. 2). Soon thereafter she went to his studio every day. Picasso continued to see her and their daughter Maïa, born October 5, 1935, regularly even when he was involved with Dora Maar and Françoise Gilot (Gilot and Lake, p. 129).

In 1964 Gilot stated (p. 241) that "the whole series of portraits of blonde women Pablo painted between 1927 and 1935 are almost exact replicas" of Marie-Thérèse. William Rubin (p. 226) proposes the summer of 1931 for the first images of Marie-Thérèse, and Alan Bowness refers to *The Sculptor* (Z. VII. 346), which bears the date of December 7, 1931, as the earliest representation of her (*Picasso in Retrospect,* New York, 1973, p. 141). However, her profile is recognizable in *Woman, Sculpture and Vase of Flowers,* which bears the date of April 24, 1929 (Z. VII. 259; 76 x 51 in., 193 x 129.5 cm., Collection Mr. and Mrs. Nathan Cummings).

The Thannhauser picture is dated December 27, 1931. Chronologically it belongs with three other paintings of Marie-Thérèse (Z. VII. 334, 346, 358) and a drawing (dated Feb. 4, 1931; Duncan, 1961, p. 214, repr.). Another painting, known from a photograph Cecil Beaton took of Picasso at 25, rue la Boétie in 1931, provides two im-ages of Marie-Thérèse—one a sleeping figure, the other a sculpture (not in Z.; Rubin, p. 226, repr.).

Marie-Thérèse remembers Picasso's always saying: *"Ne ris pas, ferme les yeux"* (Cabanne, p. 7). He preferred the image of her sleeping. She is seen asleep in the present picture as well as in many others (Z. VII. 331, 332, 348-50, 359, 360, 362-64,

377, 378, 382-84, 387, 388, 390, 396-403, and 407-9 among works from the years 1931-32). In fact, the identical sleeping pose with head facing down cradled in her arms is found in Z. VII. 378 (*Le Miroir*, Mar. 14, 1932), 382 (*Femme nue couchée sur un cousin rouge*, May 22, 1932), 398 (drawing, dated July 30, 1932), 399 (drawing, 1932), and a painting in Picasso's collection (Duncan, p. 215, dated May 16, 1932).

In these works, the sleeping figure is expressed in lush rounded forms. The arms lack articulation and taper off rather than terminating in hands. Robert Rosenblum refers to the "shades of lavender and purple, nocturnal colours that, in the thirties, often convey for Picasso a growing intensity of sleep and inwardness that would vanish under the physical light of day" ("Picasso as a Surrealist," in The Art Gallery of Toronto, *Picasso and Man,* exh. cat., 1964, p. 16).

EXHIBITIONS:

New York, The Museum of Modern Art, *Picasso: Forty Years of His Art,* Nov. 15, 1939-Jan. 7, 1940, no. 250 (*Woman Sleeping,* 1932), traveled to The Art Institute of Chicago, Feb. 1-Mar. 3, San Francisco Museum of Art, June 25-July 22; Buffalo, Albright Art Gallery, *French Paintings of the Twentieth Century, 1900-1939,* Dec. 6-31, 1944, no. 50 (*Woman Sleeping*), traveled to The Cincinnati Art Museum, Jan. 18-Feb. 18, 1945, City Art Museum of St. Louis, Mar. 8-Apr. 16; Santa Barbara Museum of Art, *Fiesta Exhibition, 1953: Picasso, Gris, Miró, Dali,* Aug. 4-30, 1953, no. 29 (*Woman Sleeping,* 1932).

REFERENCES:

J. Cassou, *Picasso,* New York, 1940, p. 137, repr. on its side; Zervos, 1955, vol. VII, no. 333 and pl. 138 (*La Femme aux cheveux jaunes,* 1931); P. de Champris, *Picasso: Ombre et soleil,* Paris, 1960, pp. 128 and 290, and pl. 132 (*Femme endormie,* 1931); *Masterpieces,* 1972, p. 70, repr.; W. Rubin, *Picasso in the Collection of The Museum of Modern Art,* New York, 1972, p. 226, fig. 108 (*Woman with Blond Hair,* 1931); D. Porzio and M. Valsecchi, *Understanding Picasso,* New York, 1974, p. 10, repr. (*Woman with Yellow Hair,* 1931-32); Daix, 1977, p. 237, fn. 10 and pl. 32.

60   Classical Figures. 1933-34
(Personnages classiques; Minerve;
Composition)

Charcoal on wove paper, 10¹⁵⁄₁₆ x 12¹³⁄₁₆
(26.2 x 32.5)

Signed l.l.: *Picasso*   Not dated.

PROVENANCE:
J. K. Thannhauser by 1940.

The woman's features are those of Marie-Thérèse Walter (see cat. no. 59). Although Christian Zervos titled the present drawing *Minerve,* after the Roman goddess, there is nothing specifically Roman about the helmets, shield, or architecture.

    The drawing belongs to a group representing classical personages, many of whom wear helmets and are armed with a shield or sword, which were executed at the end of 1933 and the beginning of 1934: Z. VIII. 155-61, 169, 170, 198-203. Closest in technique and style are VIII. 157 and 169. It also resembles two drawings identified by W. Boeck and J. Sabartés as "Illustrations for *Lysistrata,* 1934" (*Picasso,* New York, 1955, pp. 50-51, repr.). In January 1934, Picasso executed the six etchings to illustrate a new version of Aristophanes' *Lysistrata* adapted by Gilbert Seldes (New York, 1934). See B. Geiser, *Picasso: Peintre-Graveur,* Bern, 1968, vol. II, nos. 387-92 for actual illustrations and nos. 393-402 for related work.

REFERENCES:

J. Cassou, *Picasso,* New York, 1940, p. 23, repr. (*Composition,* photo Thannhauser); Zervos, 1957, vol. VIII, no. 158, pl. 69 (*Minerve,* 1933); *Masterpieces,* 1972, p. 71, repr. (*Minerve,* 1933).

61   Still Life: Fruit Dish and Pitcher.
      January 21-22, 1937
      *(Nature morte: compotier et cruche; Table
      bleue, orange, jaune et blanche)*

Enamel on canvas, 19⅝ x 23¹⁵/₁₆ (49.8 x 60.8)

Signed and dated u.l.: *21 janvier XXXVII / Picasso;* dated on stretcher u.r.: *22 janvier XXXVII.*

PROVENANCE:

Purchased from the artist by Paul Rosenberg, Paris, 1938 (correspondence with A. Rosenberg, Dec. 1974); on consignment to Bignou Gallery, New York, c. 1939; purchased from Paul Rosenberg, New York, by Vladimir Golschmann between Feb. 1944 and Oct. 1947 (correspondence with A. Rosenberg); Mary Callery, probably late 1947 or 1948-56 (correspondence with Callery,[1] Apr. 1974); Perls Galleries, New York, Apr. 1956-57 (correspondence with K. G. Perls, Jan. 1974); purchased from Perls Galleries by J. K. Thannhauser, Feb. 1957.

CONDITION:

Not lined. Repair at upper left in fruit dish (May 1975).

Picasso painted *Still Life: Fruit Dish and Pitcher* on Thursday, January 21, 1937, and, according to the inscription on the reverse, on the following day. Pierre Daix confirms that Picasso did it at Le Tremblay-sur-Mauldre, near Versailles, where he often spent three or four days a week at a farmhouse and studio owned by Ambroise Vollard (p. 273, fn. 9). Later Marie-Thérèse Walter recalled that Picasso generally went there from Thursday to Sunday night (P. Cabanne, "Picasso et les joies de la paternité," *L'Oeil,* no. 226, May 1974, p. 7).

The series of still lifes painted at Le Tremblay from late 1936 to 1938 are characterized by their subdued color and by the simplicity of the objects (jug, cup, candle, plate, knife, pitcher) represented. Jaime Sabartés emphasizes that in spirit these still lifes are set apart from other work. "The same objects painted in the city would have had a different aspect. One felt that he had seen them breathing pure air, free from extraneous worries" (*Picasso: An Intimate Portrait,* trans. A. Flores, New York, 1948, p. 142).

On January 22 Picasso painted another version of the present composition with only minor changes in the pitcher and more simplified forms in the compotier (19⅝ x 24 in., 49.8 x 61 cm.; Duncan, 1961, p. 220, repr.). In a still life, *Nature morte au pichet,* dated January 20 (Z. VIII. 326), the pitcher had been treated in a representational manner. Yet the shapes of the base, body, handle, and mouth of the pitcher, which later become abstract designs, are already accentuated. Likewise, the "figure eight" designs at the base of and across the fruit dish are suggested in the January 20 painting, developed in the January 21 version, and modified slightly in that of January 22. This distinctive configuration of fruit appeared in 1931 in Braque's still lifes (N. Mangin, *Catalogue de l'oeuvre de Georges Braque: peintures 1928-1935,* Paris, 1962, pls. 73-74).

Picasso had painted still lifes with a compotier on the left and a pitcher on the right the month before (December 8; Z. VIII. 328; Duncan, p. 219; and December 14,

1. Callery (correspondence, Apr. 1974) remembered purchasing the painting from Paul Rosenberg, New York, during World War II. Rosenberg's records indicate otherwise.

1936; not in Z.). In a picture dated January 16 (Z. VIII. 327; *La Renaissance de l'art français et des industries de luxe,* vol. XXI, Jan. 1939, foll. p. 16, color repr.), the same objects are quite clearly described without emphasis on abstract shapes.

The division of the background and the differentiation of planes in the table through color are developed further in still lifes with pitchers painted in April 1937 (Z. VIII. 358, 359, 364-67).

EXHIBITIONS:

New York, The Museum of Modern Art, *Picasso: Forty Years of His Art,* Nov. 15, 1939-Jan. 7, 1940, no. 277 *(Still Life,* dated Jan. 21, 1937, lent by the Bignou Gallery, on consignment from Paul Rosenberg), traveled to The Art Institute of Chicago, Feb. 1-Mar. 3; Cincinnati Modern Art Society, *Golschmann Collection,* Apr. 30-June 1, 1947 (probably *Still Life,* 1937, oil); New York, Rosenberg Galleries, *Vladimir Golschmann Collection,* Oct. 6-25, 1947, no. 14 *(Table bleue, orange, jaune et blanche,* 1937, 19½ x 23¾ in.); New York, The Museum of Modern Art, *Picasso: 75th Anniversary Exhibition,* May 22-Sept. 8, 1957, Addenda p. 115, repr. *(Fruit Dish and Pitcher),* traveled to The Art Institute of Chicago, Oct. 29-Dec. 8; Philadelphia Museum of Art, *Picasso,* Jan. 8-Feb. 23, 1958, no. 192.

REFERENCES:

J. Merli, *Picasso, el artista y la obra de nuestro tiempo,* rev. ed., Buenos Aires, 1948, pl. 447; Zervos, 1957, vol. VIII, no. 329 and pl. 154 *(Nature morte); Masterpieces,* 1972, p. 72, repr.; Daix, 1977, p. 273, fn. 9.

---

62   Head of a Woman (Dora Maar).
      March 28, 1939
      (Tête de femme; Girl with Blond Hair)

Oil on wood panel, 23⁹⁄₁₆ x 17¾ (59.8 x 45.1)

Signed and dated l.r.: *Picasso / 39;* dated on reverse: *28.3.39*

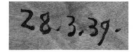

PROVENANCE:

Purchased from the artist by Paul Rosenberg, Paris, 1939 (correspondence with A. Rosenberg, Dec. 1974); purchased from Paul Rosenberg, New York, by Keith Warner, Oct. 1943;[1] G. David Thompson, Pittsburgh;[2] J. K. Thannhauser.

CONDITION:
Panel, which is warped, has veneer on each side of plywood core: total thickness is approximately one-quarter inch. The pattern of cracks follows grain of the veneer. Panel's unpainted surface visible in places in woman's hair (May 1975).

1. The present picture was not included in the sale of Warner's collection at the Parke Bernet Galleries, New York, on Mar. 16, 1950, nor in earlier auctions at Parke Bernet which contained pictures from Warner's collection (Dec. 15, 1949, and Oct. 18, 1950). Warner died in 1959.
2. Mrs. G. David Thompson confirmed that the picture was once in her husband's collection and had belonged to Warner but could not provide specific dates (correspondence with D. C. Rich, Apr. 1974). Thompson died in 1965.

Dora Maar was a photographer and, by 1934, a member of Surrealist art circles in Paris. According to Pierre Daix, Picasso was introduced to her at St. Germain-des-Prés early in 1936 by Paul Eluard, whom he had met only recently (1965, p. 157). However, Brassaï (who had known Dora since the early 1930s) states that the artist made her acquaintance in the autumn of 1935 (*Picasso and Company*, Garden City, 1966, p. 42). Picasso's earliest portraits of her date from their stay at Mougins during the autumn of 1936 (Penrose, 1958, p. 303).

Dora Maar was born in Paris of a French mother and a Yugoslav father, an architect named Markovitch. After living for years in Argentina, she was in Paris by the early 1930s. An exhibition of her photographs took place in 1937. Due to her association with Picasso, she turned increasingly to painting, which she showed in the 1940s and 1950s.

The present painting was executed when Dora Maar was twenty-nine years old (*Time*, vol. XXXIII, Feb. 13, 1939, p. 46. A photograph of Picasso by Dora Maar is on the cover). Her hair was brown rather than blond as Picasso has chosen to portray it here. Her eyes were "dark and beautiful" and "her quick decisive speech and low-pitched voice were an immediate indication of character and intelligence" (Penrose, p. 260). She appears in Picasso's work until 1945.

In spite of the dislocation of the features, the painting resembles the sitter. Photographs of her are reproduced in A. Fermigier, ed., *Picasso*, Paris, 1967, p. 196; C. Beaton, "Picasso's Studio 1944," *Horizon* (London), vol. XI, Jan. 1945, opp. p. 49; and R. Penrose, *Portrait of Picasso*, rev. ed., New York, 1971, pp. 64-65.

This panel is one of several very similar pictures of the sitter, all the same size, painted late in March 1939 at the time of the fall of Madrid. These include works of March 27 (The Art Gallery of Toronto, *Picasso and Man*, exh. cat., 1964, no. 229, repr.); March 28 (Z. IX. 276 and pl. 129); March 29 (not in Z.; New York, Parke Bernet, *The Collection of . . . the Late G. David Thompson*, Mar. 24, 1966, no. 69, color repr.); March 29 (not in Z.; Duncan, 1961, p. 240, repr.); and March ? (Duncan, p. 240, repr.). Her image also appears in monotypes dated March 22 (Z. IX. 270-73, 277).

EXHIBITIONS:

New York, The Museum of Modern Art, *Picasso: Forty Years of His Art*, Nov. 15, 1939 - Jan. 7, 1940, no. 360 (*Girl with Blond Hair*, Paris, dated Mar. 28, 1939, lent by Rosenberg and Helft, Ltd.), traveled to The Art Institute of Chicago, Feb. 1 - Mar. 3, San Francisco Museum of Art, June 25 - July 22.

REFERENCE:

Masterpieces, 1972, p. 75, repr.

63   Françoise Gilot. September 9, 1947

Sanguine on wove paper, 25¹⁵⁄₁₆ x 19⅞
(65.9 x 50.5)

Signed and dated l.l.: *Golfe-Juan 9 septem-
bre 47   Picasso.*

PROVENANCE:

Purchased from the artist by J. K. Thannhauser, Sept. 1947.

In September 1947, while in southern France, Justin Thannhauser stopped to visit Picasso at Golfe-Juan. At that time Picasso drew for him this festive, decorative image of Françoise Gilot.

Picasso, Gilot, and their infant son Claude, born May 15, 1947, had come to Golfe-Juan in August, where they were living at Louis Fort's house. During that month M. and Mme Georges Ramié invited Picasso to see the results of his first work in pottery, done the year before, which they had had fired (F. Gilot and C. Lake, *Life with Picasso*, New York, 1964, p. 183f.). By the autumn he was working every day in the late morning and all afternoon at the Madoura pottery works in Vallauris (see D. de la Souchère, *Picasso in Antibes*, New York, 1960, pls. 58 and 61, and J. Sabartés, "Picasso à Vallauris," *Cahiers d'Art*, 23e année, 1948, pp. 138, 144, and 149 for ceramics with similar faces made in October 1947).

The playfully curving lines of the present work create a motif suggestive of the sun or a flower; both images Picasso associated with Françoise. The painting *La Femme-fleur* (Z. XIV. 167) dates from May 5, 1946. Also from the same year is a lithograph of Gilot as the sun (F. Mourlot, *Picasso Lithographe*, Monte Carlo, 1949, vol. I, no. 48). In 1945 the artist returned to lithography, a medium which he had not employed since 1919. For related lithographs of Gilot, see Mourlot, vol. I, nos. 38-48, 68, and vol. II, nos. 84 and 106.

In style the Thannhauser drawing is closest to two drawings of Gilot done on July 5, 1946 (Z. XIV. 192 and 193). The designs of her hair and bodice in the July drawings are elaborated in the Thannhauser work in the shapes of the chin and cheeks. Picasso's treatment of the cheeks and chin resembles representations of the sun. Even the curls and waves of the hair suggest the sun rather than Gilot's hair, which was straight (see photographs of her at that time in Gilot and Lake, pp. 33, 169, and 176).

Françoise Gilot, a young painter born November 26, 1921, met Picasso in May 1943. From 1946-53 she occupied an important place in his life and art.

REFERENCES:

Zervos, 1965, vol. XV, no. 73 and pl. 43 *(Tête de femme)*; *Masterpieces*, 1972, p. 74, repr.

---

64   Garden in Vallauris. June 10, 1953
(Jardin à Vallauris; Pine Tree and Palm Tree; Paysage de Vallauris)

Oil on canvas, 7⅜ x 10½ (18.7 x 26.7)

Signed l.r.: *Picasso*; dated u.r.: *10/juin/53*; inscribed on reverse: *1*

PROVENANCE:

Acquired from the artist by Galerie Louise Leiris, Paris, 1953; purchased from Galerie Leiris by Curt Valentin, New York, Jan. 1954 (correspondence with Galerie Leiris, June 1975); purchased from Valentin by J. K. Thannhauser shortly thereafter.

CONDITION:

Not varnished (May 1975).

Garden in Vallauris and *Houses at Vallauris* (cat. no. 65) are two of thirteen canvases Picasso painted of a transformer station during June 1953. Trees and building are common elements in all; yet the composition differs in each painting.

On the reverse of *Garden in Vallauris,* written in black paint, is the number 1, indicating that it was executed before the other two paintings also dated June 10. This would contradict Klaus Gallwitz's placing *Le Transformateur* (Z. XV. 273) first in the series followed by another version (XV. 274) and the present picture (XV. 272; pp. 66-67).

In the 1950s at Vallauris Picasso told Alexander Liberman: "I never do a painting as a work of art. All of them are researches. I search incessantly and there is a logical sequence in all this research. That is why I number them. It's an experiment in time. I number them and date them. Maybe one day someone will be grateful, he added laughingly" (quoted in D. Ashton, ed., *Picasso on Art: A Selection of Views,* New York, 1972, p. 72).

EXHIBITION:

New York, Curt Valentin Gallery, *Pablo Picasso 1950-1953,* Nov. 24-Dec. 19, 1953, no. 24 *(Pinetree and Palmtree, 1953, 7½ x 11 in.).*

REFERENCES:

Curt Valentin Gallery, New York, *Picasso,* n.d., vol. IV of unpublished "Black Albums" of photographs on deposit at The Museum of Modern Art, New York [p. 61], repr. (no. 15722, *Pine Tree and Palm Tree);* Zervos, 1965, vol. XV, no. 272 and pl. 150 *(Paysage de Vallauris);* K. Gallwitz, *Picasso at 90: The Late Work,* New York, 1971, p. 66, pl. 67 *(Pine and Palm); Masterpieces,* 1972, p. 75, repr.

65   Houses at Vallauris.   June 25, 1953
      (Maisons à Vallauris)

Oil on canvas, 19⅝ x 24 (49.8 x 61)

Signed and dated l.l.: *Picasso / 25 juin 53*.

PROVENANCE:

Acquired from the artist by Galerie Louise
Leiris, Paris, 1953; purchased from Galerie

Leiris by Curt Valentin, New York, Nov.
1953 (correspondence with Galerie Leiris,
June 1975); purchased from Valentin by
J. K. Thannhauser.

Picasso selected only certain elements from the view of the transformer station at
Vallauris (see cat. no. 64): the building on a hill, the pine tree, and the building
with a balustrade. While concentrating on a much more restricted representation,
he has painted it on a larger canvas than the preceding picture.

The painting most closely resembles *Landscape with Pine* of June 15 (Z. XV. 280)
as well as *The Hill* of June 24 (Z. XV. 281). No canvases of this scene date from June
17 through June 23, and the last one was done on July 1, 1953 (Z. XV. 285).

For several years Picasso had painted landscapes of Vallauris and its distinctive
houses and gardens (photographs in J. Sabartés, *Picasso: Documents iconographiques*,
Geneva, 1954, pls. 154, 175, 176; see also Z. XV. 174, 185-89). Vallauris, a pottery
center prior to Roman times, was located three miles from Golfe-Juan. It was in the
1930s that Picasso first discovered it with Paul and Nusch Eluard (Daix, 1965, p. 163).
He began working in ceramics there in 1947, and from May 1948 to 1954 he lived
at the Villa La Galloise. He also had a studio with separate areas for painting and
sculpture in an old factory in rue du Fournas in Vallauris from 1949 on (F. Gilot and
C. Lake, *Life with Picasso*, New York, 1964, pp. 253-54).

EXHIBITION:

New York, Curt Valentin Gallery, *Pablo Picasso 1950-1953*, Nov. 24-Dec. 19, 1953, no.
23 (*Houses in Vallauris*, 1953, 20 x 24½ in.).

REFERENCES:

Curt Valentin Gallery, New York, *Picasso*, n.d., vol. IV of unpublished "Black Albums" of
photographs on deposit at The Museum of Modern Art, New York [p. 46], repr. (no.
15712, *Houses at Vallauris*); Zervos, 1965, vol. XV, no. 284 and pl. 156 *(Maisons à Vallauris)*; K. Gallwitz, *Picasso at 90: The Late Work*, New York, 1971, p. 67, pl. 75; *Masterpieces*, 1972, p. 76, repr.

66 Two Doves with Wings Spread.
March 16-19, 1960
(Deux pigeons aux ailes déployées)

Oil on linen, 23 9/16 x 28 3/4 (59.7 x 73)

Signed u.l.: *Picasso;* dated on reverse:
16.3.60
19.
 I

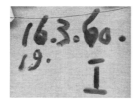

PROVENANCE:

Acquired from the artist by J. K. Thannhauser, Sept. 1960.

CONDITION:

Not varnished. In places unpainted support
visible. Considerable impasto in other
areas, especially in center between doves
(May 1975).

When Picasso signed the painting in September 1960 at La Californie, David Douglas Duncan was with him and took photographs (conversation with K. Lee of Guggenheim Museum, Jan. 1975. Prints of the photographs of Picasso signing this painting are in the Guggenheim Museum files). Picasso painted this version on March 16 and went back to it on March 19. He did another version, begun after the present picture (Z. XIX. 221). The placing of the doves perching on a ledge recurs in the two birds at the right in *Trois pigeons* (Z. XIX. 219; Mar. 20, 1960, 25 5/8 x 31 7/8 in., 65 x 81 cm.).

The paintings of doves from February and March 1960 were all done at La Californie, the villa on a hill over Cannes, where Picasso had made a dovecote on the third-floor balcony (see photograph in D. D. Duncan, *The Private World of Pablo Picasso*, New York, 1958, pp. 46-47). Earlier he had designed a poster of a dove for the 1948 Peace Congress and had made ceramic pigeons and doves in 1953 (see D.-H. Kahnweiler, *Picasso Keramik*, Hannover, 1957, pls. 36-38 and J. Sabartés, "Picasso à Vallauris," *Cahiers d'Art*, 23ᵉ année, 1948, pp. 93, 143, 168, 186).

Jaime Sabartés (*Picasso: An Intimate Portrait*, New York, 1948, pp. 7-8, 26-27) discusses not only Picasso's love of pigeons but also his father's. For painting of doves and pigeons by Picasso's father, José Ruiz Blasco, see R. Penrose, *Portrait of Picasso*, rev. ed., New York, 1971, p. 17, fig. 15 and p. 122, fig. 321.

REFERENCES:

Zervos, 1968, vol. XIX, no. 220 and pl. 65 *(Deux pigeons aux ailes déployées)*; *Masterpieces*, 1972, p. 77, repr.

Camille Pissarro

Born July 1830, Saint Thomas
Died November 1903, Paris

67   The Hermitage at Pontoise. c. 1867
*(Les Côteaux de l'Hermitage, Pontoise;
Pontoise; Hügellandschaft)*

Oil on canvas, 59⅝ x 79 (151.4 x 200.6)
Signed at l.l.: *C. Pissarro.*   Not dated.

PROVENANCE:
Acquired probably from Durand-Ruel or
from the artist by J.-B. Faure by 1876;[1] purchased from Faure by Durand-Ruel, Paris,
June 1901; sold to Cassirer, June 1901;[2]
acquired by Moderne Galerie (Heinrich
Thannhauser) by 1918.

CONDITION:
Unlined. Painting is on original stretcher.
There is a horizontal seam across the entire
width thirteen and one-half inches up from
the bottom where two pieces of canvas
were joined. Crackle patterns are prominent, especially in the sky. Scattered areas
of cleavage lower right (Dec. 1974).

The view represented is the rue du Fond de l'Hermitage (now rue Maria Deraismes)
in Pontoise. A photograph of the site as it appeared in May 1962 is reproduced in
L. Reidemeister (p. 39 and correspondence with Reidemeister, Nov. 1976). The small
square or open space at the foot of rue Maria Deraismes still exists. The houses
joined by a wall at the right and center of the painting survive as do some of those
grouped at the left. Today, a large building stands at what would be the left foreground and the trees on the hill are, of course, larger (correspondence with E. Maillet,
Musée de Pontoise, Nov. 1976). Pontoise is situated twenty-seven miles northwest
of Paris on the right bank of the Oise River.

The catalogue of the Salon of 1866 listed Pissarro's address as "à Pontoise, rue
du Fond-de-l'Ermitage; et à Paris, chez M. Guillemet, Grande-Rue, 20 (Batignolles)"
*(Explication des ouvrages de peinture, sculpture, architecture, gravure, et lithographie
des artistes vivants,* Paris, 1866, p. 199). The specific house where Pissarro lived between 1866 and 1868 remains unknown. No trace of documentation has been found
at the mayor's office or elsewhere by the Musée de Pontoise. The exact dates when
Pissarro lived in the Maison de la Sente de Cheminées, which dominates the hill,

1. Cézanne's letter of July 2, 1876 (quoted in the text), gives the terminal date. J. Rewald
kindly informed D. C. Rich that he found in L. R. Pissarro's files the following information:
"Extrait d'un carnet de notes de l'artiste: 1873 - en dépôt chez Durand-Ruel—1) Grande
T de 2m sur 1m50—'l'Hermitage' 2500 frs. vendu à Faure" (correspondence, Feb. 1975).
The dimensions and title clearly indicate the Thannhauser painting as does the fact that
it was on consignment. According to the archives of Durand-Ruel, Faure purchased two
paintings by Pissarro in 1873. One entitled *Le Palais Royal à l'Ermitage, Pontoise* (Durand-
Ruel Stock No. 2726, no date or measurements given) was sold for 2,500 francs, having
been purchased from the artist the same year (correspondence with C. Durand-Ruel, Nov.
1976). Pissarro-Venturi contains no reference to a painting of that title. Undoubtedly, the
references in the Durand-Ruel archives are to the present picture.
   Jean-Baptiste Faure, the famous baritone (1830-1914), often bought works at low prices
from Durand-Ruel and sometimes from the artists themselves. About 1873 he began col-
lecting Impressionist paintings, acquiring among others thirty-seven by Pissarro and sixty-
eight by Manet (A. Callen, "Faure and Manet," *Gazette des Beaux-Arts,* vol. LXXXIII,
Mar. 1974, p. 157). During the war, Faure, Durand-Ruel, and Pissarro were all in London.
Upon his return to Paris in 1873, Faure lived at 39, rue Neuve-des-Mathurins.
2. Durand-Ruel Stock No. 6430 (correspondence with C. Durand-Ruel, Nov. 1976).

cannot be determined. The house has survived and has recently undergone renovations (correspondence with Maillet, Nov. 1976).

There are two paintings of Pontoise that Pissarro dated 1867: *Jallais Hill, Pontoise* (Pissarro-Venturi 55; 34¼ x 45¼ in., 87 x 144.9 cm., The Metropolitan Museum of Art, New York; J. Rewald, *Camille Pissarro*, New York, 1963, p. 71, color repr.) and *Hermitage at Pontoise* (Pissarro-Venturi 56; 35⅞ x 59¼ in., 91 x 150.5 cm., Wallraf-Richartz Museum, Cologne; Champa, color pl. 21). The Thannhauser painting is closely related to both in style and subject matter and is dated c. 1867 by all sources except Kermit Champa. Another undated painting of the Hermitage which can be placed in the year 1867 is *View of the Hermitage* (Pissarro-Venturi 57; 27½ x 39⅜ in., 70 x 100 cm., present whereabouts unknown; Champa, fig. 108).

Champa views Charles-François Daubigny's *Hermitage at Pontoise* (44⅛ x 63½ in., 112 x 161.5 cm., dated 1866, Kunsthalle, Bremen; Champa, fig. 106) as the picture that "provided a schema for Pissarro's series of pictures of the same subject done between mid-1867 and the spring of 1868" (p. 75). He places the more traditional Thannhauser version latest in date, 1867 into 1868, so that it was completed in time for the Salon (conversation, Jan. 1977).

It would appear then more than a coincidence that in 1868 Daubigny interceded on Pissarro's behalf at the Salon so that two of his Pontoise landscapes were accepted. *"La Côte de Jallais"* (no. 2015) is the painting now in The Metropolitan Museum of Art. *"L'Ermitage"* (no. 2016) has never been identified with certainty although Pissarro and Venturi (vol. I, p. 86) stated that it was probably the Thannhauser picture. Without providing proof, Champa says that it was in the Salon (p. 76). John Rewald thinks that Pissarro may have sent it to the Salon since it is a large painting. However, the fact that two works were accepted could indicate that both were smaller in size (correspondence, Nov. 1973).

Both Emile Zola and Jules Antoine Castagnary complained that Pissarro's paintings were hung too high (Castagnary, *Salons [1867-1870]*, Paris, 1892, vol. I, p. 278). Zola described the painting of the Hermitage hill in considerable detail. *"Dans l'Hermitage au premier plan, est un terrrain qui s'élargit et s'enfonce; au bout de ce terrain, se trouve un corps de bâtiment dans un bouquet de grands arbres. Rien de plus. Mais quelle terre vivante, quelle verdure pleine de sève, quel horizon vaste! Après quelques minutes d'examen, j'ai cru voir la campagne s'ouvrir devant moi"* (F. W. J. Hemmings and R. J. Niess, eds., *Salons*, Geneva and Paris, 1959, p. 128). ("In *The Hermitage* in the foreground is a terrain which becomes larger and deeper: at the end of this terrain is a group of buildings within a grove of large trees. Nothing more. But what vibrant earth, what greenery full of vitality, what a vast horizon! After studying it for several minutes, I thought I saw the very countryside open up before me.") Zola went on to state his preference for *La Côte de Jallais,* referring to specific details found in the painting in The Metropolitan Museum. Zola's description of *The Hermitage* appears to fit the picture in the Wallraf-Richartz Museum rather than that in the Thannhauser Collection. It is also quite possible that the painting exhibited as no. 2016 no longer exists since a large proportion of the paintings Pissarro stored at his house at Louveciennes were destroyed during the Franco-Prussian War.

The Thannhauser painting was admired by Cézanne, who wrote to Pissarro from L'Estaque on July 2, 1876: *"Dès que je le pourrai je passerai au moins un mois en ces lieux, car il faut faire des toiles de deux mètres au moins, comme celle par vous vendue à Faure"* (Rewald, ed., *Cézanne Correspondence,* Paris, 1937, p. 127). ("As soon as I am able I shall spend at least a month in these parts for I must do some canvases of at least two metres in size like the one by you which was sold to Faure.")

EXHIBITIONS:

Paris, Salon of 1868, no. 2016(?);[3] Berlin, Künstlerhaus (organized by the Galerien Thann-hauser), *Erste Sonderausstellung in Berlin,* Jan. 9-Feb. 15, 1927, no. 189, repr. *(Pontoise);* Paris, Musée de l'Orangerie, *Centenaire de la naissance de Camille Pissarro,* Feb.-Mar. 1930, no. 10 *(Pontoise);* Buenos Aires, Museo Nacional de Bellas Artes, *La pintura francesca de David a nuestros dias,* July-Aug. 1939, no. 106 *(Vista de Pontoise),* traveled to Montivideo, Ministero de Instruccion Publica, Apr.-May 1940 (label on reverse), and Rio de Janeiro, Museu Nacional de Belas Artes, June 29-Aug. 15 (label on reverse of frame); San Francisco, M. H. De Young Memorial Museum, *The Painting of France Since the French Revolution,* Dec. 1940-Jan. 1941, no. 82, repr.; The Art Institute of Chicago, *Masterpieces of French Art,* Apr. 10-May 20, 1941, no. 123, repr.; Los Angeles County Museum, *The Painting of France Since the French Revolution,* June-July 1941, no. 104; The Portland Art Museum, *Master-pieces of French Painting,* Sept. 3-Oct. 5, 1941, no. 86; Washington, D.C., The National Gallery of Art, on loan from Feb. 1942-June 1945 (correspondence with P. Davidock, Nov. 1973); New York, The Museum of Modern Art, on loan from Aug. 1945-July 1946 (con-versation with B. Winiker, Oct. 1976); Pittsfield (Mass.), The Berkshire Museum, *French Impressionist Painting,* Aug. 2-31, 1946, no. 13.

REFERENCES:

J. Meier-Graefe, "Camille Pissarro," *Kunst und Künstler,* Jg. 2, 1904, p. 483, repr. *(Hügel-landschaft);* W. Kirchbach, "Pissarro und Raffaëli," *Die Kunst unserer Zeit,* Jg. 15, 1904, p. 124, repr. *(Die Ermitage in Pontoise);* J.-C. Holl, *Camille Pissarro,* Paris [1911], p. 41, repr. *(Les Côteaux de l'Ermitage, Pontoise);* Munich, Moderne Galerie (Heinrich Thann-hauser), *Nachtragswerk III,* 1918, pp. 19, repr., and 119 *(Landschaft, 150 x 200 cm.);* T. Duret, *Die Impressionisten,* Berlin, 1923, p. 91, repr. *(Landschaft);* H. Osborn, "Klassiker der Fran-zösischen Moderne," *Deutsche Kunst und Dekoration,* vol. 59, Mar. 1927, p. 341, repr.; B. E. Werner, "Französische Malerei in Berlin," *Die Kunst für Alle,* Jg. 42, Apr. 1927, p. 224; L. R. Pissarro and L. Venturi, *Camille Pissarro: son art-son oeuvre,* Paris, 1939, vol. I, pp. 20, 86, no. 58, and vol. II, pl. 11 *(Les Côteaux de l'Hermitage, Pontoise, c. 1867);* J. Rewald, *The History of Impressionism,* New York, 1946, repr. opp. p. 148 *(Hermitage at Pontoise,* c. 1867); L. Reidemeister, *Auf den Spuren der Maler der Ile de France,* Berlin, 1963, p. 39, repr.; C. Kunstler, *Pissarro Cities and Landscapes,* trans. E. Kramer, Lausanne, 1967, pl. l *(Slopes at the Hermitage, Pontoise);* *Masterpieces,* 1972, p. 10, repr.; K. S. Champa, *Studies in Early Impressionism,* New Haven and London, 1973, pp. 75-77 and fig. 109 (incorrectly states that the painting was dated 1868); J. Rewald, *The History of Impressionism,* 4th ed. rev., New York, 1973, p. 159, repr. *(The Hermitage at Pontoise,* c. 1867); J. Rewald, "The Impressionist Brush," *Metropolitan Museum Bulletin,* vol. 32, 1973-74 [p. 12], repr.

3. See discussion above in text. The issue is complicated somewhat by the presence of two railway labels on the reverse of the stretcher, indicating that the picture was shipped from the Chemin de fer du Nord in Paris to Pontoise. Rewald thinks that the shipping label refers not to the stretcher alone but to the completed painting which must have been sent to Paris sometime after it was painted—c. 1867 and before 1873 (correspondence, Feb. 1975).

Pierre Auguste Renoir

Born February 1841, Limoges
Died December 1919, Cagnes

68 Woman with Parrot. 1871
(La Femme à la perruche; Femme au perroquet; Dame mit Papagei; Girl Feeding a Bird [Lise])

Oil on canvas, 36¼ x 25⅝ (92.1 x 65.1)

Signed l.r.: *A. Renoir.*   Not dated.

PROVENANCE:

C. Hoogendijk,[1] The Hague, until 1912 (Amsterdam, Frederik Muller & Cie, *Catalogue des tableaux modernes,* May 21-22, 1912, no. 57); purchased at sale by Cassirer and Bernheim-Jeune;[2] acquired by C. Tetzen Lund, Copenhagen, before 1921; Galerie Barbazanges, Paris, 1922;[3] J. K. Thannhauser by 1927.

CONDITION:

Lined at an unknown date before 1965. Moderate impasto in some areas (the sitter's head and hands and the parrot), whereas the skirt of the woman's dress is thinly painted. All edges show signs of considerable wear. Old repair at lower right. Scattered areas of cleavage in background (Jan. 1975).

The woman is Lise Tréhot, who appears in many paintings by Renoir (see Cooper, 1959, p. 169, and Daulte, 1971, p. 419). She was born at Ecquevilly (Seine-et-Oise) on March 14, 1848, and her family moved to Paris sometime after 1855. It is not known when Renoir and Lise met. Douglas Cooper proposes that it was in 1865 or early 1866 when Lise's older sister Clémence became the mistress of Renoir's friend, Jules Le Coeur (see p. 164 of Cooper for additional biographical information). Lise's association with Renoir ended before April 24, 1872, when she married Georges Brière de l'Isle (1847-1902), an architect and friend of Le Coeur. It is said that she never saw Renoir again. Lise kept two of her portraits by Renoir, but destroyed all her papers at some time before her death on March 12, 1922 (p. 171). A photograph of Lise Tréhot taken in 1864 is published in *The Burlington Magazine,* vol. CI, May 1959, p. 165, fig. 2.

In *Woman with Parrot,* Lise wears the same black silk dress with white cuffs and buttons and even the same earrings as in *Lise with a White Shawl,* which Cooper dates 1872 (21⅝ x 17¾ in., 55 x 45 cm., Collection Mr. Emery Reves; F. Fosca, *Renoir: His Life and Work,* trans. M. I. Martin, Englewood Cliffs, 1962, p. 25, color repr.).

1. Cornelis Hoogendijk (1866-1911) acquired the pictures in his collection in Paris and other European cities before 1900. He also owned another of Renoir's paintings of Lise, *Baigneuse au griffon* (73½ x 46⅛ in., 184 x 115 cm., 1870, Museu de Arte Moderna, São Paulo; Daulte, no. 54). It is not known from whom Hoogendijk purchased either picture (conversation with Henkel, Nov. 1977).
2. The painting remained with Cassirer, who sold it (correspondence with G. Gruet of Bernheim-Jeune, Nov. 1976). The fact that the painting was included in a catalogue of the Moderne Galerie (Heinrich Thannhauser) in Munich in 1916 indicates that it was with the gallery but it does not prove that Thannhauser owned the picture. J. K. Thannhauser's notes (Dec. 1972) do not add any information as to whether the Moderne Galerie owned the picture before 1927.
3. The Galerie Barbazanges lent the picture to an exhibition at the Louvre in 1922. According to the provenance in Daulte, the picture belonged to the Galerie Barbazanges after Tetzen Lund and before Thannhauser.

Woman with Parrot would have to date from before Lise's marriage in April 1872 and after Renoir's return to Paris from service in the Franco-Prussian War (July 1870-Mar. 1871). Upon his return in mid-March, Renoir rented a room in rue Dragon not far from the apartment of his friend Edmond Maître (1840-1898) in rue Taranne (Daulte, p. 36).

As Cooper has pointed out (p. 168), *Woman with Parrot* is "so close in handling and conception" to Renoir's *Portrait of Mme Maître,* which bears a date of April 1871, that a coeval date can be safely assumed (51⅜ x 32⅝ in., 130 x 83 cm., Collection Mme René Lecomte, Paris). François Daulte dates both paintings April 1871 (p. 36).

Renoir chose the theme of a woman holding a parrot for the portrait of Lise, who was his mistress, and for the portrait of Rapha, then the mistress and later the wife of his friend, Edmond Maître. The subject had been depicted in the 1860s by Courbet, Manet, and Degas. In Manet's *Woman with a Parrot* (72⅞ x 50⅝ in., 185.1 x 128.6 cm., 1866, The Metropolitan Museum of Art, New York), the woman stands beside the bird. In a drawing by Degas (9¼ x 7⅜ in., 23.5 x 18.7 cm., c. 1866, BN Carnet 8, p. 27, Bibliothèque Nationale, Paris; J. S. Boggs, *Portraits by Degas,* Berkeley and Los Angeles, 1962, no. 48, repr.), the parrot perches on the woman's finger, as it does in the Thannhauser painting.

The relationship between women and parrots can be traced back for centuries. Women were thought to share their secrets with parrots. In turn, parrots were believed to speak more readily to women and children than to men (P. Larousse, *Grand Dictionnaire universel du XIXe siècle,* Paris, 1867, vol. XII, p. 657). In nineteenth-century France, these birds were common pets (see M. Hadler, "Manet's Woman with a Parrot of 1866," *Metropolitan Museum of Art Journal,* vol. 7, 1973, pp. 115-22).

EXHIBITIONS:

Berlin, Paul Cassirer, *XV. Jahrgang I. Ausstellung,* Oct.-Nov. 1912, no. 39 (according to Gordon, 1974, vol. II, p. 619); Paris, Bernheim-Jeune, *Renoir,* Mar. 10-29, 1913, no. 2; Dresden, Galerie Arnold, *Ausstellung Französischer Malerei der XIX Jahrhunderts,* Apr.-May 1914, no. 99; Oslo, Nasjonalgalleriet (arranged by Foreningen Fransk Kunst), *Renoir,* Feb. 12-Mar. 6, 1921, no. 4 (lent by Chr. Tetzen-Lund and ex. coll. H. Cassirer), traveled to Copenhagen, Ny Carlsberg Glyptotek, Mar. 17-Apr. 10, 1921, and Stockholm, Nationalmuseum, Apr. 31-June 1;[4] Paris, Palais du Louvre, Pavillon de Marsan, *Le Décor de la vie sous le Second Empire,* May 27-July 10, 1922, no. 149 (*Femme au Perroquet,* 1869, Galerie Barbazanges); Berlin, Künstlerhaus (organized by the Galerien Thannhauser), *Erste Sonderausstellung in Berlin,* Jan. 9-Feb. 15, 1927, no. 196, repr.; Amsterdam, Stedelijk Museum, *Honderd Jaar Fransche Kunst,* July 2-Sept. 25, 1938, no. 200; Buenos Aires, Museo Nacional de Bellas Artes, *La pintura francesca de David a nuestros dias,* July-Aug. 1939, no. 113, traveled to Montevideo, Ministero de Instruccion Publica, Apr.-May 1940, and Rio de Janeiro, Museu Nacional de Belas Artes, June 29-Aug. 15; San Francisco, M. H. de Young Memorial Museum, *The Painting of France Since the French Revolution,* Dec. 1940-Jan. 1941, no. 88, repr.; The Art Institute of Chicago, *Masterpieces of French Art,* Apr. 10-May 20, 1941, no. 130, repr.; Los Angeles County Museum, *The Painting of France Since the French Revolution,* June-July 1941, no. 110; The Portland Art Museum, *Master-*

4. Information from correspondence with L. Østby, Oslo, Oct. 1976, L. Vestergaard of Statens Museum for Kunst, Copenhagen, Sept. 1976, and N. Weibull of Nationalmuseum, Stockholm, Feb. 1977.

pieces of French Painting, Sept. 3 - Oct. 5, 1941, no. 91; Washington, D.C., The National Gallery of Art, on loan from Feb. 1942 - July 1946 (correspondence with P. Davidock, Nov. 1973); Pittsfield (Mass.), The Berkshire Museum, *French Impressionist Painting,* Aug. 2 - 31, 1946, no. 20; Los Angeles County Museum, *Pierre Auguste Renoir,* July 14 - Aug. 21, 1955, no. 9, repr., traveled to San Francisco Museum of Art, Sept. 1 - Oct. 2.

REFERENCES:

O. Mirbeau, *Renoir,* Paris, Bernheim-Jeune, 1913, p. 55 and repr. opp. p. ii (*La Femme à la perruche,* 1868); W. Hausenstein, *Katalog der Modernen Galerie, Heinrich Thannhauser München,* Munich, 1916, repr. betw. pp. 20-21 *(Dame mit Papagei);* A. Vollard, "La Jeunesse de Renoir," *La Renaissance de l'art français et des industries de luxe,* vol. I, May 1918, p. 17, repr. (*La Femme au Perroquet,* 1865); M. Osborn, "Klassiker der Französischen Moderne," *Deutsche Kunst und Dekoration,* vol. 59, Mar. 1927, p. 347, repr.; A. Basler, *Pierre-Auguste Renoir,* Paris 1928, p. 15, repr. (1871); J. Meier-Graefe, *Renoir,* Leipzig, 1929, pp. 44, repr., and 437, no. 28 (1871-72); O. Thomsen, *Chr. Tetzen-Lunds Samling af moderne fransk Malerkunst,* Copenhagen, 1934, no. 97 *(Dame avec un papegai);* C. Roger-Marx, *Renoir,* Paris, 1933 and 1937, p. 31, repr. (*La Femme à la perruche,* 1871, incorrectly states Musée de Hambourg); J. Thiis, *Renoir,* Stockholm, 1944, p. 197, repr. (photo of 1921 exhibition of French art in Oslo); J. Alazard, *Auguste Renoir,* Milan and Florence, 1953, no. 7, repr. (incorrectly states Hamburg Museum); "La Jeunesse de Renoir," *Connaissance des Arts,* no. 34, Dec. 15, 1954, p. 70, repr.; D. Cooper, "Renoir, Lise and the Le Coeur Family: A Study of Renoir's Early Development—I. Lise," *The Burlington Magazine,* vol. CI, May 1959, pp. 168, 169, 171, and fig. 12 (*Girl Feeding a Bird [Lise],* 1871); F. Daulte, "Une Donation sans précédent: la collection Thannhauser," *Connaissance des Arts,* no. 171, May 1966, p. 62, repr.; Daulte, 1971, p. 36 and no. 65 (*La Femme à la perruche,* 1871); *Masterpieces,* 1972, p. 22, repr. (c. 1872).

69 **The Algerian.** 1881

(Femme algérienne)

Oil on canvas, 16¼ x 12¹¹⁄₁₆ (41.3 x 32.2)

Signed u.l.: *A. Renoir*   Not dated.

PROVENANCE:

Acquired from O. Dubourg by Bernheim-Jeune, Mar. 23, 1906;[1] sold to Jules Strauss at an unknown date and bought back Oct. 23, 1908; sold by Bernheim-Jeune at an unknown date to an unknown buyer after 1917 (correspondence with G. Gruet of Bernheim-Jeune, Nov. 1976); J. B. Stang, Oslo;[2] acquired by J. K. Thannhauser, probably in the 1930s.

CONDITION:

Lined at an unknown date before 1965 (Jan. 1975).

Renoir's first trip to Algeria took place from March 4 to April 17, 1881. He was in Algiers with Samuel Frédéric Cordey (1854-1911) and met Paul Lhote and Eugène-Pierre Lestringuez there. Upon his return to Paris, he rented a studio at 18, rue Houdon near the place Pigalle (B. E. White, *An Analysis of Renoir's Development from 1877 to 1887*, Ph.D. dissertation, Columbia University, 1965, p. 171, and Daulte, p. 45).

A pencil drawing for the Thannhauser painting, representing the same model, is contained in a sketchbook (16v) which is inscribed on the inside front cover "1881. mars avril. Alger-avec Cordey / automne-Italie-Venise-Naples" (*Renoir en Italie et en Algérie,* facsimile ed. [preface by A. André and intro. by G. Besson], Paris, 1955). The angle of the head and the arrangement of the hair and veil are identical in both works although the hand and body are omitted in the sketch. In addition, the same model appears full-length and seated in an interior in a painting entitled *L'Algérienne* (25⁹⁄₁₆ x 21¼ in., 65 x 54 cm.; Daulte, no. 370), which was destroyed by fire in 1947 when it belonged to the Earl of Jersey (notes made by D. C. Rich at the Courtauld Institute, London, Mar. 1975).

Although the drawing on 16v of the sketchbook can probably be placed in March to mid-April of 1881, the Thannhauser painting cannot be dated so precisely. The features of the model are distinctly non-European and resemble those in the sketch made in Algeria. Therefore, it is likely that the painting was done soon after the artist's return from Algeria and before his departure for Italy in the autumn. While it is possible that Renoir painted the canvas in Algeria, the brief duration of his visit makes it far from certain. Even before his first trip Renoir had treated the subject in

1. C. Durand-Ruel (correspondence, Nov. 1976) states that the present picture never was at Durand-Ruel and that Daulte (no. 369) erroneously lists in the collection history "Durand-Ruel, Paris (Vente Collection, Durand-Ruel, New York, 5 et 6 mai 1887, no. 48)," which actually refers to no. 367, *The Algerian Girl* in The Museum of Fine Arts, Boston. Daulte also states that in the Dubourg sale at the Hôtel Drouot, Nov. 24, 1903, the present picture was "adjugé 1880 fr. à Georges Petit." The painting is reproduced in the sale catalogue but was bought in at the sale (correspondence with M. C. Comerre, Compagnie des Commissaires Priseurs, Dec. 1976). It is not known when and from whom Dubourg obtained the painting.

2. According to Gaunt (p. 10) and J. K. Thannhauser. Jørgen Breder Stang (1874-1950) collected French art but was forced to sell during the early 1930s (correspondence with L. Østby, Oct. 1976). His existing records do not contain information about *The Algerian,* but it is still possible that he owned the painting, perhaps outside of Norway (correspondence with Halvor N. Astrup, Jan. 1977).

the painting *Parisians Dressed as Algerians* ($61^{13}/_{16}$ x $51^{3}/_{16}$ in., 157 x 130 cm., 1872, The National Museum of Western Art, Tokyo; Daulte, no. 84).

Algerian Girl (20 x $15^{3}/_{4}$ in., 50.5 x 40 cm., The Museum of Fine Arts, Boston; Daulte, no. 367) bears the date 81. Without providing proof, François Daulte states that Renoir painted this canvas in Algeria. The colors, predominantly blue, green, and red, are much brighter than those in the Thannhauser painting. Renoir's Algerian sketchbook seems to include a drawing of the young girl (19v) depicted in the Boston painting. Yet, in the painted version, she has blue eyes, pink cheeks, and her features look European.

Fantasia ($28^{1}/_{4}$ x $35^{1}/_{4}$ in., 71.7 x 89.6 cm., Musée du Louvre, Galerie du Jeu de Paume, Paris), which John Rewald (*The History of Impressionism,* 4th ed. rev., New York, 1973, p. 454) states that Renoir painted in Algeria in 1881, reveals a palette and style similar to the Thannhauser work. Albert André (preface to *Renoir en Italie et en Algérie* [p. 2]) and Daulte (p. 45) mention titles of paintings executed during the trip without citing documentation.

EXHIBITIONS:[3]

Geneva, Galerie Moos, *Exposition d'art français,* Dec. 1918, no. 260, repr. (correspondence with G. Moos, Nov. 1976); Los Angeles County Museum, *Pierre Auguste Renoir,* July 14-Aug. 21, 1955, no. 30 (1883, lent by J. K. Thannhauser), traveled to San Francisco Museum of Art, Sept. 1-Oct. 2.

REFERENCES:

G. Geffroy, *Catalogue de tableaux,* Paris, Hôtel Drouot, Nov. 24, 1903, pp. 13-14 and 26; W. Gaunt, *Renoir,* London, 1952, p. 10, no. 50, repr. (c. 1881-82, coll. J. B. Stang); M. Berr de Turique, *Auguste Renoir,* Paris, 1953, pl. 50 (*Femme algérienne,* c. 1881-82, coll. J. B. Stang); Daulte, 1971, no. 369 (*Femme algérienne,* 1881); *Masterpieces,* 1972, p. 23, repr. (1883).

3. Daulte incorrectly indicates that the present picture was exhibited at Galerie Paul Rosenberg, *Exposition d'art français au XIXe siècle,* June 25-July 13, 1917, no. 56.

70   Still Life: Flowers. 1885
*(Nature morte: fleurs; Blumenstilleben;
Still Life with Flowers and Pot)*

Oil on canvas, 32¼ x 25⅞ (81.9 x 65.8)

Signed and dated l.r.: *Renoir. 85.*

PROVENANCE:

Acquired by J. E. Blanche, probably from the artist;[1] Walther Halvorsen, Oslo;[2] Leicester Galleries, London, by 1926?;[3] J. K. Thannhauser by 1927.

CONDITION:

Not lined. Crackle pattern visible especially at upper left and lower left. Scattered cleavage in background area. Painted surface continues slightly over the bottom edge of the stretcher where part of a chartreuse drawer knob is visible, the rest having been lost through abrasion (Jan. 1975).

The year 1885 belongs within the period that Renoir's style became more severe and solid. From 1884 through 1887 he worked at resolving questions of line and color. In September-October 1885 Renoir wrote to Paul Durand-Ruel: *"J'ai beaucoup perdu de temps à trouver une manière dont je sois satisfait. Je pense avoir fini de trouver, et tout marchera bien"* (L. Venturi, *Les Archives de l'Impressionisme*, Paris, 1939, vol. I, p. 132). ("I've lost a great deal of time trying to find a style with which I could be satisfied. I think I have finally found it, and everything will go well.")

Although Renoir maintained a studio in Paris, he traveled considerably. In 1885 he was in Paris at the time of the birth of his son, Pierre, on March 21; at La Roche-Guyon from June 15 to July 11 (where Cézanne came to join him); in Wargemont for July; back at La Roche-Guyon during August; at Essoyes during September-October; early November at Wargemont; and from November 20-30 in Paris, where his home was at 18, rue Houdon and his studio at 37, rue de Laval.

Still Life: Flowers is closest to *Still Life: Flowers and Prickly Pears* (28¾ x 23¼ in., 73 x 56.5 cm., usually dated 1884, present whereabouts unknown; New York, Sotheby Parke Bernet, *Highly Important Impressionist . . . Paintings . . . from the Estate of the late W. W. Crocker*, Feb. 25, 1970, no. 8, color repr.), which depicts the same vase and a similar background and table. In the Thannhauser painting, Renoir omitted the fruit and cloth on the table and subdued the color and pattern of the background. The present picture is distinguished by restrained colors and firmly delineated contours. Daniel Catton Rich thought that the Thannhauser *Still Life* reflected Renoir's contact with Cézanne.

The present picture is actually dated 1885; *Gladioli*, a similar work, bears the date 1884 (26 x 21¼ in., 66 x 54 cm., ex. coll. Sam Salz, now Collection Mr. George L. Simmonds, Chicago; New York, Duveen Galleries, *Renoir Centennial Loan Exhibition*, exh. cat., 1941, pl. 51). Another related version is *Roses and Gladioli* (29¼ x 21¼ in., 74.3 x 54 cm., present whereabouts unknown; New York, Bignou Gallery, *Renoir,* exh. cat., 1935, pl. 4), which is inscribed "au docteur Latty, souvenir d'amitié." Since Dr. Latty is the one who delivered Pierre in March 1885, it can be assumed that the picture was probably executed in 1885.

1. Jacques-Emile Blanche (1861-1942), once the pupil of Renoir, purchased Renoir's *Bathers* in 1889 from the artist (White, 1969, p. 344, fn. 98) and sold it in 1928.

2. According to notes made by J. K. Thannhauser, Dec. 1972. See also cat. no. 24, fn. 4.

3. See EXHIBITIONS. However, it is not known whether the painting belonged to the Leicester Galleries.

EXHIBITIONS:

London, Leicester Galleries, *Catalogue of the Renoir Exhibition,* July-Aug. 1926, no. 3, repr. *(Fleurs,* dated 1885); Berlin, Künstlerhaus (organized by the Galerien Thannhauser), *Erste Sonderausstellung in Berlin,* Jan. 9-Feb. 15, 1927, no. 198, repr. *(Blumenstilleben);* Los Angeles County Museum, *Pierre Auguste Renoir,* July 14-Aug. 21, 1955, no. 33, traveled to San Francisco Museum of Art, Sept. 1-Oct. 2; Santa Barbara Museum of Art, *Fruits and Flowers in Painting,* Aug. 12-Sept. 14, 1958, no. 50, repr.

REFERENCES:

J. Meier-Graefe, *Renoir,* Leipzig, 1929, pp. 177, repr., and 441, no. 171 *(Blumen,* 1885); B. E. White, "Renoir's Trip to Italy," *The Art Bulletin,* vol. LI, Dec. 1969, pp. 344-45, fn. 99; *Masterpieces,* 1972, p. 26, repr.; B. E. White, "The Bathers of 1887 and Renoir's Anti-Impressionism," *The Art Bulletin,* vol. LV, Mar. 1973, p. 107, fn. 8.

Georges Rouault

Born May 1871, Paris
Died February 1958, Paris

71   Christ and the Fishermen. c. 1938
      (Christ et pêcheurs; Paysage)

Oil on paper mounted on canvas, 20¾ x
29⅝ (52.7 x 75.2)

Signed l.l.: *G Rouault*   Not dated.

PROVENANCE:

Purchased from Galerie Pétridès, Paris,[1] by
Henry Pearlman, 1948; acquired from
Pearlman by J. K. Thannhauser in the mid-
1950s (correspondence with Pearlman,
Nov. 1973).

CONDITION:

The paper support has been glue mounted
on canvas. Varnish is present both in the
medium and on the surface (Jan. 1975).

Rouault treated the theme of Christ and the Fishermen frequently from 1937 into
the 1940s (see P. Courthion, *Georges Rouault*, New York, 1961, cat. nos. 227, 230,
234, 327, and 423). The Thannhauser version resembles the large canvas in the Musée
d'Art Moderne de la Ville de Paris (26¾ x 50½ in., 68 x 128 cm.; Courthion cat.
no. 327, where it is dated 1937) in composition, figure groups, and in the presence of
a sun and clouds in the sky. The composition of the Paris painting is more fully developed, and the colors are richer and more luminous than those in the present picture.

Isabelle Rouault concurs on the title of the painting and, on the basis of photographs, prefers a date of 1938 (correspondence, Apr. 1977).

EXHIBITIONS:

Paris, Galerie O. Pétridès, *Exposition Rouault*, Feb. 28-Mar. 1939, no. 9 (no cat.; label on
reverse reads: *Paysage* 54 x 74); New York, Feigl Gallery, *Modern European Masters*,
summer 1948, no. 3, repr.

REFERENCE:

Masterpieces, 1972, p. 42, repr. (c. 1930-40).

1. Paul Pétridès (correspondence, June 1977) remembers also that Pearlman acquired it but
   has not been able to find records regarding the picture. It is not known from whom
   Pétridès obtained the work. Isabelle Rouault thinks that her father did not sell directly
   to Pétridès but that around 1937-38 most works went to Ambroise Vollard (correspondence, Apr. 1977).

Chaim Soutine

Born ? 1893,[1] Smilovitchi, Lithuania
Died August 1943, Paris

72   The Venetian. c. 1926
      (La Vénitienne; Figure)

Oil on canvas, 31¹⁵⁄₁₆ x 21½ (76.1 x 54.7)

Signed l.r.:² *C. Soutine*   Not dated.

PROVENANCE:

Probably acquired from the artist by Paul Guillaume; Paris; purchased from Guillaume by C. W. Kraushaar Art Galleries, New York, 1930 (correspondence with A. Kraushaar, Aug. 1974); acquired from Kraushaar by The Toledo Museum of Art, Dec. 1936; acquired through exchange by J. K. Thannhauser, Dec. 1954 (correspondence with O. Wittmann, Nov. 1973).

CONDITION:

Lined with wax resin at an unrecorded date before 1965 (Jan. 1975).

The present title is not the artist's since the painting was called *Figure* when Paul Guillaume sold it in 1930.

Maurice Tuchman (correspondence, Nov. 1973) dates the picture c. 1926 and relates it to the painting *Woman with Green Necklace* (35½ x 31¾ in., 90.2 x 80.6 cm., Collection Mr. and Mrs. Sydney R. Barlow, Beverly Hills; Los Angeles County Museum of Art, *Chaim Soutine,* exh. cat., 1968, no. 47, color repr.). The sitter is not identical and neither has been identified. Soutine always painted from a model and in the mid-1920s he lived and worked primarily in Paris.

EXHIBITIONS:

New York, C. W. Kraushaar Art Galleries, *Exhibition of Modern French Paintings, Water Colors and Drawings,* Oct. 2-28, 1930, no. 27 *(Venetian Lady);* San Francisco, The California Palace of the Legion of Honor, *Exhibition of French Painting,* June 8-July 8, 1934, no. 236 *(Portrait of a Venetian Lady,* lent by C. W. Kraushaar Galleries); The Buffalo Fine Arts Academy, Albright Art Gallery, *The Art of Today,* Jan. 3-31, 1936, no. 112 *(The Venetian);* The Toledo Museum of Art, *Portraits and Portraiture Throughout the Ages,* Oct. 3-31, 1937, no. 51 *(Venetian);* West Palm Beach, The Norton Gallery, *An Exhibition of French Painting: David to Cézanne,* Feb. 4-Mar. 1, 1953, no. 41 *(The Venetian),* traveled to Coral Gables, The University of Miami, The Lowe Gallery, Mar. 15-Apr. 5.

REFERENCES:

The Toledo Museum of Art, *Catalogue of European Paintings,* 1939, pp. 268-69, repr. *(The Venetian);* P. Courthion, *Soutine: Peintre du déchirant,* Lausanne, 1972, p. 262, fig. B *(La Vénitienne,* dated 1926-27); *Masterpieces,* 1972, p. 82, repr. (1921-31).

1. See Courthion, p. 161.
2. M. Tuchman (correspondence, Aug. 1977) knows of no paintings after 1924 on which the signature is authentic, and he thinks that most earlier signatures are not by the artist. See also Courthion, p. 171.

Henri-Marie-Raymond de Toulouse-Lautrec-Monfa

Born November 1864, Albi (Tarn)
Died September 1901, Château of Malromé (Gironde)

73   Au Salon. 1893
      (Intérieur; Im Salon)

Pastel, gouache, and pencil on cardboard, 20⅞ x 31⅜ (53 x 79.7)

Signed l.r.: *H. T. Lautrec*   Not dated.

PROVENANCE:

Heim, Munich,[1] until 1913 (Paris, Hôtel Drouot, *Catalogue de tableaux . . . par H. de Toulouse-Lautrec,* Apr. 30, 1913, no. 3, repr. *[Au Salon]*); acquired at sale by Georges Bernheim, Paris; S. Sévadjian until 1920 (Paris, Hôtel Drouot, *Catalogue des tableaux modernes . . . formant la collection de M.S. . . . S . . . ,* Mar. 22, 1920, no. 22, repr. *[Intérieur,* 52 x 80 cm.]); Baron Lafaurie by 1926; Mlle Lucie Callot (acc. to Dortu); J. K. Thannhauser.

The salon depicted is that of a brothel in Paris, probably the one at 24, rue des Moulins (see D. Cooper, *Henri de Toulouse-Lautrec,* New York, 1956, p. 118, and J. Bouret, *Toulouse-Lautrec,* Paris, 1963, p. 137 and 140). From 1892 through 1895 Lautrec frequently represented scenes from the brothels and even lived in one for a time.

The red circular divan appears also in *In the Salon* (Dortu P.502; 23⅝ x 31½ in., 60 x 80 cm., Museu de Arte, São Paulo, Brazil) and in *Women Playing Cards* (Dortu P.505; 22¾ x 18⅛ in., 57.5 x 46 cm., Collection Dr. Hahnloser, Bern). The woman in the middle of the Thannhauser picture is seen frontally in the center of the São Paolo version. This model (with her hair pulled up in a bun on top of her head) can be found again at the far right in *Ces dames au réfectoire* (Dortu P.499; 24⅛ x 32 in., 61 x 81 cm., The Museum of Fine Arts, Budapest; F. Novotny, *Toulouse-Lautrec,* London, 1969, color pl. 76). In the present picture and in the related works, all generally dated 1893, Lautrec conveys the boredom experienced by the prostitutes.

There are drawings for the women in the foreground of the Thannhauser pastel. The woman at the left appears in the same pose in a blue pencil drawing in a private collection (5⅞ x 9¼ in., 14.7 x 23.2 cm.; Dortu, vol. VI, D.4.046, where it is incorrectly identified as *Femme assise de dos, au theatre* and dated c. 1895). Likewise, three drawings for the woman seen in profile in the center should be related to the present picture (D.4.045, 4.047, and 4.048 in Dortu, vol. VI, pp. 692-93, where they are dated c. 1895 rather than 1893).

EXHIBITIONS:

Kunsthaus Zürich, *Ausländische Kunst in Zürich,* July 25 - Sept. 26, 1943, no. 694[2] (*Au Salon,* 80 x 52.7 cm.); New York, The Museum of Modern Art, *Toulouse-Lautrec,* Mar. 20 - May 6, 1956, no. 27 (*The Salon,* 1893).

REFERENCES:

T. Joyant, *Henri de Toulouse-Lautrec,* Paris, 1926, p. 283 (*Au Salon,* 1893); G. Jedlicka, *Henri de Toulouse-Lautrec,* Zürich, 1943, opp. p. 207, repr. (*Im Salon,* 1893); E. Fougerat, *Toulouse- Lautrec,* Paris [1955], pl. vii; F. Daulte, "Une Donation sans précédent: la collection Thannhauser," *Connaissance des Arts,* no. 171, May 1966, p. 67, repr.; M. G. Dortu, *Toulouse-Lautrec et son oeuvre,* New York, 1971, vol. II, P.500, pp. 306-7, repr. (*Au Salon,* 1893); *Masterpieces,* 1972, p. 37, repr.; G. M. Sugana, *The Complete Paintings of Toulouse-Lautrec,* London, 1973, p. 108, no. 351 (1893).

1. Among twenty works by Toulouse-Lautrec, Heim owned two works related to the present picture (Dortu P.499 and P.505). How and when Heim obtained them is not known but they were all sold in Paris in 1913.
2. No records exist at the Kunsthaus indicating who owned the picture in 1943 (notes by E. Billeter, Feb. 1977). However, the exhibition title suggests a previous owner rather than J. K. Thannhauser.

Edouard Vuillard

Born November 1868, Cuiseaux
Died June 1940, La Baule

74   Place Vintimille. 1908-10

Distemper on cardboard mounted on canvas, left panel 78¾ x 27⅜ (200 x 69.5); right panel 78¾ x 27½ (200 x 69.9)

Not signed or dated.

PROVENANCE:

Acquired from the artist by Henry Bernstein, Paris (Georges Bernstein Gruber in conversation with D. C. Rich, Mar. 1975); purchased from family of Bernstein by J. K. Thannhauser, New York, 1948.

CONDITION:

The canvas mounts are not identical: the canvas on the left panel has a fine texture whereas that of the right panel is relatively coarse. Tack holes at corners and along vertical edges of both panels penetrate the cardboard and canvas.

Scattered losses in each panel. The condition of the left panel is good and generally stable. The right panel is fragile: recurring active cleavage in the green area of lawn and adjacent yellow tree (Dec. 1974).

The panels of *Place Vintimille* were part of a series of eight that Vuillard painted for the playwright Henry Bernstein. First installed (probably in the dining room and salon) in his bachelor apartment at 157, boulevard Haussmann, they were united in 1919 in Bernstein's dining room at 110, rue de l'Université in Paris. (We are indebted to Georges Bernstein Gruber, daughter of H. Bernstein, for this information. She remembers that her mother said they were installed as doors.) It has not been possible to locate photographs (if, in fact, any existed) of the panels in either apartment or to reconstruct their installation.

Bernstein (1876-1953) was the son of Marcel Bernstein, a French financier. His mother was the daughter of William Seligman of the New York banking family. By 1905 he was a successful playwright and, in 1908, his play *Israel,* which attacked anti-Semitism in France increased his fame while causing a furor that led to a three-year period of retirement (obituary, *The New York Times,* Nov. 28, 1953, p. 15).

Vuillard moved to 26, rue de Calais in 1907 and his apartment on the fourth floor looked down on the square (now called place Adolphe-Max). The left panel shows the side of rue de Bruxelles and the right, rue de Douai.

Understandably, the artist favored the subject. Similar views of the square include: sketches for the two Thannhauser panels (each 76½ x 26¾ in., 195 x 68 cm.; Paris, Durand-Ruel, *K. X. Roussel—Vuillard,* exh. cat., 1974, pls. 19 and 20, and Munich-Paris, *Vuillard—K.-X. Roussel,* exh. cat., 1968, nos. 137 and 138); a three-panel pastel (left and right panels each 72¹⁄₁₆ x 26³⁄₁₆ in., 183 x 66.5 cm. and center panel 74 x 18⅞ in., 188 x 48 cm.; Paris, Galerie l'Oeil, *Vuillard et son kodak,* exh. cat., 1963, p. 10, color repr.); a five-panel screen (distemper on paper, each section 98½ x 23⅝ in., 250 x 60 cm., ex. colls. Princess Bassiano and A. S. Henraux, Paris, now in a private American collection); and a painting in distemper (63½ x 90 in., 161 x 228 cm., ex. colls. M. Kapferer, Paris, and Mrs. D. Wildenstein, New York, now in the collection of Mrs. Joseph Hazen; Preston, p. 135, color repr.). (All related works are known only through photographs.)

The other six panels that belonged to Bernstein (private collection) include a panel representing the middle part of place Vintimille (fig. a). When a photograph of this middle part is placed between photographs of the Thannhauser panels, not only do the three have the same composition as the pastel mentioned above but their proportions are similar. The only difference is the repetition of a tree in the left and center panels that appears once in the pastel. A photograph of place Vintimille taken by the

fig. a.
Vuillard, *Place Vintimille,*
1908-10, distemper on
cardboard mounted on
canvas, 78¾ x 19⅝ in.,
200 x 49.8 cm., private
collection.

artist confirms the arrangement of the three panels (Galerie l'Oeil, 1963, p. 11, repr., and Preston, p. 38, repr., dated 1911).

There are, however, differences between the Thannhauser panels and the central one of place Vintimille in handling and in the greater degree to which the present pictures are elaborated. The central panel remains less heavily painted and freer in execution although not as boldly sketchy as the five street scenes which complete the Bernstein panels. (I am indebted to Margaret Potter and Olive Bragazzi for these observations and to Potter for her advice throughout.) There is no evidence of a sketch for the central panel to correspond with the sketches for the lateral ones, which the Thannhauser paintings follow closely. It is possible to speculate that the Thannhauser panels are more heavily painted and precisely detailed because Vuillard had made sketches specifically for them and not for the others. Furthermore, Vuillard's technique would allow for reworking (see Russell, pp. 137-40, and M. Davies, *French School*, rev. ed., London, 1970, pp. 142-44).

The Bernstein pictures are first documented in A. Segard, *Peintres d'aujourd'hui: les décorateurs,* Paris, 1914, vol. II, p. 321, in a list under the year 1910: "Six panneaux décoratifs exécutés à la colle, sur carton, sur le thème des rues de Paris, pour M. Henry Bernstein, 157 boulevard Haussmann." Since Achille Segard's list has proved reliable, the fact that it mentions only six panels can perhaps be explained as referring to the number of street scenes rather than to the number of panels: *La Rue, La Voiture d'arrosage, La Tour Eiffel, L'Enfant au ruisseau, Rue Lepic,* and *Place Vintimille.*

Of this list the first four titles appear as nos. 1-4 in the *Exposition Vuillard* held at Bernheim-Jeune, Paris, from November 11-24, 1908, where they are dated 1908. No mention is made of Henry Bernstein (Gordon, 1974, vol. II, p. 285). Thus, a *terminus ante quem* is established for four of the eight panels. The place Vintimille panels could not have been painted before 1907 since only then did Vuillard move to the square. Segard's date of 1910 is probably correct for the completion of the whole project. Inconsistencies in the handling of the panels reinforce the hypothesis that all were not executed at the same time.

Later in date is the five-panel screen (dated 1911 by Segard) which had to have been completed by April 1912, when it was exhibited at Bernheim-Jeune, *Edouard Vuillard,* as no. 29. The unity of the composition with its emphasis on the dense summer foliage and the activity in the street implies a knowledge of the Bernstein panels. In the painting in the Hazen collection, differences in style and alterations in the street confirm a date later than all other representations of place Vintimille mentioned.

EXHIBITION:

Paris, Galerie Charpentier, *Paris,* Dec. 1, 1944-Mar. 1, 1945, nos. 214 and 215, repr. left panel (correspondence with R. Nacenta, May 1975).

REFERENCES:

J. Salomon, *Vuillard, témoignage,* Paris, 1945, p. 57, repr. right panel (c. 1910); C. Roger-Marx, *Vuillard et son temps,* Paris, 1945, pp. 140, 149, repr. both panels, and 155-57 (1908); C. Roger-Marx, *Vuillard,* Paris, 1948, p. 55, figs. 42 and 43 (1908); C. Schweicher, *Die Bildraumgestaltung, das Decorative und das Ornamentale im Werke von Edouard Vuillard,* Zürich, 1949, pp. 83-84 (1908); C. Schweicher, *Vuillard,* Bern, 1955, p. 13; *L'Oeil,* no. 36, Dec. 1957, p. 78, repr. right panel: J. Salomon, *Vuillard admiré,* Paris, 1961, pp. 98 and 101, repr. both panels (c. 1910); J. Salomon, "Edouard Vuillard als Chronist seiner Epoch,"

Du, Jg. 22, Dec. 1962, pp. 30 and 36, color repr. both panels (c. 1910); F. Daulte, "Une Donation sans précédent: la collection Thannhauser," *Connaissance des Arts,* no. 171, May 1966, pp. 68 and 69, color repr. both panels (c. 1910); J. Dugdale, "Vuillard the Decorator; The Last Phase: The Third Claude Anet Panel and the Public Commissions," *Apollo,* vol. LXXXVI, Oct. 1967, pp. 272 and 274, figs. 5 and 6 (1908-10); J. Salomon, *Vuillard,* Paris, 1968, pp. 25, 108, 111, color repr. both panels, and 218 (c. 1910); H. H. Arnason, *History of Modern Art,* New York, 1968, pp. 97 and 98, fig. 141; Munich, Haus der Kunst, and Paris, Musée de l'Orangerie, *Edouard Vuillard—K.-X. Roussel,* exh. cat., 1968, pp. 110-11 (after 1907); J. Russell, *Vuillard,* Greenwich, 1971, pp. 48, repr. both panels, and 226 (1907-8); S. Preston, *Vuillard,* New York, 1971, p. 39, fig. 54, repr. both panels (c. 1908); *Masterpieces,* 1972, pp. 38, 39, repr. (c. 1908).

INDEX*

*Since they occur on almost every page, references to Justin K. Thannhauser and to The Solomon R. Guggenheim Museum are not included in the Index. The EXHIBITIONS and REFERENCES sections of each catalogue entry have not been indexed. Exhibitions and references have been indexed, however, when they are discussed in the text.

PHOTOGRAPHIC CREDITS

The photographs of works from the Thannhauser Collection at the Solomon R. Guggenheim Museum were made over a period of years by the following: Robert E. Mates, Paul Katz, Susan Lazarus, and Mary Donlon, New York.

Works for which no photographers are listed are reproduced by courtesy of their owners.

Mary Donlon, New York: cat. no. 37, fig. a

The Fogg Art Museum, Harvard University, Cambridge, Mass.: cat. no. 15, fig. a

Linda Konheim, New York: cat. no. 24, fig. a

General Research and Humanities Division, The New York Public Library, Astor, Lenox and Tilden Foundations: cat. no. 34, fig. a

Charles Uht, New York: cat. no. 74, fig. a

5500 copies of this catalogue, designed by Malcolm Grear Designers, typeset by Dumar Typesetting, Inc., have been printed by Eastern Press in October, 1978 for the Trustees of The Solomon R. Guggenheim Foundation.